HISTORY

OF

AFGHANISTAN

HISTORY

OF

AFGHANISTAN,

FROM THE EARLIEST PERIOD

TO THE

OUTBREAK OF THE WAR OF 1878.

BY

COLONEL G. B. MALLESON, C.S.I.

GYAN

Published by

GYAN

Gyan Publishing House
5, Ansari Road
Daryaganj, New Delhi-110002
Phone: 011-47034999, 9811692060
E-mail: books@gyanbooks.com

Distribution Network
gyanbooks.com
India, USA, Canada, UK, Australia

ISBN: 978-93-6208-100-1 (HB)
First Published, 1878

2nd Impression 2024

Printed at: Gyan Press, Delhi.

HISTORY OF AFGHANISTAN
Author: G. B. MALLESON

HISTORY

OF

AFGHANISTAN,

FROM THE EARLIEST PERIOD

TO THE

OUTBREAK OF THE WAR OF 1878.

BY

COLONEL G. B. MALLESON, C.S.I.

AUTHOR OF "HISTORICAL SKETCH OF THE NATIVE STATES OF INDIA," "HISTORY OF THE INDIAN MUTINY," ETC.

"Let us tell persons in high places that cunning is not caution, and that habitual perfidy is not high policy of State."

Mr. Disraeli's Speech, 11th April 1845.

SECOND EDITION.

LONDON:

W. H. ALLEN & CO., 13 WATERLOO PLACE,

PALL MALL, S.W.

PUBLISHERS TO THE INDIA OFFICE.

1879.

DEDICATION.

To Richard Everard Webster, Esq., Q.C.

My Dear Webster,

Fifteen years ago I saw you—to me a perfect stranger—win, under most trying circumstances—the two mile champion race at Cambridge. Little did I then think that I should one day rank you among my cherished friends.

Since we met some years later, I have watched with the keenest interest every stage of your career, and have often been reminded of that day at Cambridge.

I believe that the qualities you then displayed have in no small degree enabled you to achieve at so early an age the success which has marked your professional life.

It is, however, not because you have been successful, but because your life has been marked throughout by a generous sympathy with and a clinging to all that is good and true, and by a thorough distaste for all that is the reverse, that I ask you to become sponsor to this my youngest literary offspring on his introduction to the world. He will need a protector, for his name alone will provoke controversy.

Always most truly yours,

G. B. MALLESON.

27 *West Cromwell Road,*
16*th December* 1878.

INTRODUCTION.

In the Preface to my work—"An Historical Sketch of the Native States of India"—published in 1875, I stated that the history of the practically independent countries on the borders of India, countries such as Persia, Bilúchistán, and Afghánistán, might possibly engage my attention at some future period.

For that period, whenever it might be, I had collected notes and had drawn up a general sketch containing marginal references to the works necessary to be consulted. These I carefully stowed away, little dreaming that the time was so near at hand when I should be called upon to work them into shape.

In the latter half of the month of September last public interest was suddenly excited by the intelligence that a distinguished soldier was about to proceed with an escort on a mission to the Court of Kábul. Questions as to the country represented by that court, its history, its people, its kings, began at once to be asked. It was not so easy to answer them. The history of Afghánistán had been so interlaced with the history of Hindústán that there existed no independent record of the actions of its rulers and its people. Two very remarkable books did indeed seem to profess to supply the want. But Elphinstone's account of the kingdom of Kábul, charming as it is, confines itself mainly to a description of the people and the country as they were at the beginning of the present century—the history of the family of the then reigning dynasty being contained in an appendix: whilst Ferrier's "History of the Afgháns," full of detail as it is, contains but a very cursory reference to the Túrki, the Ghor, and the Moghol families who preceded, in the government of the country, the Ghilzais and the Abdális.

Under these circumstances, having the materials, the time, and the inclination, I resolved at the very end of September to attempt to supply the existing want. I have worked double tides, grudging no labour which might be required to present to the public a readable account of the antecedents of the country now invaded by our armies. I cannot hope that I have entirely succeeded. The mere mechanical labour of writing has been great, and the book has grown far beyond the dimensions contemplated at the outset. Such as it is, I offer it to the public. I know it has many faults; but I am equally conscious that I have spared no pains to render it an exact record of events which have passed.

I have had to consult numberless books of reference. Prominent amongst these I may mention the interesting travels of Jonas Hanway, the truth of whose detailed narrative is attested by other contemporary records; the late Sir Henry Elliot's History of India, as told by its own historians, edited by Professor Dowson; Erskine's Life of Bábar and Humáyún; Thomas's Chronicle of the Pathán Kings of Dehli; Briggs's Ferishta; Blochmann's translation of the Ain-i-Akbari. These are but a few, but they form, it may be said, the basis of the earlier part of my history. For the later period, the references were more plentiful and more easily obtainable. The histories of Elphinstone, of Ferrier, of Kaye, of Burnes, and the pages of the "Calcutta Review" have been repeatedly referred to. The description of the cities of Kábul, of Kandáhár, of Jalálábád, and of Ghazní has been taken from the same semi-official source which supplied the appendix to the life of General Nott.

I have found it impossible to describe the events which characterised the expedition of 1839 toAfghánistán, or the events which have led to the present invasion, without recording my own opinions as to the inexpediency of the one and the wisdom of the other. With regard to the policy which has been pursued towards Afghánistán, subsequently to the annexation of the Panjáb, I may observe that there seems to me to be an impassable gulf between the adoption of a principle suited to certain circumstances, and the riding that principle to death when those circumstances have changed. The policy, for instance, of masterly inactivity, admirably well adapted to the circumstances of an Afghánistán standing alone, remote from Russia, and far apparently beyond the zone of Russian ambition, becomes inarticulate folly when applied to an Afghánistán contiguous to and leaning on Russia. Under such circumstances it can only mean the resignation to Russia of a territory well described by a German writer as "the glacis of the fortress of Hindústán." A perusal of the pages of this volume will make it clear that the India of the past was really safe, really powerful, only when she had her troops cantoned beyond the passes of Afghánistán. They were so cantoned in the time of Akbar and of his earlier successors. It was when the later Moghol sovereigns had lost Kandáhár that the invasion of Hindústán became possible. Not even Nadir Shah, powerful as he was, dreamt of invading India until he had secured that important town. The fact that Kandáhár, garrisoned by Afgháns, delayed him for more than twelve months, proves the importance of its position, and gives some idea of the prominent part it may yet play as an out-work of the British Empire. The pages of this book show that the real contest for India has always taken place on the Helmand. The Helmand once passed and Kandáhár once occupied, the Indus has never stopped an invader. The quiescent attitude of Hindústán has ever proved an irresistible temptation to an ambitious and powerful people beyond Afghánistán; but no invasion was ever possible so long as Hindústán kept in her own hands the keys of her fortress—the valleys beyond the passes leading to her fertile plains.

It appears to me that England has too long acted on the principle enunciated by Lord Granville in his famous despatch—the principle of "not examining too minutely how far these arrangements were in strict accordance with the assurance given in January by Count Schouvaloff." Happily, times are changed. "The pulse of the public heart" beats higher than it did during the ministry of Mr. Gladstone. "The tone and temper" of this country are more elevated and more brave than when Lord Granville was foreign secretary. And England is to be congratulated that she possesses now a First Minister who is not afraid to announce plainly to the great disturber of the peace of the world, that "cunning is not caution, and that habitual perfidy is not high policy of State."

G. B. MALLESON.

27 *West Cromwell Road,*
16 *December* 1878.

CONTENTS.

CHAPTER I.

DESCRIPTIVE.

CHAPTER II.

THE GHAZNIVIDE PERIOD.

CHAPTER III.

The House of Ghor.

CHAPTER IV.

TRANSITION TO THE MOGHOL.

CHAPTER V.

HUMAYUN AND KAMRAN.

CHAPTER VI.

FROM MOGHOL TO AFGHAN.

CHAPTER VII.

THE GHILZAI RULE.

CHAPTER VIII.

THE DURANI RULE.

CHAPTER IX.

THE BARUKZYE PERIOD.

CHAPTER X.

THE BRITISH INVASION.

CHAPTER XI.

AFGHANISTAN FROM 1842 TO 1860.

CHAPTER XII.

RUSSIAN AND ENGLISH POLICY IN CENTRAL ASIA.

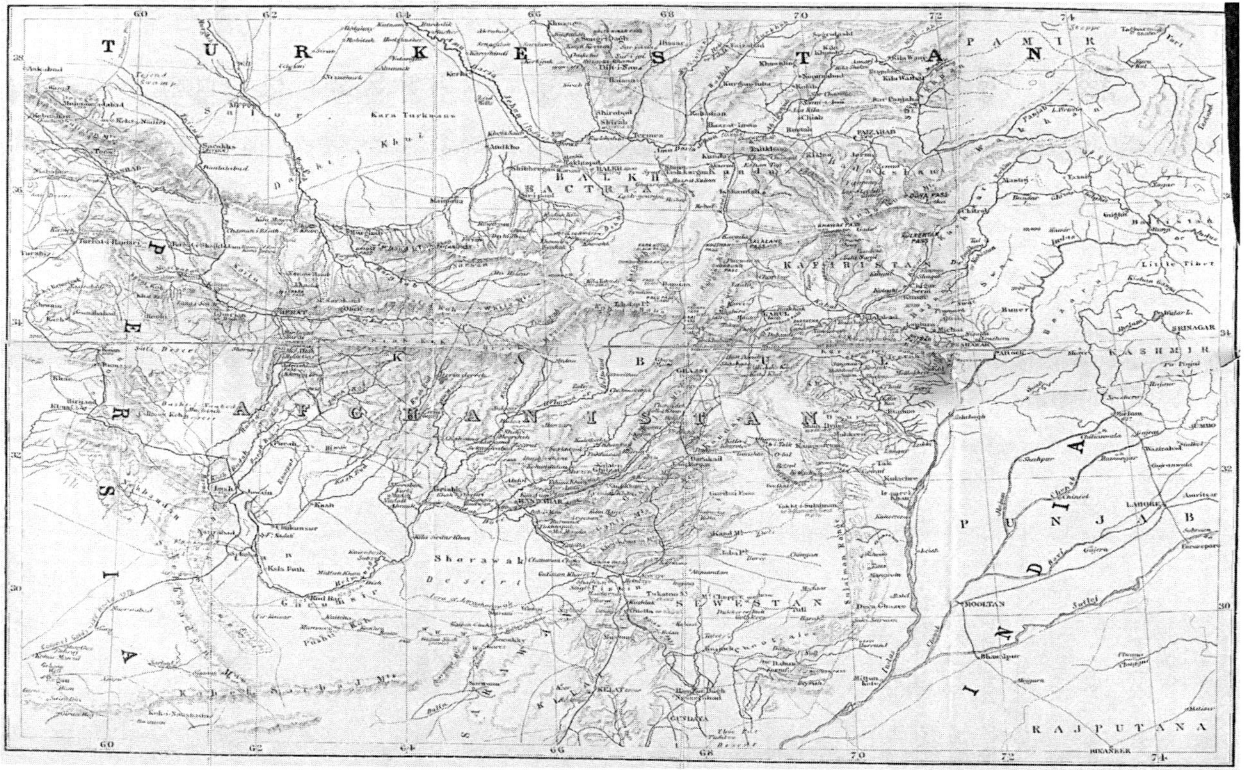
TURKESTAN
PAMIR
PERSIA
AFGHANISTAN
BALKH
BACTRIA
KAFIRISTAN
KASHMIR
PUNJAB
INDIA
SEWESTAN
RAJPUTANA
Shorawak Desert

AFGHANISTAN.

CHAPTER I.

DESCRIPTIVE.

In his work entitled "Reminiscences of a Bengal Civilian," Mr. William Edwards, then Assistant-Secretary to the Government of India in the Foreign Department, describes the departure of Amír Dost Mahammad, on the termination of the Afghán war in 1841, to resume his position as ruler of Kábul. "Just before parting," he writes, "the Amír, addressing the Governor-General in Persian, observed:—'I have seen a great deal of your Government since I came to India. Your forts, your arsenals, your ships, all are admirable. I have been down to Calcutta, and have been astonished with your wealth, your palaces, your marts, and your mint; but to me the most wonderful thing of all is, that so wise and wealthy a nation could have ever entertained the project of occupying such a country as Kábul, where there is nothing but rocks and stones.'" It will be my task to explain, in the pages which follow, the reasons which in past ages have invested, and which in the present hour particularly invest this country of rocks and stones with an importance far beyond its territorial value—an importance so vast that, in the opinion of many, the safety of India depends upon the predominance of British influence in the lands immediately beyond the British frontier.

The country inhabited by the Afgháns, and known generally as the kingdom of Kábul, is traversed from east to west by the Hindú Kúsh, and the prolongation to the westward of that mighty range. The mountains forming the prolongation branch off from the Koh-i-Bábá, a lofty range eighty miles in length, and some eighteen thousand feet high, and itself the western continuation of the Hindú Kúsh proper. Running westward, the mountains soon break into three parallel ranges—the centre and southernmost known as the Koh-i-Saféd and the Koh-i-Siáh—but all three comprehended under the general title of Paropamisan range. A line drawn nearly south from the spot where the northernmost of the three ranges referred to is touched by the Harí-rúd river, about seventy miles below Herát, to a point below the Sístán lake, and intersecting that lake, forms the western boundary of the country. The southern boundary may be roughly described as starting from the point below the Sístán lake just referred to, skirting the valleys of the Helmand and the Lora, and running then along the Shál territory to a point north-west of Déra Gházi Khán. From this point, as far as Vazírí, the Súlímán range; thence to the northern part of the Pesháwar district, the mountains overlooking the plains on the west bank of the Indus; and thence as far as the Hindú Kúsh, the wild and rugged country of unknown mountain tribes, go to form the eastern boundary.

The Hindú Kúsh, and the Paropamisan range, constitute, roughly speaking, the northern boundary of Afghánistán proper. But a portion of the country north of that range is tributary to the Amír of Kábul. This territory stretches from the westernmost spurs of the most northern branch of the Paropamisan range to the Khoja Sáleh ferry on the Oxus, along the borders of the Túrkomán desert. Thence to the great Pamír range, which constitutes the eastern limit, the Oxus forms the boundary of the tributary tribes. The eastern portion of this territory is known as Bádákshán; the western as Afghán Túrkistán.

Afghánistán has been well described as "consisting of a star of valleys radiating round the stupendous peaks of the Koh-i-Bábá, and everywhere bounded by mountains of a rugged and difficult nature."* The chiefs of these mountains is the mighty Hindú Kúsh, whose peaks, yet unexplored, are said to attain twenty thousand or twenty-one thousand feet in height. Of this range, and its prolongations westward, I have spoken. A high ridge branching from the country north of Kábul, crosses Afghánistán by way of Kándáhár and Girishk, and connects the great mountain with the Pághmán range. The Súlímán range runs from the Saféd Koh—a mountain separated from the Hindú Kúsh by the Kábul river—direct

* "Geographical Magazine," October, 1878.

south, and parallel with the British frontier. It has been described as "a mighty mountain barrier, containing in its northern section two ranges, which increase in number as they run southwards, till at its southern extremity, where the Súri breaks through, there are no less than twelve distinct ridges 'like battalions in columns of companies at quarter distance.' "*

The principal rivers in Afghánistán are the Kábul, the Helmand, the Harí-rúd, the Logar, the Múrgháb, and the A'rghand-áb. The Kábul river rises in the U'nai pass, in the south-eastern slopes of the Koh-i-Bábá, runs past Jalálábád, and through the Khaibar pass to the Indus, into which it falls near A'tak. It traverses a distance of about three hundred miles, receiving the drainage of the southern slopes of the Hindú Kúsh on the left, and the northern water-shed of the Saféd Koh (not to be confounded with the Koh-i-Saféd) on the right. Its tributaries are the Logar from the south; the Bárá, which rises in, and flows through, the Afrídí hills; the Swát; and the Panjshír, the Alishang, the Kúnar, and the Landai from the north.

The river Helmand rises also in the south-eastern slopes of the Koh-i-Bábá. It flows in a south-westerly direction to about a hundred and ten miles below Girishk. It then suddenly turns to the west, and running in that direction for about seventy miles, changes its course to the north-west, and discharges itself into the Sístán lake. The entire length of its

* "Geographical Magazine."

course exceeds seven hundred miles. Approaching Girishk it attains a breadth of at least a hundred yards, and a depth of three and a half. From this point to the Sístán lake it is considered navigable: it is extensively used for irrigation purposes.

The Harí-rúd rises in the southern slopes of the Koh-i-Siáh, shortly after it breaks away from the Koh-i-Bábá, and taking a westerly course runs south of Herát. A short distance below this turn, it takes a turn to the north, quits the Afghán territory at the point where it touches the northernmost branch of the Paropamisan range; then turning again to the north-west, it ultimately divides into two branches, and empties itself into the Tojend swamp. Herát, and the valley in which it lies, are watered by canals drawn from this river.

The Logar has been mentioned as one of the tributaries of the Kábul river. It plays an important part in the military geography of the country, prior to its junction with that river, more especially where it crosses the Ghazní and Kábul road between Shékhábád and Haidar Khail.

The Múrgháb rises in the Koh-i-Bábá range, and runs westerly to the north-west of Mérv. It is little more than a mountain stream.

More important are the Arghand-áb, a tributary of the Helmand, which rising in the range which runs in a south-westerly direction parallel with the road between Ghazní and Kandáhár, flows parallel with that range north of Kandáhár, and joins the Helmand some miles below it; the Tarnak, which follows the valley from Ghazní to Kandáhár, and joins the Arghand-áb before the latter joins the Helmand; the A'rghásán, flowing into the same river from the east, and the Dóri from the south; the Lora, another tributary of the same river, one of the heads of which rises in the Shál valley, the other just south of, and close to, Kalát, receiving the drainage of the Mústang valley.

More northerly again are the Kash-rúd, the Fáráh-rúd, and the Harút-rúd, which, rising in the southern slopes of the Koh-i-Siáh and flowing into the Sístán lake, cross the different routes between Herát and Kandáhár at various points. Other streams, such as the Zhot, the Gomal, and the Kúram, will be more specially treated of when I come to describe the passes with which they are severally connected.

Afghánistán proper may be conveniently treated of as formed of two great parts—the eastern and the western; the former represented by the towns of Kábul and Ghazní and the valley of which Jalálábád is the central point; the latter by Kándáhár and Herát. From these divisions are excepted the tribes on the eastern frontier, many of whom are independent, and who will be treated separately. To the divisions themselves, or rather to the towns which dominate them, and to the routes which connect them, I shall now turn my attention.

The city of Kábul, six thousand five hundred feet above the level of the sea, lies in a triangular gorge formed by two ranges of high and steep hills, which, running north-west and south-west, nearly meet a little to the west of the town, leaving between the two angles a narrow entrance traversed by the Kábul river and by the high road from Ghazní. The city is thus encompassed by hills on three sides.

On the southern side, indeed, there is only a narrow path between the city wall and the base of the hill. These hills are steep, bare, and rocky, and are crowned with a long line of wall, having round towers at short intervals. This line of wall is carried up the steep sides of the hills, along their summits, and across the narrow entrance which lies between them. Were it in repair, this wall would completely close all entrance from the west, but it is believed to have been allowed to fall into decay.

The city itself extends about a mile from east to west, and about half a mile from north to south. It is surrounded by a high but weak mud wall, and has no ditch.. On the top of a rocky eminence, east of the town and separated from it by a ditch, stands the Bálá Hissár, and on the slope of this acclivity are the royal palace and gardens, with an extensive bazaar, the whole surrounded by a wall and ditch.

The chief bazaars in the city itself run east and west, the largest running nearly through the centre of the town. It forms a spacious broad street of two-storied houses covered by flat roofs extending between their tops. This street is broken into three or four divisions by small squares, which have passes leading out right and left into the adjoining streets. The rest of the town is formed of narrow, dirty, and irregular streets, the houses in which are made of unburned brick. Burnes computed the population to be about sixty thousand, and this number is probably not greatly exceeded now.

The Kábul river, which enters at the north of the gorge from the west, flows eastward close under the northern wall. The river from August to October is a mere brook, but it is at times so swollen as seriously to endanger the walls of the city.

Towards the east of Kábul the country is more open than on the other sides. The two ranges of hills, separating widely to the north and south, have a broad valley lying between them, down which the road to Pesháwar runs nearly due east. This valley extends for about twenty-five miles east of Kábul, and there meets a cross chain of rugged rocks. The pass over these, called the Látá Band, is practicable only for man and horse. The valley is about ten miles broad, but at a short distance from the town a low, rocky, and barren ridge runs from west to east for about three miles, dividing the valley into two nearly equal portions.

On the northern side of the valley the Kábul river runs through a fertile tract of country. On the southern side, the river Logar, which enters it through a break in the hills, and running for some distance close at their base, crosses the valley from south to north five miles east of Kábul, and falls into the Kábul river. Their united streams pass out of the valley through a narrow opening in the Látá Band pass, already referred to.

The country on the south side of the valley on the banks of the Logar is low, marshy, and often under water. It is very fertile. So likewise is that on the northern side, where the Kábul river flows. But the centre of the valley, where the rocky range extends, is dry and barren.

To the west of Kábul lies a broad valley or plain, separated from the town by the hills through which the narrow entrance to the town passes. This plain, which is about eight miles broad by twelve in length, is a spacious amphitheatre, encircled on all sides by lofty hills, over the tops of which rises a succession of lofty hills, each higher and higher, till the view is terminated by the summits of the Hindú Kúsh. The panorama is most lovely—the plain being watered by numerous streamlets brought from the Kábul river, and covered with green fields fringed by rows of the poplar and the willow. Orchards richly stocked with fruit and flower, and vegetable gardens well laid out, diversify the landscape. The Kábul river, its banks shaded with trees, and here and there guarded by forts, runs through it. Villages and hamlets are scattered over the surface of the plain.

The country round Kábul is extremely fruitful. Grain and provisions of every kind are in abundance, whilst the most delicious fruits of every description are cheaper even than grain.

Jalálábád, formerly considered the chief town of the second district in eastern Afghánistán, is one hundred and five miles from Kábul and ninety-one from Peshávar. The line of road to it from Kábul lies for the first ten miles nearly due east, descending steeply the Kábul valley. The next ten miles, leaving the valley, commence by turning south, and proceed through a long and narrow defile between steep and lofty hills devoid of verdure. Along this defile, which is only a few yards broad, runs a noisy stream, which has to be crossed nearly twenty times. The whole breadth of the pass is covered with a mass of pebbles and boulders. At its summit the elevation is seven thousand five hundred feet above the sea. This pass is called Khúrd-Kábul. Ten miles beyond it rise the Tazín hills, still higher, having an elevation of eight thousand two hundred feet. Thence is a descent of about one thousand eight hundred feet into the small valley of Tazín. Twenty-two miles beyond this valley is the formidable Jagdalak pass.

From Jagdalak to Gandamak—as from the entrance of the Khúrd Kábul pass to Jagdalak—the road lies through a barren and inhospitable country. It is a wide waste of bare and naked hills encompassed by high and inaccessible mountains. The difficulties of transit are enormous. The road scrambles up and down steep acclivities, over long ranges of bleak hills, and through narrow defiles, bounded on each side by steep rocks. It is covered with large stones, pebbles, and rocks, and often leads the traveller down the bed of a stream. The normal inhabitants of this region are few and far between.

Gandamak itself is a great improvement on the country traversed to reach it. It stands four thousand six hundred feet above the sea-level.

For eight or nine miles after leaving Gandamak the scenery reassumes its unattractive form. The road is rough, leading the traveller across rocky beds of rivers, and over stony spurs. Three miles after passing the valley of Nimlah—itself a small oasis in the desert—a great improvement is visible. By a gradual descent the open valley of Fathábád is reached, and here are to be found almost the first symptoms of regular cultivation on this side of Khúrd-Kábul. Fathábád is eighteen miles from Gandamak.

From Fathábád to Jalálábád the distance is seventeen miles. The road makes a descent for the first eight or nine miles, over a fair though occasionally very stony country. On reaching the level ground four or five miles from Jalálábád the traveller finds himself in a fertile plain covered with high and lofty trees, under the shadow of which is often a village or a fort. Jalálábád itself stands nearly in the centre of the plain. The plain itself extends from west to east about twenty miles, and has a breadth at its broadest part of ten or twelve miles. The cultivated portion is considerably narrower, is much intersected by water cuts from the river, and is extremely swampy. The river is the Kábul river. Here it is a broad, rapid, and clear stream, having a breadth during October of a hundred yards. Its banks are low and wide apart, but during the dry season it is fordable in many places. Numerous villages are scattered along its banks, but the fertility is confined to a very narrow space; and the river, leaving the plain, soon wanders among low stony hillocks.

The town of Jalálábád is in no way remarkable. It probably remains much the same as it was when occupied by the British force in 1841–2. According to the latest accounts, its fortifications have not been restored. In 1841–2 it was described as being very small, very dirty, and very poor, surrounded by a mud wall, possessing from three to four hundred houses, and a permanent population of about two thousand. The walls, which formed an irregular quadrilateral, were surrounded on all sides by gardens, buildings, and ruins. It is believed that no improvement has been effected in this respect of late years, and it is spoken of as having been abandoned as a military post.

From Jalálábád to Pesháwar is a distance of ninety-one miles. The first forty-two of these, as far as Dáka, may be generally described as a tract of hilly country lying between two ranges of mountains, which, running in their length east and west, enclose between them a breadth of about twenty miles from north to south. This intermediate country is in no sense a valley, as it is divided into a series of small plains by cross ranges of hills which pass between the Saféd Koh* and the secondary ranges of the Himaláyas. These plains are generally barren and stony, and have a considerable slope from north to south. The river—always the Kábul river—which runs along their northern margin, has to make its way through several narrow passages in the rocks, while the only road in one of these isolated plains leads over the southern skirts of the cross ranges of hills.

About forty-four miles from Jalálábád high hills

* Not to be confounded with the western Koh-i-Saféd, previously referred to.

shoot up between the Saféd Koh and the secondary ranges of the Himaláyas, which completely block up, for about thirty miles, the valley called the valley of the Kábul. The river has to force its way through narrow gorges among the rocks, whilst the road penetrates the high hills by a defile called the Landikhána defile, just within the Khaibar pass. The following description of this part of the route is taken from the journal of an officer who traversed it in 1840, Lieut.-General Kaye :—

"14.—Landikhána, eight and a half miles.—We traversed for some two miles a stony plain, and then entered the mouth of the Khaibar pass. Just before emerging among the hills, the Saféd Koh became again visible, but was soon shut out from view. The defile into which we entered was by no means narrow (never less than fifty yards in breadth), and the hills neither steep nor difficult, but at nearly every point accessible by infantry. After about two miles of defile, the passage widened considerably to about six hundred yards, and here in the centre we passed an isolated eminence, on the summit of which was a small fort or breastwork, constructed of loose stones, and garrisoned by a company of Jezailchees. After this the pass narrowed again. We ascended considerably, but the road was by no means difficult, though everywhere stony. Stunted trees and bushes throughout the defile. Encamped on uneven ground close to the foot of the ghaut, leading over the summit of the pass. Some cultivated land rising in terraces to the summit of the hill to the south, and some rude fortifications, now dilapidated, are to be seen on the same side of the defile. Looking back, the summits of many mountains visible to the north-west, the most distant partially covered with snow. This I imagine to be the Kúner peak. We travelled towards south-east to-day.

"15.—From Landikhána, the road led up the side of the hill to the left, passing round two shoulders. The ascent not steep, but the road wound in and out, occasioned by various fissures, or water channels, in the face of the mountain. After rounding the second shoulder, we descended gently into the bed of the stream, which was previously too confined and rocky to allow of guns passing. This was the case again occasionally, necessitating the road to pass over parts of the hill; the ascents on those occasions, though short, and not very steep, difficult on account of awkward bends occurring at the very foot. Most of the carriages had to be unlimbered on this account, at three of the ascents. After about four miles we reached the summit of the pass; the hills receded right and left, and we entered on a broad extensive table-land, sloping gently towards the east, well cultivated and sprinkled with forts, hills on all sides, but not very lofty, also a few insulated eminences. The plain sometimes stretched miles across, and here and there valleys branching off right or left. After about five miles the valley narrowed, and the descent became more sensible; and as we approached Ali Masjíd, we entered into a narrow defile, enclosed by precipitous rocks; this, however, only continued for about half a mile, when we passed close under the fort of Ali Másjíd, and encamped about a mile lower down the glen. Distance marched to-day, fourteen miles.

"The Khaibar hills, and the defile through which we passed, are tolerably well wooded, but the trees are stunted, indeed, scarce anything more than bushes. On the open land, at the most elevated part of the pass, there are many forts, and much cultivation also in the valleys branching off on either side; but the forts are the worst I have met with. They have only one tower each, and that very weak. The fort of Ali Masjíd is better built and designed, but its strength consists in its situation, it being on the summit of a lofty hill, insulated and difficult of access, to the south-west of the road. The masjíd, or mosque, is in the valley below. Immediately after passing Ali Masjíd, the hills decrease in altitude and steepness. Our direction of march tortuous to-day, but generally south-east.

"16.—Jamrúd, seven miles.—From our last ground we ascended the hillside on our left by a steep, tortuous road; there was another road to the left, but we did not know of it, exceedingly easy, so we pulled the guns up the ascent; after which we proceeded for some distance over undulating ground, an elevated table-land, and passed over one narrow defile by a well-built bridge. We then descended into the bed of a stream by a good road cut in the side of the hill. The remainder of the march lay through low hills, until we debouched into the plain near Jamrúd. There is another road which continues in the defile, without ascending the hillsides; but it is very circuitous.

* * * * *

"With the exception of the hills from which we have just emerged, there is nothing to bound our view. There are ranges both north and south, but very far distant, while the plain stretches boundless to the east. Very few trees to diversify the scenery. We came about S.S.E. to-day.

"About four miles above Ali Masjíd, in the pass, there is a 'tope,' said to be Grecian, on a hill by the roadside.

"17.—To camp near Peshâwar, sixteen miles."

I turn now to the third province or division in eastern Afghánistán, that of Ghazní. The town of Ghazní lies seven thousand seven hundred and twenty-six feet above the level of the sea at the top of the valley of the Tarnak, close under the termination of a range of hills, which, running east and west, shut up this valley, and separate it from the Kábul valley. The town is ninety miles south-west by south from Kábul, on the road to Kandáhár, from which it is distant about two hundred and twenty-five miles. It is built upon an isolated ridge, on a natural mound, partly rocky and partly composed of earth. On the highest portion of the mound, which has a considerable elevation, stands the citadel, which is nearly in the centre of town, though touching the wall on the north side. The outer wall has a circuit of about a mile and a quarter. The form of the town is a sort of irregular square, the wall being built so as to suit the outline of the mound on which it rests. The foundation of this wall is little above the level of the surrounding country, and as it winds round the hill it presents to the traveller a very formidable appearance. The mound which it encircles resembles, in fact, a fortress of which the citadel is the apex. The town itself, though mean and insignificant, contains about three thousand five hundred mud houses. These houses have flat roofs, with small windows in the upper storey, and holes pierced for matchlocks, and are capable of being defended. The streets are narrow. Within the walls is stabling sufficient for a brigade of cavalry. In the citadel are houses and squares of a superior order suitable to the rank and position of the sirdars by whom they are ordinarily occupied. Formidable though Ghazní is in appearance, it is not so in reality. The town is commanded by a low hill near its north-western angle, and although the citadel soars above it, the vicinity of the hill alluded to would almost be fatal to its retention for any length of time. It is proof against escalade, and with ordinary care it could be made strong enough to defy a sudden assault, but it could not stand a protracted siege.

The valleys in the vicinity of Ghazní are fertile. Fruits and vegetables are produced in great abundance. The supply of milk and ghee is likewise plentiful.

Before descending in a south-westerly direction to Kandáhár, I propose to describe the road between Ghazní and Kábul. The distance between the two places is, as already stated, ninety miles. After quitting Ghazní, the road, three or four miles east of the town, passes over a defile in the hills which separate the Tarnak valley from that of Kábul. The summit of this pass is at least one thousand two hundred feet above Ghazní. Thence is a descent of two or three hundred feet into the Kábul valley. From this point the valley has a general slope down to the city of Kábul. It is, however, blocked up in several places by hills with steep ascents and descents, through the narrow gorges in which the Kábul and Logar rivers make their way to the more open country near Kábul. Besides the slope towards Kábul the country slopes also from east to west, on which side of the valley the river Kábul runs. The upper part of the valley is stony and barren, but fertile tracts are met with along the banks of the rivers. A very beautiful and fertile tract of land, called the valley of Maidán, occupies the Kábul valley twenty-six to thirty miles from the city. It is very rich, lies low, and is surrounded on all sides by high hills, and intersected by numerous streams.

The country between Ghazní and Kábul is blocked up with snow during several months in the year. At Ghazní itself the snow has been known to lie long beyond the vernal equinox. The atmosphere in the country between the two towns is most highly charged with electricity.

The Logar, a fine, broad, rapid river, crosses the Kábul valley about thirty miles from its head, coming out through a narrow gorge in the hills, and after crossing the valley, leaves it by another gorge. This is the strongest part of the country between Ghazní and Kábul, as the low land could be flooded by the river, and rendered nearly impassable for any but light troops, whilst the ground is high and very strong on

2

the opposite side—that nearest Kábul. This river falls into the Kábul river, but not until the latter has passed the town of Kábul.

I here append a table showing the marches and the elevations of the several halting-places between Kábul and Ghazní, with a slight description of the route:—

Name of Place.	Height above the Sea.	Distance in Miles.	General Description.
Kábul	6508	—	
Arghandi	7628	12	The road for six or seven miles runs through a highly cultivated valley abounding with orchards and fruit trees and cultivation. After leaving the Kábul valley there is an asent over a rough, stony road till within three miles of Arghandi, when there is a gradual descent to that place.
Maidán	7747	20	The road at first is hilly and somewhat difficult, keeping along the ridge of the Maidán valley; it somewhat improves as it nears Maidán.
Shékhábád	7473	18	The road rough and stony. After four miles the Kábul river is crossed. The road for many miles skirts the beautiful Maidán valley.
Haidar Khail	7637	10	The road descends into the valley of the river Logar. Here the river runs strongly and rapidly, offering an obstacle to an invader from Ghazní. About six miles from Shékhábád, the valley becomes confined and narrow, with hills rising abruptly on either side. Emerging from this defile, the road runs along the bank of a small river, which is crossed about two miles from Haidar Khail.

Name of Place.	Height above the Sea.	Distance in Miles.	General Description.
Haft Asya .	7754	10	A winding road through a narrow valley, well cultivated, and abounding with forts and villages. The country about it is dreary and desolate.
Shash Gao .	8500	9	A stony road.
Ghazní . .	7726	14	A steady ascent for three miles to the Shérdahán, or Lion's mouth, a formidable pass at an elevation of about nine thousand feet. At the entrance of this pass is built a substantial guard tower, conducting to a level plateau of considerable extent enclosed by hills. The road crosses the centre, and by an abrupt descent conducts across a second, though less extensive plateau, which stretches to Ghazní. During the winter months this pass is blocked up with snow, and communication between Ghazní and Kábu is impossible, except for foot passengers.

I propose now to return to Ghazní, and to proceed thence along the valley of the Tarnak to Kandáhár. The total distance is two hundred and twenty-five miles, and for the greater part of its length the road takes the traveller in a direction nearly from north-east to south-west. From Ghazní to Kalát-i-Ghilzai (not to be confounded with Kalát), the distance is one hundred and thirty-eight miles of gradual descent. Kalát-i-Ghilzai is a rather strong fortress on the right bank of the Tarnak, five thousand seven hundred and seventy feet above the sea level. The declension from Ghazní amounts thus to about two thousand feet. Kandáhár lies eighty-seven miles nearly due west of Kalát-i-Ghilzai.

On leaving Ghazní, the Tarnak valley is generally narrow, in some places not exceeding half a mile in breadth. As it approaches Kandáhár, however, it expands to a breadth of about thirty miles. The height of some of the peaks which hem it in is about five thousand feet. In parts of the valley there is a considerable breadth of level country, but in general it is shut in by a series of low, undulating hills rising from the banks of the Tarnak. These hills increase in size as they approach the barrier ranges. They are very bare and uninteresting, having a scanty covering of thyme and low bushes. The open portions of the valley are, however, well cultivated. The higher districts—those in the upper part of the valley—are especially so, being watered by canals brought at enormous labour from the river. These districts abound, moreover, in villages surrounded by fruit trees and cornfields. They are protected by small forts, good for defence against predatory bands.

The following route from Ghazní to Kandáhár, giving the elevations of each halting-place, and such description of each as I have been able to collect, may not be unacceptable at the present time:—

Name of Place.	Height above the Sea.	Distance in Miles.	General Description.
Ghazní . .	7726	—	Described in preceding pages.
Yárgáti . .	7502	18	The road skirts the hilly tract at the base of the Gál Koh

Name of Place.	Height above the Sea.	Distance in Miles.	General Description.
			range. The road is good, but the country barren and sandy. Yárgáti is a barren and dreary place, depending for water on subterranean aqueducts.
Karra Bagh .	7307	—	I have been unable to ascertain the exact distances from each other of the three first places mentioned. In the distance to Múklúr of forty-two miles from Yárgáti there is a descent of nearly five hundred feet, most pronounced in the last stage. The road still skirts the hilly tract at the base of the Gál Koh range. The land is still watered by means of aqueducts. The principal crops are corn and madder, and there are fruit trees, such as apples, pears, apricots, almonds, and pomegranates. At Múklúr itself the cultivation is more advanced. There are springs in the neighbourhood said to be the source of the river Tarnak.
Jamrat . .	7420	—	
Obá . . .	7325	—	
Múklúr . .	7091	44	
Ghójan . .	7068	14	The road from Múklúr to Ghójan leads over a grassy tract with hills on either side. The country round is an open plateau, skirted by low hills. It is well cultivated, and watered from the aqueducts previously mentioned.
Chasma-i-Panjak	6810	—	The road from Ghójan to Momin-Kila leads over a wilderness of an undulating character, traversed with ravines at from four to five miles distance from the right bank of the river Tarnak, along the course of which are many villages and much cultivation.
Chasma-i-Shadi.	6668	—	
Momin-Kila .	—	16	

Name of Place.	Height above the Sea.	Distance in Miles.	General Description.
Tází . . .	6321	—	From Momin-Kila to Tází, the road runs on the right bank of the river Tarnak, which, in this part of its course, is a noisy and muddy stream, about fifty or sixty feet wide, with banks one-third that height. At short intervals along the course of the stream, weirs have been thrown across, and the waters above them are led into the adjacent fields by cuttings in the banks.
Sar-i-Asp . .	5973	—	Between Tází and Kalát-i-Ghilzi the road leaves the river, and leads the traveller across a bleak and barren wilderness, the surface of which is undulating, and which is traversed by numberless ravines.
Kalát-i-Ghilzi .	5773	48	Throughout this journey of about thirty miles, the traveller is subjected, at sunrise and for an hour or two after, to a bitterly cold wind, coming according to the season from the east or west, and which carries with it particles of sand and gravel, the effects of which are often painful. There is nothing to add to the slight reference already made to Kalát-i-Ghilzi.
Jaldak . .	5396	14	The road lies over an undulating plain of, for the most part, waste land—a small strip only on either side of the river Tarnak being occupied by fields and cultivation. Jaldak lies on a sandy soil, dotted with patches of brushwood. Midway between Kalát-i-Ghilzi and Jaldak runs the boundary between the Dúráni and Ghilzi

Name of Place.	Height above the Sea.	Distance in Miles.	General Description.
			territories. The site is marked by an insignificant masonry bridge over a small rivulet which here crosses the road on its way to the Tarnak. The villages on this march, like those on the Ghazní side of Kalát-i-Ghilzi, are widely separated, and for the most part far off the high road.
Tirándáz . .	4829	17	Before reaching Tirándáz is Jaloghi, where Major Lumsden's mission halted in 1857. The character of the country unaltered.
Shahar-i-Safá .	4618	14	
Khail-i-Ákhan .	4418	15	A small hamlet of a few huts. Character of the country much the same. At this place the river Tarnak is almost exhausted, only a small stream trickling through the centre of its stony channel. Fever would seem to prevail here.
Máhmaud Kila .	3945	15	The road, soon after leaving Khail-i-Ákhan, diverges from the river, and leads across an open plain of great extent, sloping towards the west. This is the plain of Kandáhár. The water here is supplied from the subterranean aqueducts, is brackish, and so strongly impregnated with nitre as to be unwholesome.
Kandáhár . .	3500	10	The road leads across the plain already referred to. Kandáhár needs a separate description.

The town of Kandáhár, situated at the foot of the Tarnak valley, is separated from the river of that name by a short range of hills which divide the lower part of the valley, and run parallel with the river for about twenty miles. These hills are named the Torkání. Kandáhár is encompassed on three sides by high, bare, sharp-pointed rocky mountains, rising abruptly from the plain. The open side is that leading to it along the valley of the Tarnak.

A considerable portion of the plain of Kandáhár is, in ordinary seasons, fertile and well cultivated. It can boast of rich meadows clothed with green turf, of gardens and orchards filled with fruit trees, of fields of corn, of barley, of lucerne, and of clover, watered by numerous canals conveying through a break in the hills the waters of the Arghand-áb, one of the tributaries of the Helmand. These cultivated lands lie chiefly on the south and west sides of the town. Three or four miles from it to the east the traveller encounters a barren and cheerless plain, covered with stones and scantily supplied with water.

It is not that there is a deficient supply of this necessity of life. Although, in consequence of the great demand upon them for the purposes of irrigation, the rivers near Kandáhár dry up during the hot weather, there is no want of water. In the meadow land round the town it lies within two feet of the surface, and even two miles to the east it is procurable within sixteen feet.

The town of Kandáhár is large and populous. Its form is that of an oblong square, two thousand by sixteen hundred yards.

Situated on the north side of the extensive plain called after the town, about two miles from the lofty mountain called Bábá Wali, it is surrounded by a high but thin and weak wall, with numerous bastions. These walls are thirty feet high. The four principal bazaars or streets, leading from a gateway which opens nearly in the centre of each face, meet in the middle of the town in a large circular building covered with a dome about one hundred and twenty feet in diameter, and called the Chársú. This place is surrounded with shops, and it is regarded as the public market-place. The streets which converge in it divide the town into four nearly equal districts. The other streets in the town are mere lanes, formed by the narrow space between high houses—houses far more lofty than those in the principal streets.

The climate of Kandáhár is very dry, and in every respect superior to that of Híndústán. In the hot weather the wind, which is generally easterly in the morning, comes gradually round to the west by 7 or 8 o'clock, and continues in that quarter during the day. It falls about sunset, and during the night an easterly breeze springs up. In the month of June the hot wind very often continues through the night, but this is rare, and for the most part the nights are cool and the mornings very pleasant.

Grain and most of the necessaries of life are dear at Kandáhár. Firewood too is very scarce.

It is difficult to fix the number of the inhabitants. Mountstuart Elphinstone declined to make the attempt. It seems to be acknowledged, however, that the population is in excess of that of Herát. If the Herátís may be estimated, as it has been, at forty-five thousand, the Kandáhárís may possibly number sixty thousand. This, however, must be regarded merely as an approximation.

Herát, the westernmost division of Afghánistán south of the Paropamisan range, is reached from Kandáhár by way of Girishk, Farrah, and Sabzwár. The distance is about four hundred miles.

Girishk is a fort commanding the ordinary passage and summer ford of the river Helmand, which covers the fort to the east. This river, the normal width of which is about a hundred yards, rises in flood with the melting snow, and in May often attains a breadth of one mile. The village, for town it is not, is small and insignificant. The position of the fort is important, but Captain Marsh, who visited it in 1873, found it in a very dilapidated condition. The distance from Kandáhár is about seventy miles. Of these the first sixteen miles lead over a country inundated by unbridged streams; the remainder over a stony country in which water is scarce.

From Girishk to Farrah is a distance of nearly a hundred and seventy miles. The road is tolerably level, want of water being the chief drawback. Ferrier describes Farrah as "a strong and important fortress." It stands in the Sístán basin on the river Farrah, which flows to the westward of it, and which, dry for three parts of the year, attains in spring a width of one hundred and fifty yards. Farrah is enclosed by an earthern rampart, crowned with towers, and surrounded by a wide and deep ditch, which can be flooded, and with a covered way. It has the form of a parallelogram, running north and south, and has two gates.

As a military position it is important, but the climate is insalubrious. With a capacity for four thousand five hundred houses, not more than sixty were habitable when Ferrier was there in 1845. Its dilapidation has increased with each succeeding year. In 1873 Captain Marsh found but twenty huts in the town, "and those all in ruins."

Sabzwár, the next strategic point on the road to Herát, is seventy-one miles north of Farrah. The intermediate country is undulating, "a vast jumble," writes Captain Marsh, "of valleys and hills, with small plains, inhabited only by a nomadic people." It lies in a fork formed of two branches of the river of the same name, but more frequently called the Hárút, which, rising in the mountains south-east of Herát, empties itself eventually in the Sístán lake. The position is excellent, but the place itself is decayed and weak. Attached to the fort is a village containing perhaps one hundred houses.

Due north, and at a distance of ninety-three miles from Sabzwár, and severed from it by a country difficult only in the mountainous chain that has to be traversed, lies Herát, in a military sense the most important city in the territories of the Amír. It deserves, therefore, special notice. The following description is condensed from Ferrier's History of Afghánistán, published in 1858:—

"The fortified town of Herát is a quadrangle of three and a half miles long on the north and south sides, and rather more on the east and west. A thick rampart, constructed of earth brought from the interior of the city, surrounds it, and forms its defence. The height of this rampart is not everywhere equal, but the average may be about ninety feet, and it is supported on the inside by counterforts of masonry. Earth also has been taken for a distance of one hundred and eight yards beyond the ditch, and used in the construction of this work, and being a pure clay it has become exceedingly solid. The rampart has the appearance of a long hill surrounding the city, and on the crest of it a thick wall has been built about thirty-two feet high, flanked with round towers, which, as well as the curtains which connect them with each other, are loopholed for musketry. It is only in the enormous and massive towers at the angles that cannon can be mounted.

" Generally speaking, the ground from the edge of the ditch towards the country, in a radius of two hundred and fifty yards, is of a marshy nature. Water is found at a depth of from eight to ten feet, especially on the southern side of the city, for the general inclination of the ground is from north to south. Streams, which all run east and west, water the environs and supply the ditch; and it flows out on the south side opposite the large tower which forms the angle of the place called Khúrj Khákister, or Tower of Cinders.

" About three hundred yards south of the town is a canal with steep banks, supplied with water from the Hari-rúd, which is four miles distant from the city. On this canal are a great number of mills. It is fordable only at a few points. Little bridges, each of a single arch, have therefore been built at different points.

"There are five gates to the city of Herát.* To the north of it near the Meshed gate are two citadels—the New and the Old—nearly joining each other. The first commands the second, in which is an enormous round tower sometimes used as a viceregal palace.

"On the north side, likewise, parallel to the walls, and about one thousand two hundred and fifty yards from them, rises the long hill of Tálábingui forming a ridge on that side. Beyond this hill, at a distance of about one thousand yards, stands one of the most beautiful mosques ever built in Asia. It is surmounted by nine minarets, from the summit of which the interior of the town can be seen. Herát is not commanded by any of the hills in the environs; Tálábingui, which is used as a cemetry, is the highest."

So far Ferrier. Eldred Pottinger, who so nobly contributed to the defence of Herát when it was besieged by the Persians in 1837–8, gives a more vivid description of the capabilities of the place and district in his manuscript journal.† He confirms for it the title of "Gate of India." Within the country immediately about it all the great roads leading on India converge. By this route alone, he declares, could a well-equipped army make its way to the Indian frontier from the regions of the North-West.

* So also writes Captain Marsh, but the author of *Lost Among the Afghans*, who was present in Herát during its siege by the Persians in 1856–57, states that the number of the gates is seven, and that they are called after the direction to which they point, Kandáhár, Maimúna, Kábul, A'rak, Sistán, Gazargar, and Meshed.

† Kaye's "War in Afghánistán."

All the materials necessary for the organization of a great army, and for the formation of its depôts, are to be found in its neighbourhood. The plains are well watered and extraordinarily fertile. Its mines supply lead, iron, and sulphur. Saltpetre abounds. The willow and the poplar, which furnish the best charcoal, flourish in every part of the province; whilst, he adds, the population could supply a number of hardy and docile soldiers to assist an invader. The possession of Herát is in fact necessary to a successful invasion of India. Its possession by the power which rules in India would render any invasion of India dangerous to the invader; a successful invasion impossible.

Captain Marsh confirms in the main this view. After describing the city and the valley in which it lies, he adds, "as the land is fertile and the climate good, a few years would turn all this desert into a garden." Vambéry, who visited Herát in 1864, is a witness on the same side. He, too, speaks of its political importance, of the fertility of the soil surrounding it, of its ruined condition, of the hatred of its inhabitants for the Afgháns. Even Afgháns, he tells us, who settle there become invariably anti-Afghán in their sympathies.

Before dealing with the passes leading to India, I must ask the reader to return with me to Kandáhár and examine the country south-east by south of that town, that is the country between Kandáhár and Quetta.

This route leads straight from Kandáhár to the angle made by the Dórí as it bends to the westward, follows the course of that river to a point where the road strikes off to Mél Mándá: it runs thence along a narrow valley to the Gatai hills, and, crossing a long barren plain, traverses the Khojak Kótal pass down to the valleys of Kuchak and Pishin; thence the road to Quetta is easy. The distance is one hundred and fifty miles. The following is the route in detail.

Name of Place.	Elevation.	Distance.	Description.
Kandáhár . .	—	—	
Múnd Hissar .	—	12	The country between Kandáhár and Múnd Hissar is tolerably level, fertile, and well populated. The bed of the Tarnak is crossed *en route.*
Mákú . .	—	16	The route is level, though broken into ravines, and the fertility decreases. The river Árghesán, one of the tributaries of the Helmand, is crossed about midway.
Mél Mándá .	—	18	The road crosses the Bárgháná Pass at an elevation of 4,100 feet, and descends into the valley of the Dórí. Here all cultivation ceases. The waters of the river, though abundant, are slightly saline. Its banks are unfertile; there is no grass, and but little cultivation. The population is scanty. The road leaves the Dórí at Takht-i-Pál, and branches off at right angles across an undulating, though rather barren country to Mél Mándá.
Gatai . .	—	14	From Mél Mándá to Gatai is a distance of fourteen miles across a country not dissimilar. The Gatai hills are a low range, covered with stones, extremely barren, and cut up by ravines.

Name of Place.	Elevation.	Distance.	Description.
Dand-i-Guláh .	4000	6	The road runs across a barren plain; but here, sweet water, often scarce at Gatai, is to be found.
Cháokah . .	5600	19	From Dand-i-Guláh the road gradually rises, especially after passing Cháman, across an undulating plain to the foot of the hill, Cháokah. Here the temperature is very pleasant, and wild plants and fruits abound.

From this point to summit of the Khojak Kotal pass is an ascent of one thousand eight hundred and ten feet. The pass, high as it is, is commanded on either side by the Khoja A'mrán mountains. I have been assured by a very high authority, who gleaned it on the spot, that the pass can always be turned, provided the waters of the Lora do not run dry. From its summit the descent for the first two miles is very steep, but as the more level country is approached and the villages of the Dehsúri glen are reached the declension becomes much more moderate. At the distance of some twenty miles from the summit lies the village of Arámbi.

From this place runs for fifteen miles a tolerably level road across the Lora river to Haikalzai, a prosperous village on a plain of red clay, in the Pishín valley. From Haikalzai a very fair road leads across an easily traversable pass to Kachlak, a distance of eighteen miles. Kachlak is the first village situated in Balúchístán proper, in the direct road to Quetta. As to the proper boundary of that country, difference of opinion would seem to prevail; but if the Tukátú range be within the border line of Balúchístán, the actual boundary will be represented by a line drawn immediately north of that hill south-westward by west cutting the road between Haidarzai and Kachlak about midway.* From Kachlak to Quetta the distance must be about twelve miles.

Before describing the passes, I may advert for a moment to three other places of some importance, and to which reference will be made in the subsequent part of this book, mainly to mark their situation in the map. Thus, eighteen miles nearly due north of Kábul, in the Kóh Dámán, lies the town of Istálif, beautifully situated, and having, with the hamlets dependent upon it, a population of eighteen thousand. Twenty miles again north of Istálif, at the north end of the Koh Damán, is Cháríkár, with five thousand inhabitants, carrying on a brisk trade with Turkistán. Last of all, Bámián, to the north-west of Kábul beyond the Unai pass, the summit of which attains a height of eleven thousand four hundred feet, and under the soaring snow-clad peaks of the Koh-i-Bábá, eighteen thousand feet above the level of the sea.

The chief passes and routes leading from British India into Afghánistán are the Khaibar, the Kúrm, the Gomal, the Sakhi Sarwar, and the Bolan. There are others, smaller, to which it may be necessary to

* The country of Balochistán, by A. W. Hughes.

refer, but I take these in their order, entering them from British territory.

The road from Jalálábád through the Khaibar pass to Pesháwar has been described in a previous page. The entrance of the pass from the Panjáb is at Kadam, a small village, three miles westward of Jamrúd. Between this village and Pesháwar is a plain, which takes its name after that place, and makes a gradual ascent of about six hundred feet from it to Jamrúd.

The distance from Pesháwar to Jamrúd is about sixteen miles. The latter is a small village, surrounded by a mud wall, and having near it the ruins of a fort built by the Sikhs in 1837. It is in no sense profitable as a military position to an invader from India, as it is dependent for its water on the Kábul river, and the supply of it could always be cut off by the hill tribes. Three miles to the west of it is Kadam, the real gate of the pass. The approach to this is extremely formidable. Advancing to it from Jamrúd, the mountains on either side gradually close in. After entering the gorge of Kadam, the width of the valley greatly decreases. Little more than half a mile from the entrance it does not exceed four hundred and fifty feet, and it diminishes as further progress is made. The cliffs on either side are in many places steep and precipitous, in others practicable on one side or the other. Approching A'li Masjíd they are not practicable. They rise to a height of about one thousand three hundred feet above the plain.

The distance from Jamrúd to A'li Masjíd is about

eight miles. The width of the pass contracts greatly in parts, not exceeding forty feet in some places, whilst in others it covers nearly three hundred. It is narrowest in the defile leading to the fort of A'li Masjíd. Here the hills are extremely wild and precipitous; and, as previously stated, are entirely impracticable. From their sides formidable rocks jut out, commanding the entire glen below them. From that glen the heights may well seem inaccessible. The mosque from which the fortress of A'li Masjíd derives its name is in the valley below it. The main fort stands on the summit of a lofty hill, isolated and difficult of access, to the south-west of the road. It is connected by a weak wall with a smaller fort on the same hill. The southern and western faces of both are, however, commanded by two hills higher than that upon which the fortress stands. Even, then, if A'li Masjíd could not be turned, it offers no insuperable obstacle to a determined enemy. But, as I shall show presently, the fortress can be turned.

Beyond A'li Masjíd the nature of the defile remains unaltered. For half a mile its width is but little affected, but then it gradually increases, the hills maintaining their varied character, generally inaccessible, but occasionally easy. At the Látábeg valley, nearly nine miles from A'li Masjíd, the average width increases to a mile and a half. Half a mile further on, however, it diminishes to ten feet or less, with perpendicular hills on either side!

Half a mile beyond this, the Landikháná pass is traversed. The width of the road at this point is one hundred and forty feet; the hills continuing very steep, especially those on the left. From this point to the opening of the pass at Dáká, the width ranges from three hundred to two hundred feet, the hills being steep on either side. The road lies through the bed of the river, and except at the Landíkháná pass the gradient is generally easy.

Difficult as the Khaibar pass is, it can be turned. For instance, by the Tátara road, which enters the hills about nine miles north of Jamrúd, and keeping north of the Khaibar range falls into the Jalálábád road at Dáká. The Abkhána road, the Karapa road, the Sháh Bágádi road, also avoid A'li Masjíd, and are traversable.

To the west of the Khaibar is the route by the Kúrm river. Thal, the starting point for this route, is a village in the Kóhát district, sixty-six miles south-west of the station of that name, which, again, is thirty-seven miles south of Peshávar. From Banú it lies forty-two miles due north. The distance between Thal and Kábul and Thal and Ghazní are respectively one hundred and sixty-eight and one hundred and ninety-two miles. The road for the first fifty miles to the Kúrm fort lies through a fertile though unhealthy country. The fort is strong, but not defensible against modern artillery. It is a place of some importance, having been the seat of a provincial government in the time of the Ghorian sovereigns; and in a military sense it retains that importance still. From the Kúrm fort to Haidar Khail, where the route strikes into the Ghazní and Kábul road, the distance is one hundred and twenty miles: thence to Ghazní twenty-two miles. The direct road to Kábul strikes off at Kúshí, eighty miles from the Kúrm fort.

The district of Kúrm is one of the most fertile in Afghánistán.

The Gomal route is the next that deserves attention. This route leads from Derá-Ishmáil-Khán to Ghazní and to Kandáhár. From Derá-Ishmáil-Khán to Tánk within our frontier the distance is forty-two miles. The entrance to the Gomal pass is sixteen miles to the westward of Tánk. The road through the pass follows the river Gomal, which is believed not to be formidable, to Arsúk, a village on that river. From Arsúk to Ghazní, by a road skirting the Mahsúd Vazírí country, are sixteen marches; from Arsúk to Kandáhár, by a south-westerly route, eighteen marches. On both routes provisions are abundant, but the tribes might be hostile.

Of the other routes between the Gomal and the Bolan the Sakhi Sarwar seems alone to demand special notice. Sakhi Sarwar lies thirty-five miles south-west from Derá-Ghazní-Khán. From it to the further end of the pass at Rákni the distance is about sixty-seven miles. The pass is narrow and difficult. "No camels, fully laden," says MacGregor, "can travel by this route, and it is difficult even for half-laden ones; no two horsemen can go abreast up the ascent, but have to dismount and lead their beasts. . . . No supplies are procurable from the mouth of the pass until the village of Rákni, in the Khetrán country, is reached." I have been assured, however, that since this description was penned, a traversable road has been made up the pass by the British authorities at Derá Gházi Khán. A road has also been made up the Charchar pass to the Shám plain, from which table-land the country is open to the head of the Sakhi Sarwar pass. A practicable road from Rajánpúr and Mithankót to Tall Chatiáli and Pishín is thus available. Although it has never been traversed by Europeans it is highly spoken of by natives.

It is worthy to be noted that the whole of the western portion of this route passes through the lands of the Kakar Patháns. The eastern portion traverses the lands of the Laghári Bilúchis and the Khetráns—an independent tribe, half Bilúchi and half Afghán.

I come now to the Bolan. To the entrance to this pass, near Dadar, there are two routes—the one starting from Rajánpúr, and proceeding by Derá Bibrák and Sangúla; the other from Sakkar by Jacobábád. Of the Bolan pass it need only be stated that it is comparatively open and easy for all arms, and that by the possession of Quetta we command it.

Much more might be written on the subject of the minor passes, and of the passes generally. But it is sufficient, I think, to lay before the reader a general view of those routes only which are likely to be traversed by a British army. By the possession of Quetta, on the Afghán side of the Bolan, that army possesses a base from which it can operate against the most vulnerable and important portions of the territories of the Amír, the provinces indicated by the names of Kandáhár and Herát.

I turn now to the people of Afghánistán, to the tribes who occupy the country, and who command the passes. The subject has been treated at great length by Mountstuart Elphinstone, by Ferrier—who quotes largely from Abdúllah Khán, of Herát,—by Bellew, and by many others.

Following Abdúllah Khán and other Afghán writers, Ferrier is disposed to believe that the Afgháns represent the lost ten tribes, and to claim for them descent from Saul, King of Israel. Amongst other writers concurring in this view may be mentioned the honoured name of Sir William Jones. On the other hand, Professor Dorn, of Kharkov, who examined the subject at length, rejects this theory. Mountstuart Elphinstone classes it in the same category as the theory of the descent of the Romans from the Trojans. The objections to Abdúllah Khán's view have been recently expressed, fittingly and forcibly, by Professor Dowson, in a letter to the *Times*. "If," writes that gentleman, "it were worthy of consideration, it is still inconsistent with the notion that the Afgháns are descendants of the lost ten tribes. Saul was of the tribe of Benjamin, and that tribe was not one of the lost ten. There remains the question of feature. This, no doubt, has its weight, but cannot prevail against the more important question of language." Professor Dowson then proceeds to show that the Afghán language has no trace of Hebrew in it, and concludes by pronouncing the supposition that in the course of time the whole Afghán race could have changed their language as "too incredible."

The clans forming the Afghán nation proper are very numerous. Including the Patháns—who, though descended from the same stock, speaking the same language, following the same religion, observing the same customs, and inhabiting the same country, are not recognized as pure Afgháns by the Afgháns—they are said to number two million three hundred and fifty-nine thousand. The Mahomedans who are not Afgháns, to be presently referred to, number one million two hundred and fifty thousand; and the non-Mahomedans perhaps five hundred thousand. These are distinct from the feudatory tribes north of the Hindú Kúsh, who amount in number nearly to eight hundred thousand.

The Afghán genealogies trace the four tribal divisions of their nation to Sarában, Ghúrghúsht, Bítni, and Karleh, the four sons of Kyse Abd-ú-rashíd. But Afghán legends are not to be depended upon, and the fact stands out that although the names still figure in the genealogies, the divisions are no longer used.

The principal tribes are the Dúránís, the Ghilzais, the Kákars, the Wardaks, the Povindahs, and the Berdúránís, all subdivided into many branches. Of these tribes the Dúránís and the Ghilzais are the most powerful—the former from the possession by their clan of the sovereignty; the latter from their considerable numbers and their sturdy independence of character.

The Dúránís are supreme in south and south-western Afghánistán. Elphinstone makes five divisions of their territory. These are bounded on the north by the Paropamisan range, on the west by a sandy desert separating them from Persia; on the south-west by Sístán; on the south by Shorábak and the Khoja Amrán range; on the east, without possessing any natural boundary, their territory joins the lands of the Ghilzais. It thus comprises Ferrah and the places between it and Kandáhár, including, or partially including, Kandáhár itself.

Little is known of the earlier history of this tribe. Until the time of Ahmad Sháh—of him who fought and gained the third battle of Pánipat—they were known as the Abdáli, from Abdál, their reputed founder. In consequence, it is said, of a dream, Ahmad Sháh changed the name to Dúráni, taking himself the title of Sháh Dúrí Dúrán. They are divided into two great branches, the Zirek and the Panjpá, the names of the two grandsons of Abdál. From these branches sprang nine clans, four from Zirek and five from Panjpá.

Of these nine clans the Pápalzye is the chief; and it is from the eldest branch of the Pápalzye—the Sádozye, that proceeded the legitimate sovereigns who ruled Afghánistán in the seventeenth and eighteenth centuries. It is probable that from the very infancy of the tribe this branch was supreme, for their title to that supremacy was recognized by one of the first of the Safavi kings of Persia. The privileges accorded to them by the general consent of the clan were enormous. Their persons were sacred; no punishment could be inflicted upon them except by a member of the family; nor could the head of the

Abdáli clan himself pass sentence of death upon a Sádozye. But time has lessened these privileges.

The clan next in importance to the Sádozyes, and exceeding it in numbers, is the Bárukzye. The most distinguished branch of this clan is the Mahomedzye. It was the representative of this branch, Dost Mahammad Khan, who supplanted the Sadozyes, and it is its representative, Shír Ali, who now rules in Afghánistán.

The purpose of this book does not allow me to follow the remaining branches and collateral issues of the Duránís. It will suffice to state that they are the most civilized, the most tolerant, and the most popular of all the Afghán tribes ; and the rule of a member of their clan is universally acquiesced in.

Next in importance to the Duránís, in some respects even surpassing them in importance, are the Ghilzais. Stubborn, revengeful, jealous of the Duránís, yet faithful to them when warring against a foreign enemy, the Ghilzais have played, and must always continue to play, a great rôle in the history of their country. The lands they occupy include the cities of Kábul and of Ghazní. They extend from the lofty plateau north of Kandáhár eastward to the Súlimáni range, and they stretch down the Kábul river to Jalálábád. Roughly speaking, their country may be said to form a parallelogram of which the length is about a hundred and eighty and the breadth about eighty-five miles. Several of the valleys tenanted by them run up to the Hindú-Kúsh and the Saféd-Koh.

The Ghilzais have a great past. In the beginning

of the last century this tribe conquered Persia, seated a king on the throne of Ispahán, and routed the armies of the Ottoman Porte. The third king of the race was expelled from Persia by Nádir Sháh. But they did not resign all hope of ultimate victory. A representative of the clan, Abdúrahím Khán, struggled subsequently for the throne. Fortune did not favour him, and with his failure the pent-up feeling of hatred for the Duránís greatly subsided. The rivalry, which formerly extended to the whole tribe, shows itself now merely in outbreaks of personal feeling. Not only is the sovereignty of the representative of the rival clan admitted, but in all matters affecting the independence of the country that representative has had no more devoted followers than the ancient rivals of his own tribe.

The Kákars occupy a mountainous range about a hundred miles square in the south-east of the country. They are in appearance and behaviour perfect savages. It is chiefly owing to the extreme wildness and lawlessness of this tribe that the Tall Chatiálí route to India has been for so many years closed. They are said to be broken up into small sections, not acknowledging any one head, and scarcely recognizing the Amír.

The Wardaks dwell in cultivated valleys bounded on three sides by the Ghilzai country and on the west by the Ghor mountains. They are, by comparison, a quiet, obedient tribe, devoted to agriculture.

The Povindahs are a tribe of soldier merchants, numbering about 12,000. Twice every year their caravans leave Ghazní for Hindústán and return, carrying merchandise, and fighting their way, if necessary, through the passes. They carry their trade likewise to the other great centres of central Asia, such as Herát, Kandáhár, Kábul, and Bokhára. They are one of the institutions of Afghánistán, their trade having continued now, on the same basis as that on which it now exists, for nearly four hundred years.

The Baraichis occupy Shorábak, a country about sixty miles square between the Khójah Amran range and Pishín. They are a simple people, possessing many camels, which they use to draw the plough.

Pishín is inhabited by the Tor Taríns. Their principal occupation is agriculture, for which they use bullocks, though camels are plentiful. The valley is sixty miles long by thirty, and very fertile. Another tribe of the Taríns, called the Spín Taríns, possess the country extending from the vicinity of Pishín to the Súlimáni range. This country includes the long valley of Zaíourá and the open plains Tall and Chútiáli. These people are considered brave and inoffensive.

The Hazáras and the Aimaks dwell in the lofty regions of north-western Afghánistán, stretching as far as the country above Herát. The Hazáras are Tartars by descent, simple-hearted, and differ much from the Afghán tribes. In physiognomy they more resemble the Chinese. Although Mahomedans, they belong to the Shiáh persuasion, and give but a qualified allegiance to the Amír. The Aimaks are a cognate tribe, of Moghol origin. The women of both tribes have great influence, and go unveiled.

In addition to these races there dwell in Afghánistán the Kuzilbáshis, a race of Persian descent, generally resident in towns, and constituting as it were the bulk of the more intellectual middle class. They are better educated than the Afgháns. Their intelligence is apparent from the fact that the Afghán artillery is principally recruited from their ranks.

In a somewhat lower stratum of society are the Hindkis, or men of Hindú descent settled in Afghánistán; and in one lower still, are the Játs—probably a Mahomedan branch of the great family of the *Getæ*. Whilst the Kuzilbáshis are mostly merchants, traders, and physicians; and the Hindkis bankers; the Játs are farm-servants, sweepers, or musicians.

I turn now to the tribes inhabiting the north-eastern part of the country, enclosed between Hindú-Kúsh, the Indus, the Salt Range, and the Súlimáni. These tribes are comprehended under the general name of Berdúrání, but they are more often spoken of by the distinct names of the clans into which they are divided. I shall deal with them according to the order from east to west in which they occupy the country.

I must begin by reminding the reader that, using general terms, our north-west frontier may be described as an irregular line, following the forms of the mountains which separate the intervening valley from the river Indus. The tribes who occupy the western slopes of those mountains are subject to the Amír of Kábul. Those on the eastern slope, overlooking the Indus valley, are practically independent.

The Kágán valley, some twenty miles broad, occupies the space between Káshmír and the independent Kohistáni tribes, and forms the easternmost point of our frontier. The tribes located here occupy the Black Mountain, east of the Indus. They are principally the Hasanzai and Kohistánís, with a sprinkling of Chagúrzais and Swátís, emigrants from the neighbouring hills and valleys. They can collect from two thousand to three thousand fighting men; but they have shown on two occasions that as warriors they are not formidable.

Below Kágán, but west of the Indus, in the Yúsafzai country, directly opposite Hazára, at a corner of the Peshάwar valley, is the Mahában mountain. The district in which this mountain rises borders on Tanáwal, the chief town of which is Amb, on the Indus, and its ruler is tributary to the British Government. On the eastern slopes of Mahában are the Amazais, counting one thousand two hundred fighting men; on the northern slopes the Atmanzais, one thousand two hundred strong; and on the southern slopes, overlooking the Gúsapzai plain, are the Jadúns, able to muster two thousand five hundred warriors.

Immediately north of the Mahában range is the valley of Chamla. Chamla is politically a part of Búnér, to which it is joined by a spur of the Gúrú mountain. It is accessible from the Yúsafzai plain by several passes, but of these the passes of Ambéla and Malandára are the easiest. The tribes inhabiting these valleys belong to the great Yúsafzai clan. They are estimated to be able to turn out about six thousand fighting men.

Settled amongst these tribes are the Hindústání fanatics known as the Sitáná Wáhábís. They occupy the village of Sitáná, and are bitterly hostile to the British. It was to punish them that the Ambéla campaign of 1863 was undertaken. They are said to be able to muster one thousand two hundred fighting men.

North of Búnér is the extensive valley of Swát, inhabited by branches of the Akozai Yúsafzais. The Swát valley has a length of some seventy miles, and a breadth varying from a few hundred yards to ten miles. The south-western portion of it is separated from British territory by a range of hills extending from the Búnér border to the Swát river, where it emerges from the hills into the Yúsafzai plains. Of the eleven passes by which it is connected with this plain, three only, those of Mora, Shakot, and Malakhand, are considered easy. "Swát," says Dr. Bellew,* in a little pamphlet from which I have often quoted, "Swat is a very important country in connection with the approach to India from the north-west. Through it, by Bajáwar and the Hindúráj pass into Kúnar, is the main route to Jalálábád and Kábul. Alexander the Great and the Emperor Bábar both entered India by this route, and it has also been used by columns of most of the invading armies of the Ghaznívides and Moghols." The Swát valley numbers a population of about one hundred thousand, and, including the contiguous tribes of Bajáwar and Dír, can turn out eighteen thousand fighting men.

* "Our Panjáb Frontier," by a Panjáb Official. Calcutta, 1868.

Between the Kábul and Swát rivers, to the north-west of Peshawar, is the country inhabited by the Mohmands. "The low, bare hills lying between those rivers," says Bellew, "rise towards the north into the lofty Kohimor mountain which forms the boundary between the Mohmands and the Tarkilánís of Bajawar. Towards Kábul these hills open on the Jalálábád plain and the Kúnar valley, whilst towards Pesháwar they abut on the Doába plain (in the angle of the junction between the Swát and Kábul rivers), which is British territory. Towards the south the Mohmands occupy a strip of hills on the right bank of the Kábul river, which, in its course through their country, is thus entirely in their hands." Through their territory runs likewise the Abkhána and Karappa routes from Pesháwar to Jalálábád, referred to in a previous page as routes which turn or avoid the fortress of Ali Masjíd. The chief town of the Mohmands is Lálpúra, on the left bank of the Kábul river, and opposite the western entrance to the Khaibar pass. They are a very powerful clan. The six tribes into which they are divided are called the Tarakzai, the Halúnzai, the Baizai, the Khwazai, the U'tmánzai, and the Dáwézai. Their fighting strength has been calculated at from ten to sixteen thousand men. Their alliance, however, can be purchased. "The Mohmands, like all Patháns," writes Macgregor, "are very fond of talking about Pathán honour, but they are not the less amenable to golden influences, and there is no doubt they would sell or prostitute any thing, or kill anyone, for gold. As a native official, who knows them well, says, 'You have only to put a rupee in your eye and you may look at any Mohmand, man or woman.'" The Mohmands are nominally subject to the Amír, but they pay him no taxes, and are really independent.

The extensive hill region between the Kábul river, round the spurs projecting from the eastern end of the Saféd-Koh to the Kúrm valley, as far as the Pewár pass, is occupied by the Afrídís, the Arakzais, and by Zwáimukhts, Afgháns, and Torís. The Afrídí territory begins from the right bank of the Kábul river, and extends for fifty miles due south in contact with British territory the whole distance. A tongue of Afrídí territory interposes between Pesháwar and Kohát, directly interrupting the communication between the two places. This tongue is traversed by the Kohát pass, some fifteen miles in length by four in breadth. We pay the Afrídís a subsidy to keep this pass open for us, but the arrangement is a bad one. The Afrídís will not allow the road to be improved, and though neither steep nor difficult, it is much obstructed by huge rocks. The connection of the Afrídís with the English has caused much bloodshed, and has necessitated many expeditions—the last being that undertaken nearly a year ago against the Jáwáki Afrídís, who hold the eastern tower on the crest of the pass.* There is a good gun road from the crest of the pass into Kohát.

The Afrídís can send twenty thousand men into the field. They are the best armed and most warlike of

* The centre tower is held by the Bangash tribe; the western by the Sípáhs.

all the frontier tribes. They are quite independent of the Amír.

Their neighbours, the Arakzais, are nearly as numerous. They occupy the country south of the Afrídís, and spread on to the Kúrm valley, along the eastern and southern offshoots from the Saféd Koh. They can muster eighteen thousand armed men. They are independent of the Amír, and trade directly with the British.

The Zwaimukhts, the Afgháns, and the Torís, the next neighbours of the Arakzais, occupy the Kúrm valley as far as the Powar pass. They are subject to the Amír. They can bring eight thousand men into the field.

The Vazírís, who next demand attention, occupy the country to the west of the trans-Indus frontier from Thal in Míranzai to the Gomal pass. They hold both sides of this pass, which is the great route by which the trade of Afghánistán and central Asia passes into India. They muster about twenty thousand fighting men.

Below the Vazírís are the Shiránís and Ashtaránís. The former occupy the Takht-i-Súlimán, or Kaisagarh, and the hills which surround its base. They can turn out about four thousand fighting men. Agriculturists by pursuit, they are likewise plunderers by profession, and are constantly warring on their neighbours. In their country is Zárkáni, from which the great caravans start for Kandáhár.

The Ashtáránís occupy the Súlimán range from a little south of the Takht-i-Súlimán to the Khúri pass on the Déra Ishmáil frontier. They are a small tribe numbering about one thousand warriors. The Khúri pass is the southern limit of the independent Pathán tribes. South of this point come the Balúchís, who are partly independent, settled within the British border.

Such are the frontier tribes. "In general terms," writes Dr. Bellew, whose long and varied service on the frontier invests his opinion with the highest authority, "in general terms they may be described as utter barbarians (some perhaps less so than others), steeped in the grossest ignorance. By birth they are savages, by profession robbers. Beyond the care of their flocks and fields, they follow no industrial pursuits. Under no authority at home, they are constantly at feud with each other, and at hostility with their neighbours. Murder and robbery are with them mere pastimes; revenge and plunder the occupation of their lives. The circumstances under which they live have endowed them with the most opposite qualities—an odd mixture of virtues and vices.

"Thus they are hardy, brave, and proud; at the same time they are faithless, cunning, and treacherous. Frugal in their own habits, they are hospitable to the stranger and charitable to the beggar. The refugee they will protect and defend with their lives, but the innocent wayfarer they will plunder and slay for the pleasure of the act. Patriotic in a high degree, and full of pride in race, yet they will not scruple to betray for gold their most sacred interests or their nearest relations. Professedly they are Mahommedans, but their knowledge of the religion is very hazy, and they never hesitate to set aside its tenets when they happen to be opposed to their desires or interests. They are nevertheless extremely bigoted, are entirely controlled by their priests, and are at all times ready for a *jahâd* (crusade), be the infidels black or white.

"Secure in the recesses of their mountains, they have from time immemorial defied the authority of all governments (barbarous governments) that have preceded us on this frontier, and, gathering courage from their success, have for centuries been the terror of the peaceful cultivators on the plain, whose crops and cattle, whose maidens and wives, they have looked upon as fair game for plunder. Lastly, disunited by mutual jealousies and clan feuds, they are incapable by themselves of combining in a common enterprise distant from their hills; but they have never failed, on the passage of invading armies from the west, to swarm down from their mountain retreats to swell the ranks of the plunderers, in the hope of reaping a rich harvest in the plains of India."

Such is the character of the tribes. In the chapter which will be devoted to the review of the action of the Government of India on the frontier, I shall have much to say of their conduct.

CHAPTER II.

HISTORICAL.—THE GHAZNIVIDE PERIOD.

According to Hanway, the oldest European authority who treats of the Afgháns, the Abdáli tribe, then dwelling in the eastern part of Herát, embraced towards the end of the ninth century the Mahomedan religion, and communicated it to the remainder of the Afghán people.

At this period Khorásán and Transoxiána were governed by princes of the house of Sámáni. Their capital was Bokhára. The sway of this house would seem to have extended over a great part of Central Asia, including the country now known as Afghánistán. It lasted a hundred and twenty years, and it was during that period that we find the territories of which I am about to treat first coming into prominence.

Abdúlmelek, fifth prince of the house of Sámání, had raised to high honours and dignities a Túrki slave, named Alptegín, and had finally conferred upon him the government of Khorásán. Abdúlmelek died in the year 961. On his death the high officers of state assembled to choose a successor from the members of the royal family. Every chief, with the exception of Alptegín, voted for Mansúr. Mansúr consequently ascended the throne. He at once showed his sense of Alptegín's adverse vote by depriving him of his government.

Other persecutions followed this arbitrary act, and Alptegín, finding his life threatened, rebelled. Followed by some three thousand Túrkís he escaped to Ghazní, and proclaiming himself independent, bade defiance to the Sámánís. The inhabitants of Herát, of Sístán, and of Balkh, remained faithful to the Sámánís; but those of the eastern parts rallied round Alptegín, and enabled him to bid defiance to his liege lord. For fourteen years he maintained and strengthened his position.

On the death of Alptegín, in A.D. 976, a Túrkí slave, named Sabaktagín, who, it is said, had married his daughter, succeeded him.* It was in the reign of this prince that the countries now known as Afghánistán and India came first into contact. Whatever may have been the provocation, the invasion came from the side of India.

At that time Jaipál was Rájá of the country now known as the Panjáb, but then called Láhor. His rule extended from Múltán to Kashmír, and from Sirhind to the plain of Peshâwar. It would appear that the establishment of an independent Mahomedan kingdom at Ghazní had alarmed this Hindú ruler for the

* Ferishta states that Isaak, son of Alptegín, was his immediate successor; but that he lived only two years, leaving the kingdom to his brother-in-law, Sabaktegín.

security of his dominions, and this alarm had been increased by the continued and unchecked raids of his neighbours. He determined, therefore, to anticipate more active proceedings on their part by becoming himself the invader. He crossed the Indus, then, with his army, and moved over the plain which separates Pesháwar from Jamrúd. There he was met by Sabaktagín. Before, however, the two armies could engage a furious tempest supervened. This storm so disconcerted Jaipál that he offered to treat for peace. Sabaktagín was at first unwilling, but in the end he agreed to permit his enemy to retire across the Indus, on condition of yielding at once fifty elephants, and paying, on his return to Láhor, a considerable sum for the expenses of the war. Jaipál complied with the first condition, but evaded the second.

Indignant at this breach of faith, Sabaktagín, who had returned to Ghazní, resolved to enforce the condition. He therefore once again marched towards Pesháwar. To meet the coming danger, Jaipál invoked the aid of the Rájás of Dehli, of Ajmír, of Kálinjar, and of Kanáoj. This aid was readily afforded, and at the head of a large and well-appointed force, Jaipál marched to the Pesháwar plain, and took up a position at Laghmán. Upon him here encamped Sabaktagín issued from the Khaibar pass. The force of the Ghazní chieftain consisted largely of cavalry. Keeping the enemy's wings in check with his marksmen, Sabaktagín made repeated and continuous charges with his horse on their centre. When he thought this sufficiently shaken he ordered a general assault along the whole line. The effect was decisive. The Indian army was beaten; their camp fell into the hands of the victor, and by him the country up to the banks of the Indus was annexed. A trusted officer, at the head of ten thousand horse, was appointed Governor of Pesháwar.*

Thus secure on his eastern frontier, Sabaktagín set to work to extend and settle his own dominions. Kandáhár was occupied and annexed. Shortly afterwards he was summoned to Bokhára by Nóh, or Noah, the representative of the Sámání kings, to quell a rebellion in that country. By the intervention of Sabaktagín the rebellion was quelled, and whilst he himself was confirmed by the Sámáni in his own government, that of Khorásán was confided to his son Máhmúd. Sabaktagín died when returning from this expedition.

"Sabaktagín," writes Ferrier, quoting, as I understand, from Abdúllah Khán, of Herát, "may be considered as the first sovereign who reigned over Afghánistán properly so called; but the Afgháns, in consequence of his Tartar origin, looked upon him and his descendants as tyrants and usurpers, and thought little of his good deeds and the benefits he conferred upon them." The truth of this judgment is borne witness to by the revolt of the Ghilzais occurring in the reign of his successor.

The natural successor of Sabaktagín was his eldest son Mahmúd, then in his thirtieth year. But Mahmúd was absent from the capital at his government of

* Briggs's "Ferishta," vol. i.

Nishápor (in Khorásán); and the younger brother, Ishmáil, seized the reins of power. The possession of the treasury enabled him to obtain from the leading men of the government oaths of allegiance and promises of support.

But Mahmúd was a very capable prince: hardy, active, a warrior from his cradle, accustomed to deal with men, and conscious of his own innate power. He offered at first no violent opposition to his brother. He contented himself by pointing out to him that the task of governing the wild tribes who had obeyed his father would be too much for him, but that he might manage Balkh and Khorásán: that if he would yield the remainder he might have those. Ishmáil refused; whereupon Mahmúd marched upon Ghazní. Ishmáil hastened from Balkh to cover his capital. In the battle which followed Mahmúd was the victor. Ishmáil, who was taken prisoner, passed the remainder of his days in confinement. His relationship to the conqueror shut him out from any position but a prison or a throne, and he had refused the latter. He was treated in other respects with kindness and consideration.

The ruler of Ghazní was still nominally a vassal of the king of Bokhára. On the death of Sabaktagín, the sovereign of that country, Abúl Mansúr, encouraged by the contest raging between the two brothers, nominated a creature of his own, Amír Túzan Bég, to the governorship of Ghazní. Mahmúd remonstrated. In reply he was informed that he had already Balkh, Húrmúz, and Herát, and that the favours of his suzerain must be divided; that, on that account, he had deemed it right to bestow Ghazní upon one who had always been a good and faithful servant to his lord. This conduct on the part of Abúl Mansúr was fraught with ruin to the house of which he was the representative.* Whilst Mahmúd, failing again in a conciliatory policy, raised an army to watch events, treason was busily at work in the camp of his rash and inflated suzerain. The "good and faithful servant," Túzan Bég, to whom he had given the government of Ghazní, conspired with the minister against him, put out his eyes, and raised his brother, a minor, to the throne. The conspirators hurried on to Mérv, where they were attacked and defeated by Mahmúd. This misfortune was not solitary. I'lák Khán, ruler of Káshgár, seized the opportunity to march on Bokhára, slay the boy sovereign, and annex the whole of Transoxiána. With the boy's death the house of Sámáni ceased to exist.

Mahmúd was now independent ruler of Afghánistán, including the countries now known as Afghán Turkistán and Badákshán. His first care was to settle his own territories. He then turned his attention to the country conquered by his father from Rájá Jaipál, on the west bank of the Indus. Into these he introduced order, strengthening the forts, and placing in them garrisons under trusted soldiers. Returning then to Ghazní, he cemented a firm alliance with the king of Bokhára by a marriage with his daughter. At

* The house of Sámáni.

the same time he paid attention to the organization of courts of civil and criminal justice throughout his territories.

No sooner had Mahmúd arranged these matters to his satisfaction than his soaring spirit began to pant for new fields of glory. Instinctively he turned his thoughts to India. He had served with his father in the campaign against Jaipál. He had witnessed the ease with which the vast hosts of the enemy had been overthrown by his hardy troopers: and he believed that those vast hosts, or others not one whit their superior, were the sole defenders of the fabled riches of India. Mahmúd was the ruler of the country which was rich only in rocks and stones; but India boasted of wealthy cities, of fertile plains, of temples piled up with gold and precious stones. Rich in these respects as India then was, the imagination painted her as richer still. What wonder, then, that Mahmúd, young, daring, and ambitious, living in an age and in a country when the right of the strongest was recognized as the highest law; what wonder that he, having settled the affairs of his house and of his country, should resolve to invade that land of bright promise!

He invaded it. In the month of August 1001,* Mahmúd set out with ten thousand chosen horse from

* Professor Dowson ("Elliot's History of India," Appendix, Note D.) refers to a story, in which he says there is no improbability, that Mahmúd made a successful expedition to the frontier towns of India in the year preceding. But the accounts are very vague.

Ghazní. But his father's old antagonist, Jaipál, had already levied an army and had crossed the Indus. The rivals met on the 27th of November in the plain of Peshávar. The forces were unequal. Jaipál is said to have disposed of thirty thousand infantry, twelve thousand horse, and three hundred elephants. Mahmúd had only ten thousand horse. But whilst the latter were proved warriors it is easy to conjecture that two-thirds of the Indian army were soldiers merely for the occasion. The result was fatal to Jaipál. Not only was he defeated with great slaughter, but he himself, with fifteen of his principal chiefs, was taken prisoner. Released on the promise of the payment of a yearly tribute, Jaipál returned to Láhor and resigned his crown to his son A'nand-pál. He then placed himself on a funeral pile, and, lighting it with his own hands, perished in the flames.

Mahmúd pursued his advantage over the Indians, took and plundered Waihind, an important town on the Indus, some fifteen miles above A'tok, and often the seat of the court of the King of Láhor,* and then returned to Ghazní. In November of the year following, 1002, he made a successful expedition to Sístán.

A'nand-pál, meanwhile, continued to pay his tribute; but one of his feudatories, the Rájá of Bhéra, a town on the left bank of the Jailam under the

* Professor Dowson effectually disposes of the fable that Mahmúd crossed the Satlaj, and marched on Batinda. Waihind is the modern Húnd. *Vide* "Elliot's History," Appendix, Note D.

Salt Range, was not so compliant. The walls of Bhéra were high; the ditches were deep. Behind these the Rájá thought he could safely bid defiance to the Túrki cavalry. But Mahmúd was not the man to brook defiance. He set forth at the head of his troops (1004), and marching by the valley of Banú, and following the course of the Khúram, crossed the Indus near I'sákhél and the old town of Rorí, and, passing the Sind-Ságar Doáb, through Mitta Tiwána, reached Bhéra by way of Kusháb and Shahpúr.*

The defiant Rájá, Bijai Singh by name, was a brave and skilful soldier. He had taken care to fortify and strengthen the outlying posts leading to Bhéra, and he had garrisoned them with his bravest soldiers. Mahmúd was not accustomed to the warfare thus imposed upon him. His soldiers suffered, and—for the first time—they murmured. For three days the detached forts barred their progress, and strewed the ground with dead. The abandonment of the enterprise was discussed. But on the fourth day victory crowned the assailants in an attack led by Mahmúd in person.

Still the town with its high walls and its deep ditch remained. Mahmúd appeared before it, and, in spite of every obstacle, succeeded in filling up the ditch. Disheartened, Bijai Singh determined to retire from the town with his main force, leaving only a small detachment to defend it. But Mahmúd received notice of

* Professor Dowson, *ut supra.*

his enemy's designs. He intercepted the retreat. The enemy's soldiers, surprised, attempted to escape. The Rájá, to avoid being taken prisoner, turned his sword against his breast. The same night the town was stormed, and, with its dependencies, was added to the kingdom of Ghazní.

The following year, 1005, the ruler of Múltán, Abú-l Fath Dáúd, incurred the displeasure of Mahmúd by encouraging deviations from the true faith of the Mahommedans. Mahmúd at once marched to bring him to reason, On hearing of this, Abú-l Fath Dáúd implored the assistance of A'nand-pál, Rájá of Láhor. A'nand-pál came to his assistance, but, meeting his former conqueror on the fatal plain of Pesháwar, was defeated and pursued with great slaughter as far as Sódra, near Wazírábád. Mahmúd marched at once on Múltán, brought its refractory ruler to terms, and then accorded peace to A'nand-pál on condition of the latter becoming a tributary of Ghazní.

Peace had scarcely been concluded when Mahmúd was called away to meet an invasion of Afghán Turkistán by Ilák Khan, his father-in-law, King of Káshgár and of Bokhára. Leaving as his vicegerent on the east of the Indus, oneSéwakpál, or Súkhpál, a Hindú chief who, taken prisoner in some previous raid, had embraced Mahomedanism, he hastened with the bulk of his army to the north-west, and met his father-in-law about twelve miles from Balkh. A desperate battle ensued, accompanied in its course by varied fortune. But again the star of Mahmúd prevailed. The enemy were totally defeated, and so humbled that the baffled Ilak Khán never appeared again in the battle-field during the life of Mahmúd.

But there was no rest for the conqueror. Hardly had the pursuit of his enemy ended than intelligence reached him that Séwakpál, the renegade whom he had left as his vicegerent in the Panjáb, had renounced his new creed and had revolted. Hurrying back by forced marches, Mahmúd surprised, defeated, and made prisoner the rebel. The punishment awarded him was a heavy fine and imprisonment for life. Mahmúd then returned to Ghazní (1007).

Not, however, to remain there. It may have been that the aid given by A'nand-pál to the refractory chief of Múltán * rankled in his mind. More probable is it, I think, that having touched only the confines of the treasure-land of India, his soul longed for a more minute examination of that land of promise. This at least is certain, that in the year 1008 the fear of a new invasion from the north spread over India. A'nand-pál at once resolved that this time the Ghazní ruler should encounter no unworthy foe. He sent pressing messages to the Rájpút princes of India, telling them that their own fate was at issue; that the conquest of the borderland of the Panjáb would be but a prelude to their own destruction; that to subdue their enemy he must be met with overwhelming numbers near his own frontier. He finally appealed to their strong love for their religion to incite them to oppose that religion's greatest enemy.

* "Ferishta."

The appeal was not in vain. The Rájás responded with their armies—the soldiers animated by a deep enthusiasm. Led on by A'nand-pál they advanced towards the Indus, and encamped on a plain on its left bank. Mahmúd crossed to meet them there, but seeing their numbers, and noting their enthusiasm, he covered his position with intrenchments, and endeavoured by all the means in his power to lure the Hindús to an attack.

At last he succeeded. Six thousand archers sent to the front, discharging their arrows and then retiring, drew out the enemy. The battle then joined. But whilst it was yet raging furiously, thirty thousand Gakk'hars* penetrated on two sides into the Ghaznívide lines, and forcing their way into the midst of the cavalry, cut down men and horse with their swords, daggers, and spears, so that, in a few minutes, they slaughtered three or four thousand of them. They carried their success so far that Mahmúd, noticing their fury and the disorder they were spreading, and unable to stop them, thought for a moment of retreat. Never had he been so near defeat. But, at this crisis, fortune befriended him. The elephant upon which A'nand-pál was riding became suddenly uncontrollable from the effects of the naphtha balls and arrows discharged at him by the archers, and turning

* The Gakk'hars were a people inhabiting the hilly parts of the Ráwal Pindí and Jailam districts, from Khánpúr, on the borders of the Hazárah district, along the lower range of hills skirting the Tahsíls of Ráwal Pindí, Kahúta, and Gájar Khán, as far as Doméli in the Jailam district.

suddenly, dashed with his rider through the ranks far from the battle-field. The Hindús, noticing the sudden disappearance of their leader, regarded it as a signal for flight. Abandoning then the victory within their grasp they turned and fled. The Gakkhars followed. Mahmúd pursued them without delay for two days, killed eight thousand of them, and captured thirty elephants, and booty not to be counted.*

Mahmúd pushed on to Nagarkót, the modern Kót Kángra, a strongly fortified place, guarding a temple greatly reputed for its wealth.

Nagarkót might easily have been defended by a small force in the days when gunpowder and cannon were unknown. But the movements of Mahmúd had been so rapid that the enemy had had no time to throw a garrison into it. Mahmúd found it guarded by priests; and these peaceful recluses were only too happy to come to an arrangement by which their lives should be assured to them. On the third day after Mahmúd had appeared before it they surrendered the temple—and its contents.

Those contents must have satisfied Mahmúd—possibly they whetted his desire to explore further. According to the Persian and Arabic historians the plunder amounted to one thousand four hundred pounds of gold and silver plate, four hundred pounds of golden ingots, four thousand pounds of silver bullion, forty pounds weight of pearls, corals, diamonds,

* "Ferishta": *vide* also Professor Dowson, *ut supra.*

and rubies, and specie to the value of three hundred and thirteen thousand three hundred and thirty-three pounds sterling.* With this booty Mahmúd returned towards Ghazní (1009).

The next exploit in the life of Mahmúd is specially worthy of notice, inasmuch as it brings him in contact with the most numerous tribe of Afgháns of our own day—the Ghilzais.

According to Hanway, the Ghilzais, learning that the troops of Mahmúd were returning to Ghazní in detachments, laden with plunder, laid wait for them in the mountain passes and succeeded in cutting off several of them. They had imagined that, winter being at hand, operations against them would be delayed till the spring, by which time they would be in safety in their haunts in the Ghor mountains, north-east of Herát. But they reckoned without—Mahmúd. That prince, hearing of the insult, collected a small body of troops, and pushing beyond Kandáhár, pursued the rebels without intermission. The season was January, 1010. The severity of the weather denied to the Ghilzais refuge in the mountains. They were forced to descend into the plain. There Mahmúd attacked and slaughtered them. Indeed, he killed all on whom he could lay his sword. A few families only succeeded in escaping into the more habitable recesses of the mountains. For the moment, for years to come, they were utterly crushed. The survivors had lost everything but the power of retri-

* Brigg's "Ferishta." The computation is made according to the lowest scale.

bution. That, at least, remained to them. And it was, finally, one of their number who gave the death-blow to the house of Mahmúd and supplanted it on the throne.*

Having crushed the Ghilzais, Mahmúd hurried the same year to Múltán to crush in the bud the rebellion of the chief he had reduced and restored in 1004—Abú-l Fath Lodi. The insurrection was easily quelled, and Mahmúd returned to Ghazní, bringing Abú-l Fath Lodi as a prisoner.

It was probably cupidity alone that induced the next raid of Mahmúd into India. The Hindú Rájás were submissive, and paid regularly their tributes. But the wealth of the temple of Nagarkót had but whetted his appetite. The fame of the riches of Thánésar had reached him. He was resolved to clutch them.

Thánésar is in the province of Sirhind, on the road between Karnál and Ambála, about one hundred miles north of Dehlí. Mahmúd made no secret of his intentions. He sent messengers to A'nand-pál, requesting him to arrange for the transit of his army through his territories. The Hindú Prince, unprepared for resistance, earnestly pleaded for the sacred temple. He offered, if Mahmúd would but spare it, to guarantee to the invader the annual revenues of the town, to give him fifty elephants, and to pay the equivalent of a large sum in jewels. But Mahmúd was deaf alike to pro-

* This subject is again referred to at the beginning of the third chapter.

mises and to entreaties. He continued his march, sacked the town, plundered the temple, and returned to Ghazní, says Ferishta, "with two hundred thousand captives and much wealth; so that the capital appeared like an Indian city, no soldier of the camp being without wealth or without many slaves."

Mahmúd was well aware that during his march on Thánésar, A'nand-pál and the Rájpút princes of India were placing their armies on a war footing, with a view to a new confederacy against him. Before, then, he had decided to return from that place to Ghazní, he felt inclined to seize upon Dehlí. But his officers represented to him that, with his position in Múltán still insecure, and with A'nand-pál on his communications, it would be the height of imprudence to draw upon himself the hostility of all the Rájás of Hindústán. Mahmúd accepted the advice, and returned to Ghazní, there to settle his domestic affairs, and to prepare for new conquests.

In the years 1013 and 1015, Máhmúd made two expeditions into Káshmír. The first was opposed by Jaipál II., son of A'nand-pal, who had lately died, but unsuccessfully. Káshmír was conquered, and many of its inhabitants were forcibly converted to Mahomedanism.* The second expedition ended unfavourably for the invader. It was undertaken to reduce some forts in the Káshmír territory, unsubdued in the previous expedition. Prominent amongst these was the

* Professor Dowson places this first expedition before the expedition to Thánésar, but it is uncertain.

fort of Lọh-kót, remarkable for its strength and the inaccessible nature of the ascent to it. All the efforts of Mahmúd to reduce this place were unavailing. The summer came and passed; the autumn followed, and still Loh-kót held out; at last winter supervened, and Mahmúd, with the snows upon him, was forced, for the first time in his life, to abandon an unfinished enterprize. His retreat was disastrous. Misled by guides, his troops became entangled in extensive morasses; numbers of them perished.

Not dispirited by this disaster, Mahmúd turned his arms the following year, 1016, in a new direction.

His father-in-law, Ilák Khán, King of Káshgár and Bokhára, had died in 1015. The countries ruled by him became at once a prey to civil war. The aid of Mahmúd was invoked by one of the contending parties. He crossed, then, the border, occupied Sámárkhánd and Bokhára, and conquered the country of Khwárizm.* He remained there some time to regulate the government of the conquered country. This he bestowed upon Altúm Tásh, giving him the title of King of Khwárizm. He then returned to Ghazní.

The year following, 1017, he undertook his ninth† invasion of India, on a scale far exceeding that of any preceding it. He had levied numbers of men in Túrkistan, in Khorásán, and in Khwárizm, and at the head of these he set out from Ghazní. His aim was Kanáoj,

* The country north of Persia, between the eastern shores of the Caspian and the sea of Aral, now known generally as Khiva.

† According to some, the twelfth.

distant three months' march, but then reputed to be the wealthiest and most beautiful city in India.

Kanáoj was situated on the Ganges,* in the district now known as Farrakhábád. To reach it, then, it was necessary for Mahmúd to penetrate into the very heart of India, exposing his communications and his flanks. But he acted with consummate prudence. Disposing of an army, stated by Ferishta to have numbered one hundred thousand chosen horse and twenty thousand foot, Mahmúd marched along the southern slopes of the Himaláyas. Then crossing the Jamná, he marched upon and captured Baran, the modern Balandshahr. Moving then in the direction of Mathurá, he captured the fort of Mahában, on the Jamná, and only eight miles distant from Mathurá. On that place, the Bethlehem of the Hindús, he next marched. No resistance was made to him. But the town was not the less given up to plunder, and the temples were fired. The booty was enormous, alike in gold, in silver, and in precious stones.

Re-crossing the Jamná, Mahmúd now marched on Kanáoj. According to Ferishta, the Rájá of this splendid city, terrified by the arrival of the Mahomedans, and having no means to oppose them, submitted with himself and family to Mahmúd, and obtained the friendship of that monarch. In the *Táríkh-i-Yamíní*,† on the other hand, it is stated that he took Kanáoj and its seven detached forts. He stayed there three

* This river flows now two miles east of the ruins of Kanáoj.

† Professor Dowson.

days, and marched then to Manj, a town identified by Professor Dowson as the old town of Manjháwan, or Majháwan, the ruins of which are still visible on the Pandú river, ten miles south of Kánhpúr. Here the Brahman garrison bravely resisted him for twenty-five days, and not one of them survived the capture of the place.

From Majháwan, moving down the Ganges to Asni, he took the fort of Chandar Rao, a Hindú chief. Thence, turning from a point near Fathpúr into the Bandalkhand hills, he captured one or two other places, and then marched towards Ghazní, "loaded with spoil and encumbered with captives."

He reached Ghazní in safety. The booty he is said to have brought into the treasury amounted to close upon four hundred and twenty thousand pounds in specie, besides jewels, pearls, and precious stones. It was not thrown away. Mahmúd had some magnificent ideas, and he devoted a great portion of this plunder to carry them into execution, in a manner that should tend to educate his nobles. He built in Ghazní a magnificent mosque of marble and granite. In close vicinity to it he erected a university, and, after supplying it with books in various languages, and a fine museum, he endowed it for the benefit of the rising youth of the country. His nobles were not slow to follow his example. Palaces, mosques, fountains, aqueducts, and cisterns, sprung up in every quarter of the city. Mahmúd had found Ghazní stone. With the aid of the Indian gold he made it marble.

The next year and the year following Mahmúd did

not quit his capital, but in 1021 information reached him from India that the Rájá of Kanáoj had been denounced by his brother Rájás of Hindú blood as a friend and ally of the great enemy of the Hindú faith, and had been attacked in consequence. Mahmúd at once set out with an army to his assistance. Before he could arrive, however, the Rájá of Kálinjar in Bandalkhand had attacked, defeated, and killed the Rájá of Kanáoj. Mahmúd resolved then to revenge his fate on the Rájá of Kálinjar.

The route which he took on this occasion is not known. The Ghaznívide prince is brought direct to the banks of the Jamná, the passage of which was opposed by Jaipál II., son of A'nand-pál. To cross the river in the face of an opposing army was difficult; but, according to the Mahomedan writers, the daring of a few men averted the danger. The tale is difficult to believe, but there are no Hindú historians to controvert it. Eight of the royal guard of Mahmúd's army, says Ferishta—and his account is confirmed by Nizám-úd-Din*—swam across the river, and, entering the enemy's camp one morning by surprise, struck such a panic into his troops, that the Hindús saved themselves by flight. At all events, Mahmúd crossed the Jamná.

He then marched against the Rájá of Kálinjar, and came in sight of his army, numerous, well appointed, and strongly posted. So formidable did it appear from the eminence whence Mahmúd viewed it, that

* Elliot's "History of India," Appendix D.

he quite despaired of beating it. It is probable that on this occasion his fame as a warrior stood him in good stead. Our modern life is full of examples of the effect produced by a reputation not so well founded as was that of Mahmúd. But, however this may have been, this at least is certain, that the enemy fled during the night, leaving their camp with all its booty and five hundred and eighty elephants a prey to the Ghaznívide. Mahmúd returned at once to his capital.

After his return to Ghazní, Mahmúd made an expedition to the countries of Swát, Bajáor, and part of Káfiristán, to bring to the true faith the Buddhist inhabitants of those regions. Sending one of his generals against Núr, he first overawed the wild tribes on the banks of the Kábul river, and then marching into Káshmír, made for the second time a demonstration against the fort of Loh-kót. But, finding this impregnable, he marched on Láhor, sacked it, and finally annexed the country of which it was the capital, having there a Mahomedan governor and Mahomedan officers. His general, meanwhile, had taken Núr, and, building a fort there, had carried away captive those of the inhabitants who refused to accept the faith of the Prophet.

Mahmúd could not remain at rest. In 1023, he again marched from Ghazní to Láhor, and thence into Bandalkhand, his object being to defeat the Rájá of Kálinjar. Passing on his way the fortress of Gwáliár, he sat down before it. But the chief holding it having propitiated him by timely presents, Mahmúd broke up and pursued his way to Kálinjar. But the Rájá of that place, in consequence, probably, of the success of the policy adopted by the chief of Gwáliár, humbled himself by submission and costly presents. Mahmúd, pleased and flattered, confirmed him in his government, and even added other forts to his domains.

The next expedition undertaken by Mahmúd was at once the most famous and the most unfortunate of his life. Nearly eight hundred years later, the recollection of it, acting on the imagination of a Governor-General of India, induced him to recall the event, in a "song of triumph," to the minds of the princes whose temples Mahmúd had then despoiled. I mean the expedition to Somnáth.*

Somnáth was a temple in the Káthwár peninsula, famous for its wealth, its sanctity, and the enthusiasm of its countless devotees. In the eyes of a man so covetous of wealth, and so devoutly pious as was Máhmúd, these were faults it was necessary to correct. In the month of September 1024, then, he set out from Ghazní with an army of thirty thousand horse, besides volunteers, marching on Múltán. Thence to the western peninsula his route lay across the desert country lying between the Satlaj and Rájpútáná. He took with him then innumerable camels and vast stores of supplies. At last he reached Ajmír. He sacked the town—its Rájá having abandoned it—and laid waste the country; but left the fort un-

* In the interval between the expedition to Kalinjar, and this now to be recorded, Mahmúd proceeded to Balkh to punish the governor of the province for his oppression.

molested, fearing that a siege would delay too long his onward progress. He pushed on therefore, taking many forts on his way, marching through desert districts barren of water, till at last on one Thursday morning he found himself in front of the famous temple. "Here he saw," says Ferishta, "a fortification on a narrow peninsula, washed on three sides by the sea, on the battlements of which appeared a vast host of people in arms, who, making a signal for a herald to approach, proclaimed to him that their great idol, Somnáth, had drawn the Mahomedans thither to blast them in a moment, and to avenge the destruction of the gods of India." Mahmúd smiled at the prediction, cleared the battlements the following morning with his archers, and then led his men to the assault. The Túrki soldiers mounted the walls by escalade, but the Hindús, exhorted by their priests and animated by religious exultation, pushed the assailants down. When the day closed, the latter had made no footing.

They returned the next morning to the assault; but again with the same result. Indeed, the defenders, encouraged by their success of the previous day, fought with greater fury than before. No lodgment was effected.

The third day * the assault succeeded. Some state that the Rájá of Nehrwálá, the capital of Gújrát, came with an army to relieve the place. It is more probable that some of the Hindú garrison, elated with their success in repelling the assailants, had the temerity to

* According to Ferishta. Ibn Asír, in his "Kámilu-i-Táwárikh," states that the assailants succeeded on the second day.

attack them in the open. Defeated there, the defenders on the walls became panic-stricken, and the place was carried. Step by step the garrison was forced back to the gate of the temple. Then followed a terrible slaughter. "Band after band of the defenders," says Ibn-Asír, "entered the temple to Somnáth, and with their hands clasped round their necks, wept, and passionately entreated him. Then again they issued forth to fight, till they were slain, and but few were left alive. These took to the sea in boats to make their escape, but the Músulmáns overtook them, and some were killed and some were drowned."

The treasures found in the temple were priceless. "The King of Ghazní," says Ferishta, "found in it a greater quantity of jewels or gold than it is thought any royal treasury ever contained before."

Mahmúd stayed a year in Gájrát, delighted with its climate. Then, leaving a Hindú prince there as tributary governor, he set out on his return. He found, however, the route by Ajmír barred against him by the Hindú Rájá of that country. His army had suffered too much to permit him to count upon a decisive victory against a numerous enemy; and victory, unless decisive, would be useless. He therefore determined to try a new route by the sands to the east of Sind. But want of forage, want of water, terrific heat, and the perfidy or incompetence of the guides, combined to make this march fatal to great numbers of his army. Their sufferings from thirst and from the sun were terrible. Before Múltán was reached, Somnáth had indeed been avenged. From Múltán to Ghážní the journey was easy. Máhmúd arrived there in the earlier part of the year 1026.

After a short rest at Ghazní, Máhmúd once again set forth to punish the Játs, who had been prominent in molesting his army on its return from Samnáth. These Játs are supposed to have been a horde of Tartars of the same stock as the Getæ, and who occupied the country now known as Bahâwalpúr. On the approach of the king, the Játs took refuge in the islands enclosed by the smaller channels of the Indus, and where they believed they would be able to elude attack. But Mahmúd had had the foresight to provide himself with boats. Embarking a portion of his army in these, he was able to force the position of the enemy, of whom having made a sufficient example, he returned to Ghazní.

He made no more incursions into India. After having been all his life the invader, he was himself to be invaded. Founder of the Ghaznívide monarchy, he was destined not to descend to the tomb without meeting in the field the clan that was ever after to harass and to weaken his own.

This enemy was the Séljúk Turks. It seems probable that this horde, separating itself from its Tartar overlord, had emigrated, under their Séljúk chief, to Jáúnd on the left bank of the Jaxartes. The sons of this leader had accepted the overlordship of Mahmúd, and some of the members of the family had even held high office in his army. Indeed, one of them, Amír bin Kádr Séljúkí, had so far gained his confidence that he had left him in 1021 in command of a garrison in India. Mahmúd had, in fact, fostered the military and aggressive instincts of the horde.

But now those instincts turned against himself. The Séljúk crossed the Oxus, invaded his northern provinces, defeated his generals, and plundered his districts. He was compelled to move against them. He came up with them, defeated them, and wrung from them a promise of obedience. During the remainder of his reign they did not molest him.

The next conquest of Mahmúd was his last, and certainly not the least in importance. Persia, originally forming a portion of the territories ruled over by the Sámánís, had been severed from the remainder and formed into an independent kingdom by the family of Boyá, also called the Dailamites, in the year 932. At the time of Mahmúd's accession, Persia had just fallen under the sway of a woman—the widow of the deceased and the guardian of the minor monarch. During the administration of the widow, Mahmúd, touched, it is said, by an appeal she had made to his more generous instincts, respected her dominions. But the rule of her son gave him an opportunity he could not resist. That rule was a long succession of maladministration, brought at last to such a pitch that the interposition of Mahmúd was sought for. He at once set out (1027), enticed the ruler into his power, and annexed the county to his already overgrown empire.

Nearly two years later, 29th April 1030, Mahmúd died, leaving a name which still lives in the veneration of the Mahomedans of Asia. As a mere conqueror, he deserved all the fame which he acquired, for he never was beaten. As an encourager of learning, he deserves to be mentioned with respect, for not only did he employ the treasures brought him by his wars to foster among his nobles a love of art; to found a university; to endow seminaries; to provide scholarships; and to set apart a sum to furnish pensions to learned men; but he invited all those who were distinguished for their acquirements to his capital, and did his utmost to form a national literature. As the founder of a dynasty, he was a failure. He failed from the same cause that brought about the failure of his great modern prototype—he failed because he extended the area of his conquests before the ground on which he rested, and which he might have retained, had had time to settle and harden. Even under his immediate successor it began to melt away.

Mahmúd left two sons, twins, Mahammad and Masáúd, the former of a gentle and docile nature, the latter high-spirited, daring, and fond of power. In obedience to the expressed wishes of Mahmúd, Mahammad succeeded to the throne and dignity of his father. His reign did not last long. About fifty days after his accession his household troops, corrupted by Masáúd, started off to join that prince, who was hastening from his government of Persia towards Khorásán. Mahammad sent in pursuit of these household troops a body of Hindú cavalry in his service; but the Hindús, after a desperate contest, in which they inflicted considerable loss upon the rebels, were repulsed, and their leader was killed. On being reinforced by the household troops, Masáúd despatched to his brother a proposal, which but thinly veiled his claim to supreme power. Mahammad unhesitatingly rejected it, and prepared for war.

But Mahammad was not a general. He forgot that to suppress a rebellion a king must act promptly. He lost the confidence of his army by his delays, and when, on a solemn occasion, the crown fell accidentally from his head, the omen decided his generals to bring to an issue projects which had been slowly maturing. On the night of the 26th October 1030, the conspirators, composed of his leading nobles, surrounded the king's tents, possessed themselves of his person, sent him as a prisoner to the fortress of Wálí, and then marched to join Prince Masáúd at Herát. Masáúd was then proclaimed king. One of his first acts was to cause his twin brother to be deprived of his eyesight.

Masáúd, though not the equal of his father, possessed many of the qualities which had made him the founder of an empire. But it was his fortune to have to encounter trials and difficulties more severe than any which had been imposed upon Mahmúd. Mahmúd had made the empire. Masáúd had to defend it against vast hordes of fierce and barbarous warriors.

These warriors were the Séljúkí Turks.

We have seen how the attempt made by this horde of warriors had been foiled by Mahmúd. The death of that prince, and the civil war which followed it, offered to their leader an opportunity which he did not forego. Masáúd had scarcely settled matters within his own dominions, and had arrived at Herát from Ghazní, when he was beset by complaints of the ravages inflicted on the inhabitants of his northern frontier by the Séljúks. It happened that just about this time a conflict between claimants to the provinces of Mekrán and Kachhi had been decided by the intervention of Masáúd, but he deemed his presence necessary at Herát to regulate the final settlement. He did not, therefore, go in person against the Séljúks, but sent his general, Abdúl Ráis, to chastise them. But Abdúl Ráis not only failed in his object: he could not prevent the invaders from possessing themselves of the important towns of Sámárkhánd and Bokhárá.

Still engaged in the designs regarding Mekrán and Kachhi, Masáúd refrained from attacking the Séljúks in person, but ordered thither from Khwárizm his best general, Altím Tásh, reinforcing his already numerous army with fifteen thousand cavalry from Ghazní. Altím Tásh crossed the river Oxus, recovered Bokhárá, and marched on Sámárkhánd. Alítagín Séljúk, the leader of the Séljúks, withdrew his army from the city on the approach of the enemy, and took up a position he had before carefully reconnoitred. The position was extremely strong. His centre occupied a village; his right was covered by a river and a thick wood; his left by a lofty mountain. But this was not all. Behind a hill on his left front, and far enough from the battle-field to prevent it from becoming an object of suspicion to the enemy, he had placed in ambush a large body of cavalry.

The battle about to ensue was to be remarkable for the valour and the devotion of the Ghaznívide general, and the fierce resolution of his soldiers. Caring little for the strength of the Séljúk position, he boldly attacked it in front. He had already made a great impression upon it, when he was suddenly assailed in the rear by the cavalry placed in ambush. But he did not falter. Still pressing his attack in front he faced the intruders with another division of his army. The contest was desperate; he received a mortal wound; but he put the Séljúks to flight and forced the position. His own wound Altím Tásh had concealed, as best he could, from his men whilst the contest was raging. But after the victory had been gained, he assembled his officers, and telling them he had not long to live, counselled peace with the Séljúks. The offer was made and agreed to. Peace was made, but by one of its conditions Sámárkhánd was severed from the Ghaznívide empire.

The following year, 1033, Masáúd made an expedition into Káshmír, with the intention of penetrating into Hindústán. It would seem, however, from the meagre accounts of the expedition that remain, that he contented himself with storming the fort of Sarsatí, in the Káshmír hills. It is probable that his further progress was stopped by a severe drought and famine which prevailed this year throughout Asia, and especially in Persia and Hindústán.

The year following was noteworthy for a renewal of the war with the Séljúks. Once again Masáúd, instead of marching against them himself, sent his generals, Boghtadi and Húsén, to oppose them. When the two armies were in presence, the Séljúks sent a message to the king's generals to the effect that they were ready to abstain from depredations provided an annual subsidy were assured to them. This message having received a contemptuous reply the Séljúks attacked the Ghaznívide camp. They were, however, repulsed and defeated, with the loss of their camp, their baggage, their wives, and their children. The greatness of the victory having, however, caused the Ghaznívide army to disperse for plunder, a compact body of the Séljúks, who had taken no part in the contest, suddenly attacked them, and changed their victory into an absolute and complete defeat. The Séljúks were then left for a time to continue their depredations unhindered.

Leaving them unmolested, Masáúd made, in 1036, his first expedition into India. Crossing the Satlaj he moved direct on Hánsí, then considered impregnable. On the sixth day of the siege Masáúd took it by escalade, and found in it enormous treasures.

Thence he marched to Súnpat, fifty-one miles from Dehli, the fort and temples of which, with their treasure, fell into his hands. He returned to Ghazní, viâ Láhor, leaving at that place, as governor of his possessions on the left bank of the Indus, his son Modúd.

But the depredations of the Séljúks had been increasing; they were now threatening Balkh and Khorásán. At last, 1037, Masáúd resolved to attack them in person. All his nobles urgently pressed this step upon him. One of those of Khorásán especially, anxious to show his sense of the fatal result of further temporising, sent him a copy of verses, in which the moral was pointed that "the Séljúks, who were once but ants, have now become little adders; and if they are not soon destroyed, they may in a short time become dragons."

Masáúd's first movement against the enemy was unfortunate. He set out from Balkh at the end of the year, crossed the Oxus, and occupied the province of Mawúr-úl-Kehr. But an unusually cold winter, accompanied by a more than ordinary snowfall, forced him to retreat to Ghazní—a movement he accomplished only with great difficulty. Meanwhile, one of the Séljúk chiefs, Jákar Bég, had taken advantage of his retrogade movement to threaten Balkh. Masáúd, then, had hardly reached Ghazní when be received a messenger from the Governor of Balkh with a pressing demand for reinforcements.

The king set out with his army for Balkh. But no sooner had the other Séljúk chief, Toghral Bég, learned his departure from Ghazní, than, making forced marches, he appeared before that place, plundered the suburbs, emptied the king's stables, and effected great damage before he could be repulsed. Jákar Bég, on his side, did not await the king before Balkh, but retreated to Mérv. The distance between the two places is a hundred and eighty miles. The king followed him thither. On his way the Séljúks offered him terms—to cease from depredations on condition of receiving a tract of territory for their maintenance.

The king accepted, and alienated a tract for the purpose.

It was like stopping the rapid flow of a river with a mud wall. The Séljúks did not keep their engagements for a single week. On the king's retrogade march to Herát, they attacked his rear guard and plundered his own baggage, cutting down the soldiers who defended it. Masáúd turned, and avenged himself; then passing through Herát and Nishápor (in Khorásán) he moved on to Tús (near the modern Meshed). At this place the Séljúks again attacked him, and again he defeated them. But no sooner were they defeated in one place than they appeared in another.

Masáúd passed the following winter in Nishápor. In the spring he marched with a large army in the direction of Mérv with the intention of coming to a final settlement with his enemies. The Séljúks were not less willing to bring matters to an issue. They assembled a large army, under their most famous leader, Toghral Bég, in the neighbourhood of Mérv. Amusing the king by allowing him an easy conquest over some minor chieftains, they enticed him on to Dandúnáken, the passes on either side of which they had secured. They then attacked the Ghaznívide army. The shouts of their men, and the number of their horsemen, startled some of the Ghaznívide leaders, and many of them left the field in a panic. The king was not one of these. He fought till all but his own personal guards had fled or been killed. With these he could not hope for victory. He cut his way through the enemy and escaped to Mérv. But he had lost his empire.

He felt this, as he rode from Mérv to Ghor, and from Ghor to Ghazní. He felt that he had received a blow from which, by the aid only of his empire west of the Indus, he could not rally. But he had India—India the fertile, the prolific, the unexhausted—and as far as the Satlaj India was his own. To India, then, he resolved, on reaching Ghazní, to retreat, there to recruit fresh forces to restore his fortunes.

For India, then, after having punished the leaders who had abandoned him, he set out. One son, Modúd, he left at Balkh, to offer some resistance to the enemy; another, Mádúd, he despatched to hold Múltán; a third, Yazídyár, he left at Ghazní, to keep down the Afgháns, the Abdális, and the Ghilzais,* who were showing their head.

Taking with him all the valuables he could collect, and loading them on camels, and accompanied by his blind brother, Mahammad, Masáúd set out for Láhor. But he had soon to learn by experience that an Oriental army can support neither defeat nor retreat. Arrived on the banks of the river Jailam, his household troops conspired with the camel drivers to distribute the king's treasure amongst themselves. Masáúd, enraged, appealed to the other troops to bring the others to reason. But it is probable that these had been "squared." A valid pretext was at hand to justify their disobedience. This was skilfully used. The blind Mahámmad was released from confinement, and

* This is the first mention in the record of this tribe subsequent to its slaughter by Mahmúd in 1009.

declared to be the lawful ruler. The whole army welcomed him with shouts. Masáúd was seized and brought to the new sovereign for judgment. With a leniency typical of his character, Mahammad permitted him to choose as his residence some fort into which he might retire with his family.

Mahammad, considering that his blindness unfitted him for the supervision of affairs, placed the authority in the hands of his son Ahmad, reserving to himself only the regal title. For some time the father and son remained in the Panjáb, engaged in organizing their army. Meanwhile, Modúd, the son of Masáúd, who was governing the province of which Balkh was the capital, had heard of his father's fate, had hastened to Ghazní, and had been welcomed there as a sovereign. He marched with all convenient speed against his uncle and cousin, met them on the banks of the Indus, and defeated them. Mahammad, and three of his sons, Ahmad, Abdúl Rahmán, and Abdúl Rahím, were taken prisoners, and, with the exception of the last-named, who owed his life to the fact of having showed respect to King Masáúd while he was in confinement, were put to death. Another son of Mahammad, who had been appointed by his father governor of Múltán, was then attacked, defeated, and slain.

But King Masáúd had left another son, Mádúd, and Mádúd was then in possession of Láhor and its dependencies, and refused to acknowledge his brother. The two brothers met, then, near that capital, to decide the question of empire or death. Fortune seemed to avour Mádúd, for on the eve of the day for which the battle had been set, whole battalions of his brother's army came over to him. But treachery worked for his brother. The following morning Mádúd was found dead in his bed. The whole army then followed Modúd, who thus became undisputed sovereign of the Ghaznívide empire.

He was called upon almost immediately to deal with the Séljúks. These ever-encroaching barbarians had, after their defeat of Masáúd, occupied the provinces of Herát, Ghor, and Sístán, and placed them under a chief of their own race as an independent kingdom. And now another clan of the same horde had captured Balkh, occupied Túrkistán (the country now known as Afghán Túrkistán), and had forced the Ghaznívide general to fall back, by way of Kábul, on Ghazní. The following year, 1044, they threatened Ghazní itself, but the Ghaznívide general, Toghral Bég, defeated them and drove them out of the country. Toghral followed up his victory against the Séljúks by marching on Kandáhár, which had been occupied by the Kuzilbáshis, and by defeating them. He then put the climax to his services by rebelling against his sovereign. A timely appeal made by Modúd to the loyalty of his officers, suppressed, however, the rebellion and the rebel.

Complications meanwhile had been occurring in Hindústán. It had happened that the contests between different relations for the Ghaznívide empire had induced in the minds of many Hindú sovereigns the belief that they could recover the independence of which the power and genius of Mahmúd had deprived them. The Rájá of Dehli was the first to give the signal. Setting his army in motion, he drove the lieutenants of the Ghaznívide from Hánsi, from Thánésar, and from their dependencies. He then marched on Kángra and took it. This success incited other dispossessed Rájás to follow his example. Joining their forces, they marched on Láhor. For seven months they sat before that capital, reducing its garrison to extremities. Finding themselves at the end of their resources, the defenders then resolved, as a last resource, to die fighting valiantly. They accordingly made a sortie, and attacked the besiegers with all the fury of despair. Their efforts succeeded beyond their hopes. The Hindús, surprised and panic stricken, gave way and fled in disorder.

It was when the Ghaznívide empire was thus being hemmed in; when the Séljúks had occupied Persia, Sístán, and the provinces west of Kandáhár; when many towns in India and the Panjáb had been lost; that Modúd, on his way to oppose the insatiable Séljúks in the west, suddenly died, leaving behind him a diminished and threatened empire.

The death of Modúd gave rise to new internal dissensions. After a short interval, in the course of which a son of Modúd, aged four years, was proclaimed under the title of Masáúd II., only to be at once deposed, the sovereignty was seized by his uncle, Abú-l-Hásán, who endeavoured to fortify his claim by marrying the widow of the deceased monarch. Disturbances and insurrection followed this usurpation. Of these, Abú-l-Rashíd, a son of Mahmúd of Ghazní, took advantage to raise his own standard and drive Abú-l-Hásan from the throne (1052). The new king at once sent two armies—the one to recover the revolted cities of the Panjáb; the other, under Toghral Hájib, to reconquer Sístán. Both armies succeeded. Toghral Hájib, however, was a strong supporter of the principle that "might is right." No sooner, then, had he succeeded in Sístán than he marched on Ghazní, seized the king, put him to death, and with him all the representatives of the house of Sabaktagín on whom he could lay hand. Three only escaped his vigilant search.

Toghral Hájib survived the perpetration of these murders but forty days. He was assassinated as he was ascending the throne to give public audience. His head was then brought out, placed on a pole, and carried round the city. Farókzád, one of the three members of the Sabaktagín line who had escaped, was then chosen by lot to be king.

Farókzád was a capable man. But, feeling his want of experience, he appointed as his vizier, Noshtigín Hájib, the general who had recovered the Panjáb for Abú-l-Rashíd, and sent him to oppose the Séljúks, who, taking advantage of the late disturbances, were again marching on Ghazní. The two armies met not far from the capital. The battle that followed is said to have been unprecedented for the severity with which it was contested. It began with the rising of the sun, and when that orb set it was yet undecided. At last the discipline of the Ghaznívides prevailed, and their victory was assured.

Farókzád was encouraged by this great deliverance to attempt to recover the country of Khorásan from the Séljúks. His generals defeated these in a great battle, but the defeat was more than retrieved a little later by the most famous of the Séljúk leaders—the redoubtable A'lp Arslan—so that Khorásan remained permanently alienated.

After a reign of six years, Farókzád died. He was peaceably succeeded by his brother Ibráhim, described by the historian, Minháju-s-Siráj,* as "a great king—wise, just, good, God-fearing, and kind, a patron of letters, a supporter of religion, and a pious man." He certainly was the very opposite of his ancestor Mahmúd, being a lover of peace and of the pleasures of the harem. The length of his reign is variously estimated at thirty-one and forty-two years. He made peace with the Séljúks by confirming them in all their conquests, and caused his son, Masáúd, to marry a Séljúk princess.

During his reign an expedition was made to India by one of his generals, and subsequently, it would seem, by the king in person. Accurate details of it are wanting. It is only known that it was successful. Ibráhim died in the year 1098, have begotten thirty-six sons and forty daughters.

His son Masáúd succeeded him. This prince, known in history as Masáúd III., was the worthiest representative of the Ghaznívide family. He was a lover of justice, a reformer of the laws, a remitter of taxation.

* Tabakát-i-Násirí. Elliot's "History of India," vol. ii.

His mind seems to have been mainly bent upon securing to his people a fair and just administration.

Like all the capable members of his family, he was firmly resolved to maintain and strengthen his hold on India. The better to superintend the operations of his generals, he established, for a time, his court at Láhor, become by the annexations of the Séljúks a central part of his dominions. His generals are said to have carried his arms further into Hindústán than any since the time of Mahmúd, and to have returned laden with booty; but accurate details of these invasions seem altogether wanting. Masáúd III. died in 1115, after reigning seventeen years.

On the death of Masáúd III. civil war again supervened. Arslán, one of his sons, "famous," according to the Mahomedan historian of the *Tabakát-i-Násirí*, "for his magnanimity and energy, courage and bravery," was yet strongly sensible of the evils likely to arise from a disputed succession. To prevent these evils he seized and confined all his brothers, and appropriated to himself the crown. Unfortunately for the success of his plan one of his brothers, Bahrám,* escaped. Bahrám made his way, very naturally, to the court of his relative, Súltán Said Sanjar, the Séljúk Governor of Khorásan. A war ensued—a war tantamount to a Séljúk invasion of the Ghaznívide territory. After various fluctuations of fortune, it ended in the victory of Bahrám, who at once secured his position

* "Ferishta" calls Bahrám the brother of Arslán. Minháju-s-Siráj speaks of him as his uncle. Other writers agree with Ferishta.

by putting Arslán to death. The civil war had lasted two years.

Bahrám was a great patron of literature. He encouraged poets and poetry. The great Persian poet, Nizámi, resided at his court, and dedicated to him one of his poems. Ferishta mentions more than one instance of his patronage of literature and the arts.

Bahrám made two expeditions into Hindústán to quell rebellion on the part of the Mahomedan viceroy commanding there. He succeeded. Soon after his return to Ghazní, after the success of the second expedition, he committed an act which, by its results, brought about the destruction of the Ghaznívide empire. The act is thus stated by Ferishta: "He soon after publicly executed Kútb-u-Dín Mahammad Ghori, Afghán, to whom he had given his daughter in marriage." This Afghán prince was the brother of the ruler of the Afghán tribe which had ruled in Ghor, and which submitting to Súltán Mahmúd, and subsequently to the Séljúks, had recently regained its independence. The act of Bahrám in beheading a man of so much consideration, so closely allied to himself, and the brother of the ruler of a powerful tribe, must have been caused by some pressing motive. What that motive was has never been clearly established. But the act was fatal to him.

The deceased man's brother, Saif-u-Dín Súr, Prince of Ghor, at once marched with an army upon Ghazní. Bahrám fled from the city towards the Panjáb. Ghazní was then occupied by the Prince of Ghor, and he, preferring to remain there, sent his brother, Alla-u-Dín Súr to represent him at Ghor. But the people of Ghazní would not have his rule. All his efforts to render himself popular with them were fruitless, and they secretly informed Bahrám as to the opportunities that were likely to offer to re-establish his throne. Profiting by these advices Bahrám suddenly appeared before Ghazní in the winter, at a time when he knew the city to be denuded of Afghán troops. The Ghorian prince, unable to meet Bahrám with his own troops, yielded to the solicitations of the treacherous inhabitants of Ghazní to avail himself of their services. At the head of a force composed, then, mainly of Ghazní soldiers, he went out to meet Bahrám. But hardly were the two armies in face than the Ghazní soldiers seized upon the Afghán prince, and made him over to his enemy. Bahrám entered Ghazní as a conqueror. But he tarnished his victory and blasted the prospects of his house by his treatment of the vanquished prince. "The unhappy captive," says Ferishta, "had his forehead blackened, and was seated astride on a bullock, with his face towards the tail. In this manner he was led round the whole city, amid the shouts and insults of the mob; after which, being put to torture, his head was cut off and sent to Súltán Sánjár Súlkúkí; while his vizier, Syud Majd-u-Dín, was impaled."

Such treatment roused Alla-u-Dín to fury. Vowing vengeance against the house of Ghazní he set out with an army for that city. In vain did Bahrám attempt to frighten him. "The threats of Bahrám, he said, "are as impotent as his arms." He pressed on, fury in his heart, towards Ghazní. As he approached the town Bahrám led out his army to meet him. He had superior numbers, but the "morale" was with the hardy assailants. At last the battle joined. Again and again did the Ghaznívides bear down the Afgháns by the weight of their numbers; again and again did the Afgháns rally and return to the onslaught. One charge more desperate than the rest decided the victory. With his own spear, Alla-u-Dín transfixed the son of Bahrám. The elephant bestridden by the latter was killed; Bahrám, however, extricating himself, succeeded in mounting a horse, and fled for his life.

Alla-u-Dín then entered Ghazní. The city, beautified by Mahmúd and his successors, was given up to flame, to slaughter, and to devastation. All the monuments of the Ghaznívide kings were destroyed, and every trace of them effaced—the tombs of Mahmúd, Masáúd I., and Ibráhím excepted. For seven days the massacre, the pillage, the burning continued, and "as if insatiate of revenge," says Ferishta, "Alla-u-Dín, when he left, carried a number of the most venerable and learned men in chains to Firóz-Koh, to adorn his triumph, when he ordered their throats to be cut, tempering earth with their blood, with which he plastered the walls of his native city." He annexed Ghazní to his principality of Ghor. Bahrám died on his way to, or on reaching, Láhor. He was succeeded there by his son Khúsrú (1157).

Khúsrú reigned seven years, the greater number of which were occupied by attempts to recover the lost capital of his fathers. He waited at Láhor until he heard that Alla-u-Dín had returned to Ghor. He then marched for Ghazní, hoping for the co-operation of Súltán Sanjar Séljúk. But the Séljúki empire in northern Asia, so long the persistent enemy of the Ghaznívide power, was tottering to its downfall. The lieutenants of the Séljúk Súltán in Khwárizm had revolted, and he himself was shortly afterwards defeated and dispossessed by the Túrkmáns of Ghiza. As these victors at once marched upon and occupied Ghazní, Khúsrú was forced to return to Láhor. That he made another attempt on Ghazní is improbable. Although the statement is made by Ferishta, the contrary is implied by Minháju-s-Siráj, and it is certain that after an occupation of Ghazní for two years by the Ghiza Túrkmáns they were expelled by Sáid Ghíyás-u-Dín Mahammad, the representative of the house of Ghor.

Khúsrú, dying in 1157, was succeeded by his son, Khúsrú Malik. He was the last of the Ghaznívide kings. Mild, liberal, and fond of pleasure, he was not formed of the stuff that resuscitates an empire. During the whole of his reign, Ghíyás-u-Dín Ghori made gradual but continued encroachments on the remnants of his dominions. Pesháwar fell, then the country between the Indus and the Chináb. At last Láhor itself was attacked (1181). Láhor bought her safety by surrendering the country occupied by the invader, and the son of her king as hostage. It would appear that the Ghorian monarch, under the pretext that the conditions made by Khúsrú Malik had not been fulfilled, returned subsequently to Láhor, but was repulsed and compelled to withdraw. In his absence, Khusrú Malik, making an alliance with the Gakk'hars of the hills, made a raid upon Siálkôt, but was repulsed. This enterprise demonstrated to the Ghorian monarch the necessity of bringing the whole matter to a prompt conclusion. Feigning a desire to negotiate peace, he enticed Khúsrú and his army away from Láhor; then suddenly interposing between him and that city he made prisoner of the one and occupied the other. Khúsrú and his son were doomed to imprisonment for life, but a little later they were murdered. With the deposition of Khúsrú terminated the rule of the Ghaznívide dynasty (1187.)

CHAPTER III.

HISTORICAL.—THE HOUSE OF GHOR.

THE descent of the house of Ghor has been discussed by Professor Dorn, by Mountstuart Elphinstone, by De Gingues, and by other eminent authorities. The balance of opinion is in favour of their pure Afghán origin, and I cannot but think it most probable that they were descended from the survivors of the tribe which attempted to plunder the soldiers of Mahmúd on their return from India, laden with booty, in 1010, and who were attacked and nearly exterminated by that prince "in the strong country of Ghor," some months later.*

On the disappearance from the scene of the last scion of the Ghaznívide house the Ghorians invaded India. Ghíyás-u-Dín Ghori had early associated with himself in the government his brother, Mohammad Shaháb-u-Dín, and it was this brother who had

* *Vide* "Hanway's Travels," vol. ii. page 98. Compare Elphinstone's "History of India," vol. ii. pages 550 and 559, and note. *Vide* also Brigg's "Ferishta," vol. i. page 161.

conducted the final operations against Khúsrú Malik, described in the previous chapter, and who commanded the army ordered to operate in India. As he subsequently ascended the throne with the title of Mahammad Ghori, it will save confusion if I refer to him under that name.

The Panjáb having been annexed, Mahammad Ghori settled the country, and returned to Ghazní. Two years later (1189) he set out on his first expedition across the Satlaj. He knew that the enemy he would have to encounter was no mean one, that the Rájá of all Rájásthán, Prithi Rájá, disposed of the troops of Rájpútáná and of Dehli, and that the kingdom of Kanáoj had recovered its ancient power and splendour. He knew that the Rájpúts whom he would have to encounter were better trained, better disciplined, and better commanded than the soldiers who had followed Jaipál and A'nand-pál; that they had profited by the experience they had had of Mahomedan soldiers, and would be ready to look them in the face. But he was bent on permanent conquest, and he went prepared to enforce it.

Crossing the Satlaj, he marched on Bitanda,* in Patiála, then a town of some consideration, occupied it; advanced to Thánésar, occupied that; and then marched on Dehli by way of Karnál. The distance between Thánésar and Karnál is twenty-three miles;

* Ferishta states that he first marched into Ajmír, where he took the town of Batanda. But there is no such town in Ajmír, and there is no record that Mahammad Ghóri made at this particular time any other conquest in that country.

the country is a broad plain. At Tiráori, midway between the two places, he was met by the armies of Prithi Rae, Rájá of Rájásthán, of Cháwand Ráe, Viceroy of Dehli, and of other vassal princes, amounting to two hundred thousand men, with three thousand elephants. The army of Mahammad Ghori was smaller in numbers but it was a well-tried and unbeaten force. With it he believed he could effectually put in practice the old Ghaznívide plan of disheartening the enemy by a succession of charges, and then breaking them by one general assault. He tried it on this occasion, sending squadron on squadron in quick succession against the Hindú centre, which appeared weakened by the great length to which the line extended. But its weakness was not real. Behind the first line the Hindú leaders had placed their best infantry, and they had planned that whilst these should offer to the onslaught of the Moslems a stern and stubborn resistance, their wings should lap over and enclose them. So it happened. The Hindú centre remained firm and solid, proof against repeated attacks. Then the wings, wheeling inwards, took the enemy in flank and rear. The followers of Mahammad Ghori saw that defeat was inevitable and began to flee. He saw that defeat was inevitable but did not flee. Despair added fury to his normal courage. He dashed through the enemy, and came so near to the Viceroy of Dehli that he wounded him in the mouth with his lance. He would have pressed on, but the Viceroy, a brave man, delivered a counter blow which almost drove him to the ground. Some of the few attendants who had followed Mahammad managed then to mount him upon a horse and carry him from the field. But the rout was complete. His army was pursued for forty miles. The remnants, however, collected at Bitanda,* where they were besieged for thirteen months. At the end of that time they were granted terms.

Mahammad Ghori proceeded after his defeat to Ghor, there to visit his brother. He then returned to Ghazní. The disgrace he had met with rankled in his heart, and, though he devoted some time to pleasure, in the hope of driving it from his memory, it would not leave him. There was but one mode of atoning for it, and that was to avenge it.

Accordingly, he raised another army, and, two years after his first defeat, he again set out (1191). The court poet of the day, Hásán Nizámi, thus describes him at the moment of his departure :—†

> "His standards proclaim victory.
> Indeed, they are almost prepared to write the book of victory,
> His ensigns and black umbrella are full of adornment,
> How beautiful on the face of time are the curls and freckles of the State!"

He marched, says Ferishta, by way of Pesháwar, Múltán, and Láhor, and advanced to the river Sarasvati, on the other bank of which the Hindú host was encamped. The Sarasvati is a small river in Sirhind,

* The retreat on Batanda, nowhere disputed, and the fact, presently to be recorded, that the next battle was fought on the Sarasvati river, seem clearly to show that the Bitanda referred to was the town of that name in Patiála.

† Elliot's "History of India," vol. ii. page 212.

rising in the slopes of the Himálayas, losing itself in the great sandy desert, and, except during the rainy season, is merely "a small thread of running water." It is regarded with peculiar veneration by the Hindús. At the time of which I am writing, it was swollen beyond its ordinary depth.

The Rájpút chiefs were so confident of success that they offered terms to the enemy. Mahammad Ghori replied in such a manner as to induce the belief that he was aware of his own weakness but that he could not act without his brother's orders. This answer had the effect of causing the Hindú leaders to abate their wonted caution. Mahammad Ghori, who had anticipated this, was thus able to cross the river a little before dawn, and to attack them in their camp. Their great numbers enabled them, however, to hold the Mahomedans in check whilst they were changing their front and forming up. They succeeded in accomplishing this manœuvre.

Mahammad Ghori had, meanwhile, drawn up his men to oppose the new order of the enemy. His plan was still to weary out the enemy by charges of cavalry, but, to prevent himself from being surrounded, the charges were to be made, as it were, in retreat. That is, each division, after charging and firing its arrows, had orders to wheel to the rear, its place being at once taken by the next division, to which similar orders were issued. In this manner he fought the battle till sunset, drawing the enemy on, then checking them, then drawing them on again, always fatiguing them, but never letting them get behind him. By sunset he thought he had sufficiently worn out the Hindús. Placing himself, then, at the head of twelve thousand of his best horsemen, he charged their centre—this time not to let it go. The assault was so tremendous, and his grip was so firm, that it decided the battle. The centre gave way, the wings followed, and in a few minutes the entire Hindú army was fleeing in confusion.

The Viceroy of Dehli was killed on the field. The King of Rájásthán, Prithi Ráj, was taken prisoner, and put to death. The royal tents and camp equipage, and their contents, were taken. Mahammad Ghori marched at once on Ajmír, taking many important places, among others Hánsi, on his way. Arriving at Ajmír he put several thousands of the inhabitants to the sword and made slaves of many others. He then laid on the country a heavy tribute, and returned to Ghazní. Behind him he left "his faithful friend and slave," afterwards his successor, Malik Kutb-u-Dín Aibak, who, in his absence, took possession of Mirath, of Aligarh, and of Dehli.*

But there was another Hindú sovereign yet unsubdued, the Rájá of Kanáoj. This Rájá was the greatest in India. According to the Mahomedan historian, Ibn Asír, his territories "extended lengthways from the borders of China to the province of Málwá, and in breadth from the sea to within ten days journey of Láhor." Though this is a poetical description it is

* It is owing to this circumstance, says "Ferishta," that foreign nations say: "The empire of Dehli was founded by a slave."

certain that the territories of the Rájás of Kanáoj were very considerable, extending probably from Aligarh to below Banáras, and embracing a considerable tract to the west of the Jamná. It is probable that this king, who is called Jai Chand, had been considerably alarmed for his own safety by the capture of Dehli and Aligarh, for it is asserted* that it was he who collected his forces and became the aggressor. It was to punish this aggression that Mahammad Ghori came down once more with an army from Ghazní.

The two armies met at Itáwah. The vanguard of the Ghorian army was led by Kutb-u-Dín, and the onslaught of that vanguard sufficed to put to flight the Hindú host. But the defeat was not the less crushing because so easily won. The slaughter was immense; ninety elephants were captured, and the King of Kanáoj † was left dead on the field. As one great consequence of it Banáras fell into the victor's hands, and saw her temples desecrated, and her treasures carried off "upon fourteen hundred camels." Nor was this all. The great kingdom of Kanáoj never recovered from the shock. The Mahomedan dominion was soon to extend beyond even its borders into Bihár.

Mahammad Ghori returned to Ghazní, leaving at

* Elliot's "History of India," vol. ii. page 251.

† The death of this Rájá afforded the first known instance of the use of artificial teeth. "The Hindú king," writes Ibn Asír, "was slain, and no one would have recognised his corpse but for the fact of his teeth, which were weak at their roots, being fastened in with golden wire."—Elliot's "History of India," vol. ii.

Aligarh, Kutb-u-Dín as his viceroy, to complete his work. Some disturbances in Ajmír, quelled without difficulty, afforded to the viceroy the opportunity of penetrating into Gújrát, the scene of Mahmúd's triumph. He was re-called thence by pressing orders from Ghazní.

Mahammad Ghori, in fact, was on his way to Hindústán, and needed all his forces. This prince, anxious to consolidate his authority in central India, marched on Biána, an important place about fifty miles from Agra, took it, and planted there an Afghán colony, naming Bahá-u-Dín as its governor. He was about to march against the fortress of Gwáliár—the fortress on the hill still existing—when the outbreak of troubles in Khorásán re-called him to Ghazní. The siege was consequently prosecuted by his lieutenants. Gwáliár fell; but Kutb-u-Dín advancing far into Ajmír to support the Hindú tributary prince he had placed there on the throne, was assailed in such force by the combined Hindú forces of Gújrát, Nágor, and Mhérwárá, that he was forced to retreat on the town. The following year, however, he not only avenged his defeat, but succeeded in taking the forts of Kálinjar and of Kálpí and in conquering Rohilkhand.

Meanwhile, Mahammad Ghori had not only quelled the troubles in Khorásán, but had re-annexed to the Ghazní sovereignty Herát and its dependencies. Whilst engaged in making these conquests he had become, by the death of his brother, the sole reigning king.

Almost his first act, after he had been crowned, was

to attempt to recover the kingdoms of Khwárizm,—that important appanage that had been severed by the Séljúks from the Ghaznívide monarchy. He advanced into the country, conquered it, and forced its sovereign to take refuge in his capital, the only place remaining to him. Here he besieged him. But the King of Khwárizm defended himself with so much ability and resolution that the besiegers lost many men without gaining any corresponding advantage. The King of Khwárizm had, meanwhile, sent pressing letters to the Khitan Tartars—the same tribe which had, after the overthrow of the Séljúks in Khorásán, momentarily occupied Ghazní—and these were now responding to his call. They advanced in such force, and so suddenly, that Mahammad Ghori, to save himself and his army from absolute destruction, was obliged to fight at a great disadvantage. Never did he display more skill or greater courage—but the odds against him were altogether out of proportion, and he was completely defeated.

He fled towards Ghazní, but his retreat was cut off. Of his whole army scarcely more than a hundred clung to him. But with these he made a desperate charge, fairly to be ranked with that made on the overwhelming Hindú force at Tiráori. It had the same success. He cut his way through the enemy with his following, and gained the fort of Andkhó.*

But in Andkhó he was enclosed. There was no

* Andkhó is now an important place just within the frontier of Afghán Túrkistán, not far from Khojá Sáleh.

escape. Resistance was futile. His presence too was required at his capital. He agreed, then, willingly, to purchase his freedom by the payment of a large sum of money.

His presence was indeed required at the capital. The total defeat of his army had spread dismay. The report of his death following hard upon the news of his defeat incited disorder. One of his officers seized Múltán. His favourite slave proclaimed himself in Ghazní. Suddenly the released monarch appeared on the scene. Ghazní refused to open her gates to him. He marched, therefore, on Múltán, took it, enlisted troops on the Indian borders, and returned to Ghazní, which, as abject now as it had been insolent before, yielded to him without a blow. Concluding, then, a peace with the King of Khwárizm, he marched into the Panjáb to punish the Gakk'hars of the hills, who had invaded and plundered that province. Attacked by the king from the direction of Afghánistán, and by his faithful lieutenant, Kutb-u-Dín, from that of India, these marauders were soon subdued. Mahammad Ghori then proceeded to reside at Láhor.

Whilst residing here he planned a final expedition to Khwárizm—an expedition which he was resolved to make decisive. He marched then towards Ghazní. He had reached the Indus, and had laid himself to rest on his bed in a tent on the banks of that river, when some Gakk'hars noticing his exposed situation, resolved to make away with him. They crossed the river in the dead of night, entered his tent unopposed, and murdered him as he slept.

The titular successor of Mahammad Ghori, was his nephew, Mahmúd; but the influence and authority of Kutb-u-Dín preponderated over the ties of blood. Mahmúd himself, seeing how vain would be his opposition to such a man, resigned to him the ensigns of sovereignty at Láhor, and returned to his ancestral home in the mountains of Ghor (1206). The real successor then was Kutb-u-Dín.

But with the accession of Kutb-u-Dín, the history of Afghánistán as an independent kingdom temporarily ceases. The slave king elected to be ruler of the Hindústán which he had conquered, and took up his abode at Dehli. With the eclipse of the house of Ghor Ghazní was forgotten.

CHAPTER IV.

HISTORICAL.—THE TRANSITION TO THE MOGHOL.

KUTB-U-DIN had transferred the seat of government to Hindústán. Immediately, his father-in-law, Táj-u-Dín Eldóz—the slave who had shut the gates of Ghazní against Mahammad Ghori after his defeat in Khwárizm, and who had been subsequently pardoned by his master—was proclaimed King of Ghazní by Mahmúd, Mahmúd retaining for himself the mountain throne of Ghor, and with it the overlordship over Afghánistán. The united forces of both princes succeeded in reducing Herát and the country—now forming the western boundary of Afghánistán—between it and Sístán. But here their success ended. Attempting to recover the northern districts now known as Afghán Túrkistán, they were defeated by Mahammad Khán, King of Khwárizm, and were even forced to yield up Ghazní. In the height of his distress, Táj-u-Dín fell back on the post of Kúrm.* It would

* In the text Kirmán. In his "Chronicles of the Pathán Kings of Dehli," page 26, Mr. Edward Thomas advances an ingenious argument to show the identity of Kirmán with Kúrm, the fort on

seem that at this place Táj-u-Dín made peace with his conqueror, for he is next heard of as raising troops to attack Láhor and India. He actually penetrated as far as Thánésar; but there he was defeated and taken prisoner by Shams-u-Dín Altmásh, the son-in-law of Kutb-u-Dín, and at that time King of Dehli (1215). He died a prisoner.

Meanwhile Afghánistán had fallen under the domination of Mahammad Khán, King of Khwárizm. The events of the reigns of this prince and his successor are so completely absorbed in the greater career of the new Attila of the north, the far-famed leader of the Moghols, Chingiz Khán, that I pass over the lesser to deal with the greater subject.

For many ages the Tartar tribes in the north of Asia, occupying the wild desert and mountainous country north and north-west of the kingdom of Khwárizm, "had carried on war with each other, unknown to or unregarded by the conterminous nations, or known to their Chinese and Túrki neighbours alone."* One of these tribes was the Mongol, Múghúl, or as it is generally spelt, Moghol. They were an ugly race, with yellow complexions, high cheek-bones, small eyes, and large mouths. But they had in them the stuff out of which were made the devastators of

the river of that name. I have not space for that part of the argument which deals with the orthographic question. But I may be permitted to state my opinion that Mr. Thomas has clearly established that the geographical requirements of Kirmán are met by the actual position of Kúrm.

* Erskine's "History of India," Introduction.

the earth, and they only wanted a leader. Suddenly that leader appeared in the person of Chinghiz Khán. Writing being then unknown to the Moghol race, it is impossible to fix accurately the date of the birth of this conqueror. Historical events sufficiently demonstrate, however, that it occurred about the year 1155. The death of his father, when he had attained the age of thirteen years, brought him into rude contact with the world. He had many rivals with whom to contend, and his first experiences were of the severest. Now buffeted by fortune, now rising superior to all the arts of his enemies, he finally established his supremacy by two acts. The first was the complete defeat of his rivals on the field of battle, with an army counting only one-fourth of the number of theirs; the second, a deed of atrocious cruelty with which he crowned his victory. It is asserted that having taken many prisoners, he prepared eighty huge cauldrons, filled them with boiling water, and in them cast his still living captives. Far from alienating the barbarous tribes in the midst of whom he lived, this atrocious act cowed and subdued them. In the perpetrator they recognised their master.

The power thus established by cruelty was consolidated by the display of a force of character, of a capacity to influence men's minds, to bend them to one resolute will, such as has been rarely surpassed. In the course of a few years, Chinghiz Khán had established his supremacy over the vast country bordered in the east by China, in the north and west by the Volga and the Caspian. Proclaimed the Great Khán of the Tartars, having conquered Western China, and penetrated as far as Pekin, Chinghiz Khán found the kingdom of Khwárizm a bar to further conquests to the south.

At that time (1219) Mahammad Khán was King of Khwárizm. The dominions of this prince included the countries of Bokhára, Samarkand, Khokand, Káshgár, Persia, Afghánistán and Belúchistán, down to the Indus. Suddenly, Chinghiz Khán attacked him with three armies. The first, following to a certain point the course of the Jaxartes, descended upon Khiva; the second, ascending that river, occupied Khojind, and conquered the country now known as Ferghána; the third, commanded by Chinghiz Khán in person, crossed the river, and penetrating into the country, took Bokhára and Samarkand. In a few days the entire territory north of the Oxus was in the hands of the conqueror.

Meanwhile, the king, Mahammad Khán, sensible of his inability to oppose the Moghol horde, had retreated to Nishápor in Khorásán. Chinghiz Khán, occupied with Samarkand, sent a corps of twenty thousand men, under two of his generals, to pursue him. Mahammad Khán fled. The Moghol generals arriving at Nishápor, and finding their prey had escaped, then conceived and executed one of the most daring projects that ever entered into the heart even of a Moghol. They ravaged the whole of Western Persia, conquered Trans-Caucasia, crossed then the range of the Caucasus, occupied Derbend, defeated there an army composed of the various peoples of the countries they had traversed and were traversing, and drove them beyond the Dnieper. Some of the fugitives even crossed the Danube in their terror. So great and so general was the alarm, that the inhabitants of the Russian provinces of Kief, of Smolensko, and of Tchernigov, dreading lest they too should be attacked in their turn, combined to attempt to drive the enemy from the country he had but just gained. In the battle on the banks of the Dnieper that followed, the allied patriots were defeated. The Moghols then crossed that river, and penetrated into Bulgaria. Thence they returned to rejoin the main army.

Meanwhile, Mahammad Khán, despairing of safety on the mainland, had fled for refuge to one of the small islands of the Caspian. There he died (1220). His son and successor, Jalál-u-Dín, was a man of very different temper. In Khwárizm when he heard of his father's death, he at once assembled his adherents, attacked and dispersed the troops sent to oppose him, and leaving in that province a sufficient body of troops under his brothers, pushed on to Nishápor, there to endeavour to recruit a new army. Chinghiz Khán, meanwhile, on the first news of the outbreak in Khwárizm, had hastened to that province, had suppressed the rebellion, killing in battle the two brothers of Jalál-u-Dín, and had then marched southward, capturing in succession Balkh, Mérv, Herát, Nishápor, and Tús (near the site of the modern Meshed). An army corps of thirty thousand men which he had sent to watch Jalál-u-Dín, was, however, defeated by that prince, who had succeeded in raising double that number. Chinghiz Khán, indignant at this reverse, dashed at once in pursuit of the victor, who, abandoned by some of his generals, was making the best of his way to India. Chinghiz overtook him at the Indus, totally defeated his army, Jalál-u-Dín himself owing his escape solely to the daring with which he cut through his enemies and swam the river. The Moghol army then ravaged the Panjáb, and returned to Tartary (1224). Subsequently Chinghiz completed the conquest of China, and there died (1227).

Jalál-u-Dín, meanwhile, escaped from the battlefield on the Indus, had, after many adventures, re-established his authority in Persia. But Afghánistán remained until the year 1251 under the rule of Chinghiz Khán and successors. During that period the enslaved country had no history.

In that year, Shír Khán, the governor of the Panjáb for the King of Dehli, Násir-u-Dín Mahmúd, invaded Afghánistán, seized upon Ghazní and Kábul, and annexed them to the Dehli monarchy. It is probable that they were speedily recovered, for not only, in subsequent years, do we find the Moghols making repeated incursions into India, but in the year 1336 traces appear of a new Afghán dynasty seated on the throne of Ghazní, owning subordination to, and acknowledging the suzerainty of, the Moghols of Central Asia.

This Afghán dynasty, like that which preceded it, came from Ghor. Probably it was the chief of the Afghán tribe in the Ghor mountains to whom the Moghol suzerain delegated his authority. They ruled from 1336 to 1383. The first sovereign, Shams-u-Dín Ghori, and his two immediate successors, Rúkh-u-Dín, and Fakhrúdín Ghori, accepted the position and performed the duties assigned to them. The fourth of the race on the throne, Ghíyas-u-Dín Ghori, asserted his independence, and handed it down to his successors, Shams-u-Dín, Malek Háfiz, Moez-u-Dín Hásén, and Ghíyas-u-Dín. But in the reign of the last-named prince the dynasty and the independence came alike to an untimely end.

Taimúr, known also in history as Tamerlane, was born at Késh, near Samarkand, about the year 1336. His family had been settled there for two hundred years, and had held high positions. Taimúr possessed very much the same organising genius as Chinghiz Khán, from whom, in the female line, he was descended; he almost equalled him in ferocity, and surpassed him in perfidy, whilst his aims, if as vast, were at least as reckless. At an early age he had succeeded in gathering in his own hands the guiding-reins of the Tartar tribes in Central Asia, and finding himself master, he began at once to carry terror and devastation into neighbouring countries. Afghánistán and Persia at once fell before him. He then carried his arms into Circassia, Georgia, Mesopatamia, and the southern parts of Russia. Having laid waste these countries, he prepared to invade India by way of the Hindú Kúsh, Kábul, Banú, and Dínkót, on the Indus. Into that expedition, little affecting Afghánistán, I do not propose to follow him. It will suffice to state that from the first invasion of Taimúr, 1383, until after the accession of Bábar, Afghánistán had no history of her own. Portions of her territory are occasionally mentioned for some or other specific quality by the historians. Thus, Herát is spoken of during the fifty years prior to the accession of Bábar, as having been the most magnificent city in the East, celebrated not merely for the beauty and splendour of its court, the architectural beauty of its mosques, tombs, colleges, and palaces, but as being the resort of the greatest divines, philosophers, poets, and historians of the age. At this time Herát was the capital of Khorásán, and that province was governed by Húsén Mirza, the most powerful of the princes of the House of Taimúr.* Kábul and Ghazní were then likewise ruled over by a prince of the same house, Súltán U'lúgh Mirza, but of the internal administration of the country, and of the conduct and character of its people, I have been unable to find any trace whatever. With the death of U'lúgh Mirza, however, the dry bones of its history suddenly recover their vitality.

The vast dominions of Taimúr, divided after his death, had been reunited into one kingdom by his great-grandson Abúsaid, fourth from him in order of succession. On the death of Abúsaid the empire was again partitioned. Whilst the three elder sons divided the countries north of the Oxus, the youngest son, U'lúgh Mirza, was allotted Kábul and Ghazní:—the adjoining territory of Khorásán, with Herát as its capital, falling to a more distant relation—the Húsén Mirza previously referred to.

* "Erskine's History of India." Memoirs of Bábar.

U'lúgh Mirza, Prince of Ghazní and Kábul, died in the year 1502. His death was the signal for intrigues and assassinations, one usurper following another, when in 1504, Prince Bábar, who but three months before had been forced to leave his kingdom of Ferghána as a homeless exile, appeared before Kábul and took it.

Space will not permit me to do more than give a short summary of the previous career of this extraordinary man. The sixth in descent from Taimúr, he was born in 1482. At the age of twelve he inherited by the death of his father the kingdom of Ferghána.* He was not yet fifteen when the troubles in Samarkand induced him to attempt the conquest of that province. He conquered and occupied the capital; but the task of governing and maintaining the country was beyond the means at his disposal, and after an occupation of little more than three months he was compelled to evacuate it, and fall back on Ferghána. His absence from that province had, however, proved fatal to him. Plots against him had been fomented, and he discovered one morning that he was a king without a kingdom.

By the means common in those days, he was able to raise a sufficient force to recover Ferghánà, and he was even meditating another raid against Samarkand, when the Uzbég Tartars invaded Central Asia and forced Bábar to seek refuge in the mountains. Here

* A rich country on the upper course of the Jaxartes. It is also called Khokand.

he lived for some years the life of a true adventurer; now an exile in the desert; now a monarch on a throne. He gained and lost Samarkand; he was buoyed up by hopes of Ferghána; but he was always happy, always joyous, always confident in the future.

At length, however, fortune seemed to shut out from him the last hope of success, and in his twenty-third year Bábar was forced to cross the Oxus and take refuge in Kúndúz, between Balkh and Bádákshán, the governor of which was Kushrú Sháh. Here he succeeded in raising a force of Moghols. At their head, he marched on Kábul, and took it.

At the time that he conquered Kábul that country comprehended the long and narrow plains running nearly from south to north between Ghazní and the capital; the whole mountainous territory reaching to the Koh-i-Bába and the Hindú Kúsh, and thence down to the confines of what is now British territory as far as Fort Kúrm. The mountainous tribes were more predatory and more independent than they are even at the present day.

At the head of an army of freelances Bábar felt that his only chance of safety lay in engaging his followers in new adventures. He first led them against Kandáhár, which he conquered. Within two hundred and forty miles of Herát, he thought it then advisable to make a journey thither, in order, with his relative, its ruler, to concert measures against their joint enemies, the Uzbég Túrks. During his absence his brother Jahángír revolted and fled to Ghazní. Then his Moghol soldiers mutinied. No sooner had

Bábar, returning to Kábul, put an end to these disorders, than a more dangerous outbreak, instigated and abetted by the Moghols he had brought with him, took place. Bábar, escaping with difficulty from Kábul, put himself at the head of a few devoted followers, and made head against his enemies. By his courage and his activity he made up for the smallness of his following, and, ever present where he was needed, ever taking advantage of the opportunities that offered, he in the end suppressed the revolt.

The Uzbégs, meanwhile, were advancing as the other Túrki tribes had advanced before them. They swarmed into Khorásán, occupied Herát, then besieged and took Kandáhár. Ghazní and Kábul were now threatened, when, happily for Báber, the King of Persia, alarmed at the conquest of Khorásán, advanced against the Uzbégs, defeated them with great slaughter, and drove them across the Oxus.

To be safe only, was never with Bábar the supremest good. For him safety meant opportunity for fresh conquests. The defeat of the Uzbégs by the Persians re-awakened then the old longing for Samarkand. That city had been his first conquest—the scene also of his first rebuff. He must woo her once again.

He wooed and won her (1511). But again was Samarkand fickle. She welcomed back his old enemies the Uzbégs, and after a contest ranging over two years, he lost, not only her, but every other possession across the Oxus.

Thrown back then on Afghánistán, he recovered

Kandáhár. He could not, however, be content with a country of rocks and stones. Opportunely at this moment there came to him a cry for aid from Daólat Khán, the Afghán viceroy of the Panjáb for Ibráhim Lodí Afghán, King of Dehlí. Simultaneously the Ráná of Chitór sent a messenger to promise his aid if Bábar should invade India. The invitation promised too much to allow Bábar to refuse it. King of Kábul and Ghazní, he crossed the Indus (1525–26), and advanced unopposed on Láhor, defeated there the army that had been hurriedly raised to oppose him, reduced that city to ashes, and advanced towards Dehlí. The rebellion of Dáolat Khán, and the news that the Uzbégs had invaded Balkh, recalled him to the north ere he could reach the imperial city. In his absence, however, Daolat Khán was overcome, but his general advancing then incautiously on Dehlí, was defeated by its king, Ibráhim Khán Lodí, under its walls. Bábar, having driven back the Uzbégs, returned to repair this disaster. At the head of twelve thousand men he met Ibráhim, commanding one hundred thousand men, at Pánipat, a place always favourable to an invader from the north. A daring and competent general, he found himself opposed to one who was utterly ignorant of war, and who was too self-willed to be led by others. The result was never doubtful. The Indian army was defeated with great slaughter, its king was left dead on the field, Dehlí opened its gates, and Bábar marched at once on Agra, to be proclaimed there (May 10, 1526) the first Emperor of India, to enter upon a sovereignty which, as the Great Moghol, he was to transmit to a long series of descendants, and which was destined to remain in one form or other in his family till the great crisis of 1857.

CHAPTER V.

HISTORICAL.—HUMAYUN AND KAMRAN.

BA'BAR's rule of four years and a half in India belongs to the history of that country. During that period Afghánistán remained a province governed under his orders by his second son Kámrán. On the death of Bábar (December 26, 1530), whilst his eldest son, Humáyún, succeeded to the throne of Agra; Kábul, Ghazní, and Kandáhár, continued a semi-independent kingdom under the rule of Kámrán, the overlordship of Humáyún, if existing in theory, not being acknowledged in fact. In the course of the two years that followed, the new King of Kábul obtained from the weakness and the necessities of his brother, Humáyún, the cession of the Panjáb, and with it the country south-east of the Satlaj, as far as the important towns of Hissar and Hánsi.

Kámrán was a man who to a headstrong nature added an ambition which never hesitated at the means to be employed. For three years after the acquisition of the Panjáb, however, this master passion seemed to lay dormant within him. During that period he would appear to have devoted all his energies to the internal administration of his dominions, and to the formation of a well-disciplined army. But in 1535 the Sháh of Persia, Shah Tahmasp, had but just succeeded in driving the Uzbég Túrks from Khorásán, and in occupying Herát. He had bestowed the government of this place upon his brother, a man of weak nature, who, first rebelling against the Shah, then endeavoured to obtain a secure place of refuge for himself by besieging Kandáhár. Kandáhár was defended by Amír Khwája Kilán, one of the best officers of King Kámrán, with a small but well-trained garrison. For eight months he foiled all the efforts of the besiegers. Meanwhile King Kámrán, after some delay, marched with an army of twenty thousand men to relieve him. On Kámrán's approach, the Herátí army raised the siege, and took up a position some ten miles from the city. Kámrán effecting then a junction with the governor, Khwája Kilán, attacked the enemy, and, mainly in consequence of the skill and conduct of his subordinate, totally defeated him. As this defeat seemed to secure his western border, Kámrán returned to Láhor.

But he was reckoning without the ambition of his neighbour. Another invasion of the Uzbégs—an invasion followed almost instantly by the sacking by those barbarians of the beautiful city of Herát—called into Khorásán the Shah of Persia in person. Shah Tahmasp found little difficulty in driving the Uzbégs from Herát; then looking round for fresh conquests, he recalled the brother who had rebelled against him, and taking from him the plan which in his hands had miscarried, marched upon Kandáhár. Kandáhár was unprepared to resist him. She had neither provisions, nor stores, nor even a sufficient number of troops. The governor, Amír Khwája Kilán, resolved under these circumstances, as he could not defend the city, at least to save its palaces from destruction, its people from the horrors of a storm. Placing his palace in the best possible order, arranged for a royal reception, he sent a message to the Shah, to the effect that, unable to defend the place, or to meet him in the field, he had considered that the only courteous and honourable course open to him was to make Kandáhár fit for the reception of the guest whom he could not entertain in person. He then retired on Láhor. The Shah entered Kandáhár.

Kámrán could not appreciate the refined conduct of his agent. He complained that at least an attempt at resistance should have been made, and that he might then have been able once more to relieve the place. Now, he had to reconquer it. He set out as soon as possible with an army for that purpose, reached it, and sat down before it. The Shah had returned to Persia, but had left behind a sufficient garrison. The place resisted for some time, but finally surrendered, on the condition of obtaining a free departure for the garrison. Kámrán having then restored the fortifications, returned to Láhor.

Up to this time the conduct of King Kámrán had been wise and prudent. But he had not been tempted.

He was soon to show that it had been based rather on the exigencies of the moment than on a ripe and solid judgment. It happened in the year 1538–9 the empire of his brother Humáyún was in imminent danger. At the head of a dispirited army, weakened by sickness, he lay encamped at the village of Chausá, close to the point where the Karamnása falls into the Ganges, shut out from the north-west provinces by the superior army of his competitor, Shír Khán, advantageously posted in an intrenched camp. In the upper provinces, his brother, Hindal, in arms against him, occupied Agra, and was threatening to march on Dehlí. Such were the circumstances under which the aid of the King of Kábul was invoked.

It was in the power of Kámrán to restore Humáyún. He entered Hindústán, and marched on Dehlí. Finding that place holding out for Humáyún, under his cousin, he continued his progress to Agra. On his approach, Hindal abandoned the place, renounced the contest, and returned to Mewát, his government. Kámrán then advanced against Shír Khán, who continued to lie encamped in front of Humáyún's army. Kámrán had the fate of India in his hands. That knowledge ruined him. Were he to beat Shír Khán—and he felt he could beat him—he would beat him for the advantage of Humáyún. Far better, he thought, to allow the two rivals to fight it out, and then to beat the conqueror himself—for himself. So thinking, he acted—leaving Humáyún to his fate, and returning to Agra. There, two months later, he was joined by Humáyún—not in the guise of a conqueror

—but a helpless, wounded fugitive, escaped by flight from the surprise and defeat of his army by Shír Khán at Chausá on the 27th of June 1539.

Humáyún had indeed left to him of his mighty empire only Agra and Dehlí and the tract between the two cities. He did not retain these long. A good understanding between the two brothers had never existed since Kámrán had allowed ambition to overcome his better feelings. And now, though it was patent to him and to all around him that his zealous support of Humáyún would sustain the empire founded by his father, he determined to risk its ruin rather than secure the re-establishment of his brother. He could not indeed prevent some of his chiefs, more loyal than himself, from casting in their lot with Humáyún. He wasted seven months at Agra. His longing to return, added to the extreme heat of the climate, brought on a severe attack of fever. When the cessation of this enabled him to move, he returned to Láhor, leaving his brother to meet the army with which Shír Khán, after conquering the country below and to the east of Agra, was now advancing against him.

The result showed the short-sightedness of pure selfishness. In the contest that followed, Humáyún was totally defeated, and fled with a few faithful followers to Láhor. His arrival at that city as a fugitive caused the scales to fall from the eyes of Kámrán. Far from lessening his danger by his selfish conduct at Agra, he had increased it tenfold. Shír Khán, he had information, was preparing to follow

Humáyún into the Panjáb. Instead of as at Agra having against him only a pretender to the empire occupying one of its provinces, and marching against the acknowledged ruler of the remainder—that ruler supported by himself—he had now to contend with the master of Agra and Dehlí—the lord of Hindústán! And on whose behalf was he to combat this invader? On behalf of a man who, whether victorious or defeated, would use the position of elder brother to claim overlordship over, or to dispossess, himself! In this position he dreaded Humáyún even more than Shír Khán. He loathed his very presence. Thus circumstanced and thus cogitating, he resolved to endeavour, by the sacrifice of the Panjáb, to secure at least his rocky home. He therefore sent a messenger to Shír Khán, now become Shír Shah, to treat for peace, on the condition of his being allowed to retire across the Indus. The condition was accepted, and Kámrán retreated to Kábul. Humáyún, abandoned, fled by way of Múltán to Sind (1540).

The other brother, Hindal Mirza, of whom I have already spoken as being in rebellion against Humáyún, had, after the advance of Kámrán into India, and his occupation of Agra, made his submission, been pardoned, had subsequently commanded the advanced division of his brother's army in the fatal battle of Kanáoj, and at a later date had joined Humáyún in his expedition to Sind. Here he quarrelled with him because, on the occasion of a reception given by his mother, Humáyún chose to fall in love with and to betroth himself to a young lady, subsequently the mother of the illustrious Akbar. Hindal, whose loyalty had previously been lukewarm, quitted his brother, made a raid on Kandáhár, and, having gained the governor, Karácha Khán, occupied that fortress (October 1541) without striking a blow.

It may well be imagined that this high-handed procedure was by no means acceptable to the King of Kábul. Kámrán, on his arrival at his capital, had renounced the nominal overlordship of his elder brother, and had subsequently endeavoured by the conquest of Badákshán to recoup himself for the loss of the Panjáb. He had just completed his operations in that province, when intelligence reached him that his fortress of Kandáhár had surrendered to his brother Hindal. Without any delay he marched against the place and blockaded it for six months. Then Hindal, finding further defence impossible, surrendered it. Kámrán bestowed the government of the town on his brother Askari, and took Hindal with him as a prisoner to Kábul, but, subsequently pardoning him, bestowed upon him the district of Jalálábád in jághír.

Meanwhile, Humáyún, baffled in all his plans, having suffered privations of every sort in the inhospitable deserts of Sind, having had born to him, when a haphazard guest of a border chief, a son to whom he could not offer even a hovel as a home, had resolved to move on Kandáhar. He professed to invoke the compassion of his brothers, but it is probable he desired to tempt the cupidity of Askari. Askari, however, was loyal to Kámrán. This loyalty had previously prompted him to write letters to the Sind chiefs urging the assassination of Humáyún. He now marched with a force hoping to surprise that prince. The latter had but just time to mount a horse, and escape with his wife and some forty followers to Herát, then an appanage of Persia. The child, deemed unable to bear the journey, was left to the tender mercies of his uncles. Askari brought him into Kandáhár, and treated him with the care becoming his position.

The power of Kámrán, as King of Kábul, seemed firmly established. It may be said, in general terms, that excepting the territory formed hy a line drawn from the westernmost point of the Herát district to the westernmost point of Sístán, the country called in his time the kingdom of Kábul was similar in extent to the Afghánistán of our own day. Shir Sháh had crossed the Indus, and, as do the English now, had occupied the country up to the passes. North of the great range Kámrán held Bádákshán, and a strip of the southern part of the territory now known as Afghán Túrkistán. But Balkh and the northern part were in the hands of the Uzbégs. His power seemed confirmed by the fact that his eldest brother was a fugitive, his only son in his hands; that his two other brothers were serving, carefully watched, under his orders; and that he had suppressed a rebellion in Bádákshán, occasioned by his absence at Kandáhár, and that the chief of that province was his prisoner.

But in those days to have a certain tenure of power it was necessary that the ruler should combine in his own person a great many sterling qualities. To be a good soldier was much, but it was not all. The possession of a genial nature, of a strong and resolute will; of the power to impress that will upon others, to think clearly, to strike promptly; of the keen insight which marks on the instant the various currents into which interest, fickleness, lust of power, are apt to drive those around them;—these are qualities which a man in those days was bound to possess if he wished to be perfectly secure,—which in those countries I believe he is bound to possess now. Kámrán did not possess them. Never was he less secure than when apparently at the very height of his power.

Satisfied with his position as King of Kábul, he is said from the time of his return from the second expedition to Bádákshán to have given himself up entirely to pleasure, to have paid little attention to the concerns of government or to the complaints of his subjects. Even such conduct in one whose character commanded respect and affection, might in an Eastern country have been passed over. But Kámrán's was a curious, even a contradictory, character. Adored when in adversity, attracting then men whom he had previously repelled, he commanded, when in the full enjoyment of power, neither respect nor affection. Suspicious, jealous, unsocial, he did not seem to possess then a single personal friend. Personally, his courtiers disliked him; they felt no pride in him as their king and their lord, and the service they rendered was a service inspired by fear and by interest alone.

When, therefore, Kámrán, formed by nature as I have described him, relaxed his hold over public affairs to give himself to voluptuous indulgence, he committed one of those acts for which no subsequent vigilance can atone. He must have had some dim consciousness of this when he was awakened from his revels to learn that his brother, Humáyún, bringing with him a Persian army, led by the son of Shah Tahmasp, Morád Mírza, was marching on his kingdom.

Kámrán's first care was to secure the person of the young prince, Akbar, in his capital. But before this had been accomplished, he learned that Humáyún had, after a siege of a few days, captured Bost, a fort at the confluence of the Arghand-áb and Helmand, and that the garrison having joined him, he was pushing on to Kandáhár.

I have already stated that the Governor of Kandáhár was Prince Askari, the brother of Kámrán. But he was likewise brother of Humáyún, and although Askari had offended Humáyún in the grossest manner, yet the fact that he had so injured him seemed to point to the probability that so valuable a gift as the delivery of Kandáhár might be sufficient to atone for the offence. Had Kámrán possessed a good army, and had be been certain of his brother Askari, he might, by acting promptly, have conjured the storm. But his attention to pleasure had caused him to neglect his war office, and he found himself unable to raise a force which, unsupported, would have a chance of meeting the Persians in the field.

But even then, provided Prince Askari would but

hold out, the game was not up. Kámrán had a small force, a force which, so long as Kandáhár should hold out, might, well led, inflict great damage on the Persians, and possibly compel them to retire. But here came into play the jealous, suspicious temper of which I have spoken: the terrible disadvantage to a man of not having a single friend loving him for himself alone. It was this "situation" which ruined Kámrán. Suspecting everybody, he could not act at all. He adopted the worst possible policy for a man in his position—the policy of the mere watcher of the atmosphere.

Boldness would have served him far better. For it happened that when Humáyún sat down before Kandáhár, he found he had a very difficult task before him. The place was well fortified and well garrisoned. Moreover, Prince Askari had made up his mind that true policy counselled him to be faithful to Kámrán. He therefore defended the place with skill, with vigour, and with such effect, that it is more than probable that a demonstration on the part of Kámrán would have forced Humáyún to retreat.

But Kámrán made no sign. It is certain that this inactivity on his part inspired Humáyún, or one of the able men to whom he gave his confidence, with the brilliant idea of sending a special envoy to Kábul, nominally to arrange terms with Kámrán, really to corrupt the most influential of his followers. The nobleman selected for this delicate task was the most famous, the most skilful, the most trusted, and the most trustworthy of all the followers of Humáyún. His name was Bahrám Khán. He was a native of

Bádákhshán; was educated at Balkh; had entered the army of Humáyún at the age of sixteen; had distinguished himself on many occasions no less by his valour than by his unselfish devotion; had accompanied Humáyún through Sind and to Persia; had won there the confidence of the Shah, who made him a Khán; and had now returned with his master to win back the kingdom of Kábul, and with it the empire of Hindústán.*

Such was the man sent to Kábul to prepare the way for the coming of Humáyún. The dexterity with which he accomplished his mission was the greater, because the object of it was suspected by Kámrán. No sooner had he set foot in Kábul, than the king, under pretext of doing him honour, placed confidential persons to watch and to report upon his movements. Considering the surveillance thus organised to be sufficient, Kámrán placed no restriction as to the important personages whom the ambassador might desire to visit. Bahrám thus had opportunities of seeing the young prince Akbar; prince Hindal, the brother; princes Yádgár, Násir, and Ulúgh, the cousins of the king; prince Súlimán and his son, the dispossessed rulers of Bádákhshán, and others. He remained at Kábul six weeks, and when he left he carried with him the conviction that the hearts of the nobles of Kábul had been won to his master, and that it needed only

* *Vide* the "Ain-i-Akbari," translated from the original Persian, by Professor Blochmann, whose early death in the current year is the severest loss Oriental literature has sustained: "The conquest of India may justly be ascribed to Bahrám," p. 315.

an important success, such as the capture of Kandáhár, to induce them to declare themselves.

During all this time Prince Askari had been true to Kámrán. He had repulsed every assault, and he felt confident that it needed but the appearance of that prince to force the besiegers to retire.

It is probable that some dim conviction of the possibility of such a result at last forced Kámrán to move towards the beleaguered town. Had he set out before Bahrám Khán had visited Kábul, he would in all probability have succeeded. But he did not march until after Bahrám had assured the former enemies of Humáyún of more than pardon, and had raised up against Kámrán a most formidable party in his own court.

This party manifested itself so openly, that Kámrán found himself compelled to retrace his steps a very few days after he had left Kábul. "The thanes" were flying from him. Some of their foremost men, amongst them his cousin Ulúgh Bég, reached the camp of Humáyún, bringing with them letters of adherence from many others. A Hazára chieftain about the same time openly declared for that prince.

The end was now approaching. Prince Askari, deprived of all hope of assistance, reduced to his last ration, after gallantly defending Kandáhár for five months, was forced to surrender it. He had been loyal to Kámrán. But it had been a loyalty based upon a conviction that he had nought to hope for from Humáyún. It is probable, then, that the consciousness of having deserved well of Kámrán did not support him when, seated after his capture in the presence of Humáyún, there were shown to him, by order of the conqueror, the papers in his own handwriting which contained the damning instructions to murder him.

The capture of Kandáhár deprived Kámrán of his last adherent. He had been forced to release, and to send back to Bádákshán, the governor he had formerly dispossessed. His cousin, Yádgár Násir, escaped. Last of all, his brother Hindal, after playing to him the part which Prince George of Denmark played to James II., professing astonishment at the abandonment one by one of his courtiers,—last of all, Hindal left him to throw himself upon the mercy of Humáyún. Then—and then only—was the work of Bahrám Khán complete.

Still, for a great man in his position, all was not yet lost. He had possession: he had the capital: he had troops. Treason had done much, but he was still ruler in Kábul, lord also of Ghazní. His rivals, too, laboured under the enormous disadvantage of having conquered his own country with the aid of foreigners. These foreigners were now becoming clamorous. Humáyún endeavoured to appease them by making over to them the spoils of Kandáhár. But they had insisted upon having Kandáhár too, and they had occupied it. Humáyún with his own personal following was then in about as bad a position as it is possible to conceive. He had taken a fortified town with the aid of the Persians, and now the Persians had thrust him out of it, and had warned him to betake himself to a convenient distance from its walls. But he had neither horses, nor baggage, nor money, nor equipment. His following amounted to not more than five thousand men. Under these circumstances the chances of Kámrán seemed still to be preferable.

So thought, at least, some of the nobles who had deserted him for Humáyún, for they went back in increasing numbers. In the councils of Humáyún distracting counsels abounded. But they were all the counsels of despair. There seemed no possibility to advance, to retreat, to remain on the ground they then occupied; for the winter was upon them, and nearly all the grain of the country had been consumed.

But when things were at their worst, fortune came to befriend the eldest son of Bábar. The Persian troops who were garrisoning Herát had sold their horses to some merchants on their way to India. The merchants had picketed the horses outside the town. Upon them Humáyún made a sudden and successful raid. It was the only possible way of getting them, for he had no money. His sense of justice induced him, however, to give to the complaining merchants an order in full of the value they placed on the horses, payable "when his affairs would permit"—a promise which, if vague and unnegotiable, was, I believe, redeemed in the end.

He had now horses. But to every other difficulty previous existing was now added the necessity of providing fodder for those animals. All seemed dark again. But, suddenly, at the very crisis of his fate, the Persian prince who commanded in Kandáhár,

Prince Mahammad Morád, died. The presence of this prince, the son of the Shah, had alone prevented Humáyún, at an earlier date, from attempting to surprise Kandáhár. And now this obstacle had disappeared. He was not the man to forego the opportunity. By means of an ingenious stratagem he procured entrance for some of his soldiers into the town; then, after a sharp tussle with the Persian garrison, he captured it.

Having now a base of operations, he resolved to act as Kámrán should long before have acted—to move forward. The route by Kalát-i-Ghilzai and Ghazní was not open to him, those places being held for Kámrán. But, winter though it was, he followed the course of the Helmand to its source in the Koh-i-Bábá. Turning then eastward, he marched on Kábul.*

Kámrán, rousing himself from his fatal stupor, had repaired the fortifications of the capital, and now at the head of from eighteen to twenty thousand men marched with confidence to annihilate the five thousand his brother was leading against him. He had sent on a party to occupy the Khimár Pass—the approach to Kábul; but either the detachment was not strong enough, or it was badly commanded, for Humáyún not only forced it, but cleared the defile of Khwája Pushteh.

The capture of this strong pass was fatal to Kámrán. His nobles began to desert him in shoals. He stood still and let them go. He had, even yet, a chance

* By Tírí and Yúrat Shékh Ali in the territory of Paghmán and Arkandi. "Erskine's History of India," vol. ii. p. 322–3.

of victory if he would but attack. But he would not take it. Again his suspicious temper got the better of him. Fearing to trust any one, he sent in abject terms to treat with his brother. But Humáyún, suspecting that he only cared to gain time, advanced with seven hundred lancers towards his camp. This bold forward action decided Kámrán. Abandoning his army, he promptly retreated into the citadel of Kábul. Then, as soon as night fell, taking with him his son, his wife, and his family, he rode for Ghazní. Refused admittance into that town, he made for Hazára, and ultimately took refuge in Sind. For the moment he had lost a kingdom.

Only, however, for the moment. It is true that the entire kingdom of Kábul submitted to Humáyún. He and his brother had changed conditions. He was now the crowned monarch; his brother, the houseless wanderer. But misfortune had not crushed the ambition that ruled in the heart of Kámrán, whilst adversity had stimulated his energies. He was still a watcher of the atmosphere, not as before in dread, but in hope. He was watching an opportunity.

I have said that he had taken refuge in Sind. There he had been well received by Shah Húsén Arghún, the ruler of upper and lower Sind, a man of great talent and sagacity, to whose daughter he had been for some time betrothed. He used the occasion of his exile to marry her. It was one of the wisest acts of his life. She was a noble woman, a sound counsellor in prosperity, a faithful friend in adversity. She is known in history as Chúchak Bégam.

The opportunity for which Kámrán was waiting came sooner than might have been anticipated. Shortly after having been acknowledged lord of Kábul, Humáyún had set out for Bádákhshán to recover that tributary province, which, during the conflict between himself and Kámrán, had been seized by their former ruler, his cousin, Mirza Súlimán. Humáyún conquered Súlimán; then, the better to consolidate the province and its outlying dependencies, he remained three or four months in the country; subsequently, to complete his object, he resolved to winter in Kila-Zefer, north of the Koh-i-Bábá range. He was approaching that place when he was attacked by a dangerous illness. So serious was the attack, that for four days his life was despaired of. On the fifth the crisis took a favourable turn, and he recovered.

This was the opportunity that came to Kámrán. His brother's absence beyond the great range—his dangerous illness—the chances of his death! Could fortune have been more kind? By the aid of his father-in-law, he raised a thousand chosen horse, and set out for Ghazní. On his way he plundered some Afghán horse-dealers of their horses, which, by giving to many of his men a led horse in addition to those which they bestrode, enabled them to proceed faster. Sending on trusty agents ahead, he was able to communicate with those well affected to him in Ghazní, and, by their aid, to seize that fortress before the governor had any tidings of his approach. He replaced the governor, whom he killed, by an adherent of his own; then, delaying not an hour, he pushed on for

Kábul. Again, preceding the news of his arrival, he surprised that city, put the governor to death, and captured the citadel. In it he found, with some other members of his brother's family, the young prince Akbar.

Again, then, was Kámrán lord of Kábul! Such was the intelligence which reached Humáyún just at the time when, having shaken off his fever, he had been able to resume horse exercise. It was a blow—the heavier for having been totally unexpected and therefore totally unprovided for. Not Humáyún alone had left his child and family in the capital. Many of his nobles—the men who had deserted Kámrán to join him—had done the same. The love of wife and of child is a passion with almost all races, but more especially with the Oriental. Humáyún felt instinctively that he had to meet a crisis requiring all his nerve, all his decision—and above all—all his influence with his wild following.

Humáyún differed in this respect from Kámrán, that he possessed under all circumstances the divine power of attaching others to himself—for himself. No man at that epoch had more devoted friends. It was this rather than his moral power—for naturally he was indolent and wanting in energy—which stood him in stead on this occasion. He had the sense to allow himself to be guided by capable men.

Under their advice he was equal to the occasion. Notwithstanding the fact that it was winter, that he was severed from Kábul by the snows of the Hindú Kúsh, he resolved to act at once. Concluding then a treaty with Mirza Súlimán, in virtue of which Súlimán was to hold Bádákhshán as his own, recognising only the overlordship of Humáyún, he marched at once from Kila-Zefer in the direction of Kábul. On reaching Tálikán, on the river Ferkhár, he was detained several days by the violence of the rain and snow. When the storm abated, he succeeded in making his way to Kúndúz.* Here he experienced the misfortune of being deserted by many of his nobles, those especially whose families were in Kábul, and who probably deemed that the chances were in favour of Kámrán. Humáyún stayed here for some days, refreshing and encouraging his troops; then, casting his future fate on the hazard of the die, risking his all on the success of his advance, he moved forward by way of Chahárdár across the passes. The difficulties he experienced were enormous. The roads were blocked up with snow, and it was necessary to ram this down into a hard surface. Even then the energies of man, of horse, of camel, were tried, as they rarely had been tried before. But, as usual, the aphorism, that difficulties however enormous are still only obstacles to be overcome, proved its truth. The defiles and the passes of the Kara Koh were conquered, and Humáyún found himself and his followers at Saighán, still indeed on the northern side of the Hindú Kúsh, but in a good position to move on the capital.

How had Kámrán been employing the long interval?

* Kúndúz is an important town, due north of Kábul, lying in 36° 50′ N. 69° 10′ E. It possesses an earthern fort and about 1,500 inhabitants. It is in Afghán Túrkistán.

In a military point of view, Kámrán had done all that man could do. He had raised troops, fortified the passes, and had been unsparing in his attempts to gain over the influential men of the country. He employed but two methods—intimidation and interest. To those who had been false to him before, he showed no mercy. Death in every varied form of cruelty was their lot. But some very considerable men he gained over. Prominent amongst the ablest of his earlier supporters was Shír Ali, a nobleman possessing alike influence and military skill.

Between Humáyún and the capital by the direct road there now lay the Abdéreh defile leading to Zohák, thence by a pass through the Koh-i-Bábá to Chardéh, Ghorband, and Chárikár; from Chárikár by way of Istálif to Kábul. To check his advance Kámrán sent a force under Shír Ali. Unluckily the force Shír Ali took with him was too small, and the defile was forced in spite of him. But being a capable officer, and well acquainted with the country, he made his way by a circuitous path to the northern entrance of the defile, and passing through it, fell with considerable effect upon the rear of the invaders. Humáyún, notwithstanding, pushed on to Chárikár. His position even there seemed so hopeless as to cause dismay amongst his followers, and many of them, including a cousin of his own, abandoned him and fled to Kábul. Humáyún, in this extremity, held a council of war. The proverbial issue was the result of its debates. The council decided not to attack Kábul at once, but to occupy a position below it where supplies would be abundant.

This plan was about to be put into execution, when Humáyún, acting probably on the entreaties of a trusted friend, countermanded it. The avoidance of an immediate attack, and the taking up of a position below Kábul, would, he was assured, induce amongst his followers the impression that he was about to abandon the capital and march on Kandáhár, still held for him by the faithful Bahrám Khán. He therefore pushed on for Kábul.

Kámrán was waiting for him within the city. It is difficult to assign a reason for his inaction. In his case boldness would have been prudence, and he might have used his superior force with much advantage in the passes north of the city. But he preferred to wait for his brother. As soon, however, as Humáyún's forces descended from Istálif, and had reached Deh-Afghánán, one of the outlying suburbs of the city, he sent his best general, Shír Afkan, at the head of his best troops, to attack him. A hard-fought action followed. At first the soldiers of Kámrán were successful, but an unexpected attack in their flank at a critical period of the day proved fatal, and in the end they fled in disorder. Their leader, after displaying great courage, was taken prisoner, and beheaded on the field of battle. Humáyún pressed his advantage, captured the outer inclosure of the city, and planted his artillery on the hill which commanded the town.

Kámrán made a gallant defence. The fortifications were in good order, his soldiers were well trained, and he knew well that the sword was suspended over his own head. Several of his sorties were successful; others failed. Still the besiegers made no progress. As the siege continued, however, scarcity began to prevail. Then—the certain test of the current of public opinion—desertions began to take place. Cruelties perpetrated on both sides embittered the contest. And when Humáyún put to death in the presence of both parties the prisoners he had taken from a sallying party, Kámrán retaliated by the perpetration of atrocities so horrible that the pen refuses to record them. It is said also that he caused his nephew Akbar, the son of Humáyún, to be exposed on the part of the wall where the fire was the hottest.

At last even Kámrán became convinced that further resistance was becoming impossible. Food was not to be obtained, and the blockade was complete. He sent then the most submissive letters to his brother, imploring forgiveness, and full of promises of faithful service for the future. Humáyún was inclined to be merciful, to accord to him a frank and free pardon. But his trusted councillors saw too clearly how dangerous a subject a forgiven rebel—especially a rebel possessing the selfish and ambitious character of Kámrán—would become. They worked at the same time upon Kámrán—warning him of the danger of trusting to the pardon of his brother, urging him to escape, and promising to ensure his safety. Their artifice produced the effect they desired. Despairing of his future should he fall alive into the hands of Humáyún, Kámrán, on a very dark night, 27th of April 1547, left the citadel by a breach opened in the wall, traversed the trenches,* and made his way to the mountains on foot.

He was pursued. Regarding the name of the pursuer, historians are at variance. Some say his brother Hindal; others, Hájí Mahammad, an old Moghol nobleman whom he had known in his infancy. All accounts agree in stating that the pursuer overtook the fugitive ascending the mountains overlooking Kábul, and let him go. The most dramatic story is that which affirms that Hájí Mahammad was the pursuer. He overtook Kámrán, and was about to seize him, when the prince exclaimed: "Go and boast to your father that it was I who slew him." The brave heart of the man who had been a devoted servant of Bábar shrank from the implied reproach contained in the speech. He turned at once homewards.

Again were the positions of the two brothers reversed. Humáyún was lord of Kábul, Kámrán was a fugitive. Humáyún's first act was to give up the city, which had resisted him, for one night to plunder. He likewise punished some of his brother's more influential adherents. After these preliminaries he began to devote himself to the duties and indulgences of a king in his own capital. But from this pleasant life he was very soon roused, first mildly, if disagreeably; a little later far more roughly.

The indefatigable Kámrán was again the cause.

* It is said that Humáyún's two trusted councillors, Karácha Khán and Musáhib Bég, who had given to Kámrán the advice recorded in the text, had arranged that he should traverse the lines of the besiegers in safety.

We left that prince ascending, on a very dark night, a solitary fugitive, the mountains overlooking Kábul. He made his way to the neighbourhood of Istálíf to a point where he had desired his most trusted adherents to meet him. But not one of them was to be seen. Undaunted, he pushed on, attended by but one follower, by the Senjed valley. On his way he was seized by a party of Hazáras. One of them recognising him, took him to their chief, who brought him by way of Zohák to Bámián, and there left him. At Bámián he was joined by some of his trusty adherents, conspicuous among whom were Shír Ali and Mirza Bég, and he soon found himself at the head of a body of a hundred and fifty horse. With this force, small as it was, he hoped to be able to do some business. Accordingly he marched upon Gori—a town lying nearly due south of Kúndúz, and on the road to Bádákhshán—and though its governor, who had with him a garrison of a thousand horse and three hundred foot, refused him admittance, Kámrán succeeded in enticing him outside the walls, and, by a display of the most daring courage, in defeating him and capturing the town. He found it full of *matériel* of all sorts. Leaving Shír Ali to guard Gori, Kámrán pushed on with a force now considerably augmented into Bádákhshán, in the hope of persuading the governor, Mirza Súlimán, to espouse his quarrel. But rebuffed by him, he turned off to Balkh to implore the aid of the hereditary enemies of his family, the Uzbég Túrks.

This was the intelligence which brought the first symptoms of disquietude to Humáyún. It did not much trouble him. It was a movement, he thought, which might be crushed by prompt action on his part. He accordingly sent one of his most trusted chiefs, the Karácha Khán already spoken of, with a sufficient force to drive out the intruder.

Karácha Khán acted with promptitude and skill. He marched straight on Gori, and laid siege to it. Shír Ali defended it with great obstinacy for a considerable time; but at last, finding it impossible to prevent it from falling into the enemy's hands, he suddenly evacuated it with his whole force, and retired in the direction of Balkh.

His protracted defence of Gori had well served his master's cause. It had given time to Kámrán, not only to gain the Uzbég chiefs, but to induce him to put into the field a powerful force on his behalf. Shír Ali, retreating on Balkh, fell back on this force. With it he returned to Gori. Kámrán easily recovered Gori; then advancing in the direction of Kúndúz, took Bághlán and menaced Bádákhshán.

Prince Hindal was governor of Kúndúz. On the first intimation of the movement of the Uzbég Túrks in favour of Kámrán, he had effected a junction with Karácha Khán, and this general had been joined by the troops of Bádákhshán under Mírza Súlimán. But the three united forces were too weak to meet the daily increasing army of Kámrán. Hindal, then, threw himself into Kúndúz; Karácha Khán returned to Kábul for reinforcements; the Mírza withdrew into Bádákhshán to defend the passes leading into that province.

This was the second and more disagreeable awakening of Humáyún. It roused him thoroughly. At the very first news of the danger, and before Karácha Khán had returned, he levied his army and marched northwards. He had reached Ghorband when he met his general and his following in so destitute a condition that it was necessary for them to return to Kábul to refit. Humáyún moved his force to the north-east, to Gúlbehár in the Kohistán district, to enjoy the pleasures of the chase till Karácha Khán should return. When that event happened the season had advanced too far, and the passes were closed. Humáyún attempted them, but without success. He returned, baffled, to Kábul, leaving time to Kámrán to carry out his operations against Bádákhshán.

The tide of fortune was now running strongly in favour of that prince. In vain had Mirza Súlimán attempted to bar his progress. Kámrán had driven him to take refuge in the mountains. This success had brought to him some thousands of his old adherents from Kábul. Another event was preparing in that city which would bring him more.

Humáyún had returned, baffled, to Kábul. He had not been long there before his minister, commander-in-chief, and chief adviser, Karácha Khán, took offence at the refusal of his master to dismiss another minister, who, he conceived, had insulted him. It is probable that had Humáyún yielded, even slightly, in the first instance, the angry spirit of his chief minister might have been appeased. But Humáyún indolently permitted the spark to fan into a flame. Even then he might have quenched it had he chosen to sacrifice the offending minister. He preferred, however, to steer a middle course, far from honourable to himself, inasmuch as he insinuated to Karácha Khán that it would be in his power, as chief minister, to seize an opportunity to call the offender to account at a future period. Prompt dismissal he refused. Upon this Karácha Khán, accompanied by many of the most influential men of the Court, left Kábul at the head of three thousand veteran troops, and seizing the imperial stud at Khwájá Riváj made for the passes of the eastern Hindú Kúsh.

Humáyún, though completely taken by surprise, was not stunned by the blow. He hastily collected all his available troops, and following the rebels, came up with the rearguard at Kárábágh. Karácha Khán, however, pushed on, and by favour of the night succeeded in placing the bridge of Ghorband, which he broke down, between himself and the pursuers before daybreak. Humáyún then discontinued the pursuit, and Karácha Khán, leaving a force south of the Hindú Kúsh in the Panjshír valley to guard the passes and to watch the proceedings of the ruler of Kábul, crossed the mountains, and effected a junction with Kámrán in Bádákhshán. Kámrán at once occupied Tálikán, sent a force under his general Shír Ali to endeavour to gain the city of Kúndúz, and despatched another force to Andar-áb, a town commanding the northern slopes of the Hindú Kúsh at the issues of the Girdshah Pass.

It would appear that his measures were either not

very well planned, or not very well executed. Fortune certainly was against him. His general, Shír Ali, engaged in operating against Kúndúz, was taken prisoner, and at once liberated and entrusted with high command by Humáyún. The general he had left in the Panjshír valley to guard the passes was defeated and slain. Humáyún, who had collected a formidable army, and had received promise of co-operation from Mirza Súlimán of Bádákhshán, had then traversed the Girdshah pass, and occupied Ander-áb, which Kámrán's general had previously evacuated. So far, then, the star of Humáyún had seemed to be in the ascendant.

But Kámrán was very confident. He knew that his brother's next move must be against the important town of Tálikán. He had therefore garrisoned that place with the force brought by Karácha Khán from Kábul, strengthened by some of his own men. He himself lay with his main army at a distance of about fifty miles, ready to act according to circumstances, watching his opportunity.

The opportunity soon came. Talikán stands on the Férkar river near the point where it joins the Bángí. Humáyún, then, conceived the idea of sending one division of his army across the Bángí above the town, so as to cut the communication between it and the army of Kámrán, whilst he should attack it on the other side. The execution of this delicate manœuvre he entrusted to his brother Hindal. The plan, however, had not been kept very secret, for intimation of it reached Karácha Khán in sufficient time to enable him to inform Kámrán. With the speed of lightning Kámrán marched close to the vicinity of Tálikán, placed his army in observation whilst Hindal was executing his manœuvre, and, the instant that general had placed the Bángí between himself and his main army, dashed upon him. The result was never doubtful. Hindal and his force were forced back with heavy loss.

It seems that Kámrán, a man of experience himself, and supported by chieftains of proved conduct in the field, ought to have taken advantage of this victory. But, influenced by circumstances of which I am ignorant, he preferred to take up a position on a rising ground not far from Tálikán, in a certain sense covering that fort. Humáyún on this occasion showed the quality of a great leader. He had witnessed from the opposite side of the Bángí the defeat of his detachment. Knowing well the shifting nature of the allegiance of many of his followers, he was burning to wipe out the stain—and to wipe it out at once. He crossed the river, then, immediately, at a ford a mile below the town, and marched straight against the elevated ground occupied by Kámrán.

Now was Kámrán's opportunity. He had a strong position close to the fort occupied by his followers, and in the attack the enemy was bound to expose his flank. To resist until Karácha Khán should assault that flank was his clear line of action. A complete victory would probably have ridded him of Humáyún. A defeat could not have worse consequences than a retreat into a fort which must eventually surrender. He ought then to have hailed the chance of decisive action.

He did not hail it. It is hard to say why. He did not even stand the assault; but, hastily breaking up, retired into the town, leaving all his baggage in the hands of the enemy.

Humáyún at once laid siege to Tálikán. Naturally kind-hearted, and certain now of success, he offered terms to Kámrán. Kámrán refused them. But as day succeeded day, and his hopes became fainter, when the inevitable future pressed itself more and more closely upon his vision, then did he begin to lose heart. A few days more, and the arrows which he directed at his brother's camp bore with them missives expressive of contrition and of hopes for pardon. These missives touched the heart of Humáyún. He agreed to send a confidential agent into the town to arrange the terms of accommodation.

The agent arranged the terms. Kámrán consented to renounce his independence, to acknowledge the sovereignty of Humáyún, to retire to Mekka, and to yield up the rebel nobles in chains. In justice to Kámrán, it must be stated that this last condition was agreed to by him on the understanding that the lives of those nobles should be spared.

Then Kámrán surrendered (August 17, 1548). Allowed to take a few companions with him, he selected, amongst others, Bápus Bég,* one of the

* The history of this man affords a curious instance of the morals and manners of that period. Chief minister and confidential friend of Kámrán in 1545, he had deserted to Humáyún

revolted nobles, to whom he said he wished to make reparation for injuries he had inflicted on him. The small party, and it consisted of but a few men, were conducted to the frontier of Túrkistán by Háji Mahammad—the same nobleman, it will be recollected, who had overtaken and spared the life of Kámrán as he was escaping from Kábul—and were by him then dismissed on their way to exile.

At last it would seem that Humáyún was master of the kingdom of Kábul. Twice had he completely vanquished his brother; twice had he dismissed him a fugitive without an armed following; this time he had won back to himself, by his clemency, the chiefs, who must have been satisfied that Kámrán, even with many points in his favour, could not command fortune. But so strange was the social and political life of those days, that Kámrán the exile was still a power capable of striking, and striking hardly, for the throne. Constituted as was society in the sixteenth century in Afghánistán, as it is constituted now—for in our days we have witnessed events not dissimilar—there was

on the advance of the prince towards Kábul the same year. When, subsequently, in 1547, Kámrán recovered the capital in the manner stated in the text, he, under the plea that Bápus Bég had superintended the execution of some prisoners taken by Humáyún, gave that nobleman's wife to the rabble in the bazaar, by them to be dishonoured, and killed his three sons, between the ages of three and eight, throwing their bodies over the walls. Notwithstanding this act, we find Bápus, only the following year, deserting to Kámrán, moved solely by his sympathy with Karácha Khán. And now we find him willingly accompanying into exile the prince who had insulted him in his deepest affections.

no absolute safety for Humáyún but in the death of his brother. Imprisonment was not sufficient—for he could escape. Even deprivation of sight could not take away the power of the name.*

Kámrán had scarcely proceeded forty miles from the frontier, when information reached him that Humáyún, in full darbár, had pardoned the revolted nobles, and restored them to favour. Hating the idea of exile and of Mekka, it occurred to him that could he but once obtain a footing at his brother's court, everything was yet possible. The clemency shown by his brother to his companions seemed to augur that his heart might relent to him also. It was at least worth his while to try it. Accordingly he sent Bápuṣ Bég to present his humble petition to be received into favour. The answer responded to his fondest hopes. He received permission to return.

The ceremony which followed reflected the highest honour on the warm-hearted Humáyún. When his brother appeared, he bade him cast away the whip which he had placed on his neck in token of being a criminal. "What is past is past," he said, when Kámrán, after having been seated, began to make excuses for his conduct. The two brothers then rose, embraced each other, and sobbed on each other's necks. Humáyún then conducted his brother to the highest place of honour next to himself. They then dined and ate salt together amid the rejoicing of the

* Look, for instance, at the installation of the blinded Mahammad after the deposition of Masáúd I., page 87.

courtiers. The reconciliation was most complete—in appearance.

Before setting out for Kábul, Humáyún proceeded to arrange for the government of the several provinces and districts which acknowledged his sovereignty or the overlordship of his house. Bádákhshán he restored to Mirza Súlimán, and added to it the fort and district of Tálikán and the district, to the north of it, of Kishém. Prince Hindal received Kúndúz, with the towns and districts dependent on it, chief amongst which were Gori and Bághlán; Shír Ali, the old general of Kámrán, was appointed his minister. To Kámrán himself was assigned the province, or rather district, of Koláb,* across the Oxus—to the north of Kúndúz and Bádákhshán—lying between Darwáz and Shaghnán, and bordered on the north-east by the small district of Karátighín. This district was given to Prince Askari, who, it may be remembered, had submitted after the capture of Kandáhár, and had since remained in disfavour. The policy of posting in such close conjunction to each other the two brothers who had shown the most marked hostility to himself, seems to indicate weakness on the part of Humáyún. He was ever too confiding. As their lieutenant, he nominated Chákar Ali Bég, a man of proved fidelity possessing great influence in the district.

Humáyún then returned to Kábul (5th October

* The chief town of the district, Koláb, is in long. 70°, lat. 38°. The district, though north of Badakhshán, and on the other side of the Oxus, used always to be considered as belonging to Badákhshán. *Vide* Blochmann's "Ain-i-Akbari," p. 438.

1548). Before he had left his northern provinces he had meditated an expedition to drive the Uzbég Túrks from Balkh, and to secure the adherence of Kámrán he had promised to confide to him the government of the province of which Balkh was the capital. On his arrival at Kábul, the winter and early spring being before him, he set to work to push on with vigour his preparations for this expedition. They were nearly completed when he received an embassy from Mirza Haidar, the enlightened and distinguished ruler of Káshmír. The ambassador was instructed to acknowledge the overlordship of Humáyún, to invite that prince to Káshmír, and to lay before him the plans matured by Mirza Haidar for undertaking from his mountain-country an invasion of Hindústán and driving thence the family which had supplanted the dynasty of Bábar.

This was a proposition than which none could be more tempting to Humáyún. The project, too, seemed feasible. Mirza Haidar had wrested Káshmír from the son-in-law of Shir Shah, and he had shown himself the most consummate general of his age; and now he offered to place himself, his troops, his country, at the disposal of Humáyún for the recovery of the inheritance of which he had been robbed. It was a most tempting offer—an offer at which, had his hands been free, Humáyún would have eagerly clutched. But two circumstances barred his acceptance of it: these were the attitude of the Uzbég Túrks at Balkh, and the attitude of Kámrán and Askari in Koláb and Karátighín.

The Uzbég Túrks had, we have seen, assisted Kámrán in his second contest with Humáyún, not from love for Kámrán, but from a desire to see the Moghol family weakened by internecine wars. For the same reason, when, subsequently, the two brothers were fighting with apparently even chances near Tálikán, the Uzbégs had refused to assist Kámrán. After the contest had been decided, both the brothers bore the Uzbégs a grudge—Humáyún, because they had at one time assisted his brother; Kámrán, because they had subsequently refused that assistance. Besides, the position of the Uzbégs in the famous city of Balkh, south of the Oxus, could not be regarded but with great disfavour by a Moghol ruler. Humáyún had, therefore, determined to drive them across the Oxus, or at all events out of Balkh. His preparations had been made with that object, and they had been communicated to so many people that they could hardly have escaped the penetration of the Uzbég prince, who was allied to Humáyún by marriage.

The attitude of Kámrán was, moreover, not such as to inspire him with confidence. Kámrán had ruled a kingdom; he now governed a district. Koláb was to him what, in later times, Elba was to Napoleon. He chafed at the pettiness of the mountain district. Almost his first act had been to quarrel with Chákar Ali Bég, the nobleman appointed by Humáyún to act as his prime minister, and he had refused his brother's invitation to repair to Kábul to receive there the nomination to another principality. It was evident then to Humáyún that Kámrán's loyalty would scarcely be proof against the temptation which his own departure for Káshmír and India would offer him.

For these reasons Humáyún resolved to postpone his acceptance of the tempting offers of Mirza Haidar, and to carry out his plans against Balkh. In the spring of 1549 his preparations were complete. He sent then warnings to his vassal princes and nobles, to Hájí Mahammad of Ghazní, to Mirza Súlimán of Bádákhshán, to Prince Kámrán of Koláb, to Prince Askari of Karátighín, to Prince Hindal of Kúndúz,—the first to join him at once, the others to unite with him after he should have traversed the passes.

Háji Mahammad joined his sovereign at Yúrat Chálák, near Kábul. There, too, Humáyún was met by Mirza Ibráhím, the son of Mirza Súlimán of Bádákhshán. He then set out by way of Istálif and the Panjshir valley. Here he waited till he heard that the Uzbégs had taken the field; he then traversed the passes and moved by way of Andar-áb to Nárin.* From Nárin he marched through the Nílbar valley to Bághlán, being joined on his way by Prince Hindal and Mirza Súlimán.

At Bághlán Humáyún had expected the princes Kámrán and Askari; but when he found that, notwithstanding their promises and protestations, they did not appear, he began to fear that they were watching their opportunity to betray him. Still, how-

* Erskine says, "He marched down to Anderab, and thence by Tálikán to Nárin." It is difficult to understand why he should have done this, for Ander-áb is south of Nárin, and Nárin again south of Tálikán and on the road to it from Ander-áb.

ever, hoping for the best, he contented himself with detaching a force to cover Bádákhshán from any possible attack, and then pushed on to Aibak, a strong fort on the frontiers of the principality of Balkh.

Aibak, scantily provided and vigorously assailed, soon surrendered. Had Humáyún pushed on at once he would probably have carried Balkh, for the easy capture of Aibak had made a great impression on the Uzbégs. But the inaction of Kámrán paralysed him. He still hoped he might come; he feared the mischief he might effect should he himself be seriously involved with the Uzbégs. A vacillating mind, hovering between two conclusions, almost invariably decides on a middle course, exposing it to the two evils it had wished to avoid. So it was in this case. Humáyún dreaded to attack the Uzbégs lest Kámrán should act in his rear; he dreaded to order a hostile movement against Kámrán lest he should force him into revolt. He therefore sat still and waited. The result was that the two things he most dreaded happened: the Uzbégs forced him to retreat, and Kámrán revolted!

It was so, in very deed. Humáyún delayed at Aibak so long, that the Uzbégs received reinforcements from beyond the Oxus and resolved to beat up the quarters of their dilatory invader. Just at this time Humáyún had made up his mind to advance. As he entered Astáneh the Uzbégs came down on his rearguard and plundered the baggage of his army. He continued, nevertheless, his onward movement, though marching slowly, in the hope that Kámrán would arrive. When at last Balkh was reached, Kámrán was still invisible.

The part which Kámrán designed to play became now quite clear to Humáyún, and again the conviction of it paralysed him. His troops drove in, notwithstanding, the advanced force of the Uzbégs, and Balkh lay at his mercy. The object for which he had marched from Kábul was within his grasp; he had but to stretch out his hand and take it. But he feared to stretch out his hand. Why? Simply because, in possession of Balkh, exposed to the hostility of all the tribes of the Uzbégs, an opportunity would be offered to Kámrán to slip down on Kábul. He could not make up his mind to run that risk, so—he called a council of war.

A council of war never fights. It would seem that not a single voice was raised in favour of an occupation of Balkh. Neither did any member advocate the crushing of Kámrán as a preliminary measure. As might have been expected, the middle course—so dear to mediocre minds—was adopted. That was to take up a position at Déra Géz, some twelve miles distant, commanding the entrance to the passes leading to Kábul, and whence, should Kámrán prove loyal, it would be easy to return to Balkh.

This middle course met with the success it richly deserved. The conjectures of the chiefs regarding Kámrán's possible action had not been kept secret; there was scarcely one section in the army in which the question of his conduct had not been discussed. When, then, Humáyún acted on the opinion of the council of war, and ordered his troops to turn their faces towards Kábul, though only so far as Déra Géz, the rumour spread like wildfire that the army was retiring because certain news had arrived that Kámrán had started for a raid on Kábul. Instantly there was a panic and a stampede. The majority of the soldiers had left their wives, their children, their property, in Kăbul, and they knew from experience the treatment which those hostages to fortune were likely to receive from the tender mercies of Kámrán.

Meanwhile, the Uzbégs, noting the retreat of their enemies, had pressed out to harass them. They found instead of an army a disorderly rabble, bent on pressing forward. It is true, that owing to the exertions of Humáyún, whose horse was shot under him, a covering party was formed which for a time checked and ultimately repulsed the Uzbégs. But the flight was not stopped. Discipline disappeared. Each man pressed on for himself, bent on reaching Kábul. It was like the retreat from Moscow. All cohesion was lost. Humáyún, without a horse, almost without a following, had to cross mountains, traverse passes, a prey to hunger, thirst, and fatigue, never knowing where he should pass the morrow. When he reached Kábul it was rather as a fugitive than as a king.

What, meanwhile, had Kámrán been doing? That Kámrán had throughout this period been watching his opportunity, that he had avoided joining his brother, in order to mar his plans, is clear from his subsequent conduct. But Kámrán had made no attempt on Kábul. He had not moved out of Koláb. It would have been better for Humáyún, then, had he continued his operations against Balkh. The phantom conjured up to prevent his occupation of that place had been in very deed a phantom.

But his disorderly retreat on Kábul, the dispersion of his chiefs and of his soldiers, gave Kámrán the chance for which he had been watching. Kámrán shone more in politics than in war. In the former he never, in the latter he very often, missed the moment when to strike. And now he struck. Summoning his brother Askari to Koláb, he marched into Bádákhshán.

Mirza Súlimán had found his way to that province after the disastrous retreat from Balkh. But he had no army capable of coping with that of Kámrán. He could not, then, prevent the town of Tálikán from falling into his hands; but he threw a garrison into the fortress of Kila-Zefer, and then with his small force occupied a very strong position, guarding the passes, close to the town of Jérm.

It formed no part of Kámrán's plan to waste his time in a mountain warfare with Mirza Súlimán. Leaving, then, a garrison under Bápus Bég in Talikán, he marched on Kúndúz, held by his brother Hindal, who had escaped from the disastrous retreat of the royal army, of which he had commanded, with distinguished gallantry, the rearguard. Kámrán used every endeavour to induce Hindal to transfer his allegiance to himself; but as Hindal refused, he sat down before the place.

In his attempt to take Kúndúz, Kámrán was baffled by the skill and the artifice of Hindal, and he was already despairing of success when he received intelligence that Chákar Ali Bég, the Kolábi minister with whom he had quarrelled, had invaded Koláb, defeated his brother Askari, and had laid siege to the town. He heard also that Mirza Súlimán had advanced from the hills, and was threatening to cut him off. He therefore raised the siege of Kúndúz, and sending a party to keep Súlimán in check, set out to return to Koláb.

But the tide of his misfortunes was at its flow. Kámrán relieved Koláb, was joined by Askari, and drove away Chákar Ali. Then, marching against Súlimán, he reached the banks of the river Kokcha, and encamped near the town of Rostak. When lying there his camp was suddenly set upon and plundered by a large body of Uzbégs who happened to be passing by. There was no time for resistance. The attack was utterly unexpected, the more so as the leader of the Uzbégs, Syad Uzbég, was in alliance with Kámrán. It subsequently appeared that the Uzbégs had not waited to ask to whom the camp belonged before they attacked it. However, the mischief was done. Kámrán, Askarí, and a few others escaped, but the army had disappeared; there appeared no chance of reuniting it, for Súlimán was now marching, joined by Hindal, against the revolted brothers.

This accumulation of disaster was too much for Kámrán. He threw up the cards, made the best of his way to Khost, intending to proceed thence by way of Zohák and Bámián into the Hazára country, to act then according to the information which might reach him from his friends in Kábul.

But though his fortunes seemed at their lowest, a strong tide was already flowing in his favour. The rule of of Humáyún in Kábul since his return from Balkh had given great dissatisfaction to some of the great nobles who were the main supports of his throne. Prominent amongst these was Karácha Khán, of whom mention has already been made. But important personage though he was, he was but one of a large number. Cold and stern as they knew Kámrán to be, they yet preferred him to the softer nature of the often thoughtless Humáyún.

No sooner then was it known in Kábul that Kámrán was crossing the mountains with but a few followers on his way to Bámián, than the conspirators sent out to him their most solemn professions of devotion to him, accompanied by specific recommendations as to the line of conduct he should pursue. He was advised to dissemble with his brother, by imploring his clemency and promising good conduct for the future. They engaged, on their part, to incense Humáyún against him, so as to induce him to send out parties to attack him on lines which he would avoid. Humáyún and Kábul would thus be left at his mercy.

Kámrán followed these directions to the letter, and the conspirators responded as they had promised. His appeals for mercy were rejected. Two considerable parties were sent to capture him: the one towards Zohák and Bámián; the other towards Sál-A'lang; Humáyún taking up a position with a small detachment near Déra Kipchák.

Before the party first in order of mention had

reached its destination, Kámrán had passed through Bámián, and had hastened by forced marches and with an increasing following to Déra Kipchák. There, too, treason had been at work for him. His friends were in the closest confidence of his brother; many of them about his person. Surprised by Kámrán, Humáyún still had about him adherents sufficient to repulse him, had they been good men and true. But when Kámrán arrived within bowshot, they refused to return the fire which he poured upon the group round his brother, and signalled to him to come on. Kámrán, somewhat hesitatingly, advanced. His brother's followers then dispersed, or fled, or came over to him. One miscreant, a man of Koláb, struck a blow at, and wounded Humáyún.* Though severe, it was not mortal, and he was carried in safety to the Sístán pass, where the following morning he was joined by the faithful Háji Mahammad Khán. Ultimately he made his way, with some difficulty, to Ander-áb.

Kámrán, noting the flight of the adherents of Humáyún, sent out all the troops he could spare to pursue them. He followed with the remainder to Chárikár. There he received evidence by the bloody cuirass of Humáyún, which had been found on the field, that his brother had been wounded. He sent the cuirass in to Kábul to be shown to the governor,

* "The man had raised his sword to repeat the blow, when Humáyún, turning round and looking his assailant sternly in the face, exclaimed, "Wretched rebel!" Babái, from surprise, suspended his blow for a moment, when Mehter Sagái interposed, and Babái drew off."—Erskine.

who had refused to surrender the place. The governor recognised the cuirass and submitted.

Kámrán was now, for the third time, master of Kábul, and with it of all the treasures of Humáyún and of the person of his son. His hopes were high, for he believed that his brother had perished, and, Humáyún once dead, there was no one to be feared. Claiming independent sovereignty, he allotted the various provinces or districts of Afghánistán to his adherents. Thus to his brother Askari he gave Jalálábád; to Karácha Khán, Ghazní; to Yásan Daolat, whom he had sent to follow up Hamáyún, the northern district of Ghorband. He continued likewise to levy troops and to endeavour to enlist on his behalf the services of the Hazáras and the Afgháns, so as to be ready for any event.

He was soon to be tried. Three months had not elapsed since he had reoccupied Kábul when information reached him that Humáyún, recovered from his wounds, had broken up from Andar-áb, and was crossing the Híndu Kúsh by the pass leading into the Panjshir valley.

It will be recollected that on previous occasions, whether at Kábul or at Talikán, Kámrán had always waited to be attacked—and had been defeated. He determined this time to avoid that error. No sooner, then, had he heard that Humáyún had broken up from Andar-áb, than, collecting all his troops and his Hazára auxiliaries; and having under him as leaders tried men such as Karácha Khán, his brother Prince Askari, and Yásán Daolat, he marched to the Panjshir valley and took up a strong position on a rising ground overlooking the southern slopes of the mountain, and barring the road by which Humáyún must pass.

That prince, meanwhile, had collected at Andar-áb all the chiefs who had remained faithful to the legitimate sovereign. Before he set out, anxious to bind them to his service, he proposed to them and their followers to take an oath of fidelity to himself under all circumstances. The wild chiefs heard the proposal without astonishment, and were on the point of acting upon it, when one among them, the faithful Háji Mahammad, already twice honourably mentioned in this history, ventured to suggest that when they had taken the oath it might be necessary for Humáyún to bind himself also, by a sacred and solemn engagement, to act as his advisers should recommend.* The bold proposition to limit the authority of the sovereign was startling in that rude age. Prince Hindal, who heard it made, fired with indignation; but Humáyún, who knew himself, and who felt how much depended on the cordial co-operation of his chiefs, yielded promptly and with grace. "Let it be," he said, "as Háji Mahammad and the other chiefs desire."† He then made the required declaration.

* The words were: "Whatever we, his well-wishers, recommend with a view to his interest, and deem indispensable for that purpose, he will consent to and perform."—Erskine, vol. ii. p. 388.

† Mr. Erskine states that Háji Mahammad's freedom on this occasion was not grateful to royal ears, and was probably never forgiven. This supposition is well founded. Soon after Humáyún's restoration Háji Mahammad was falsely accused of treason

Marching through the passes without difficulty—for it was summer—Humáyún suddenly found himself in the presence of his brother's army, drawn up on a rising ground, and barring his road. He halted his force, and, in pursuance of a predetermined plan, sent to Kámrán a messenger proposing terms of accommodation. The terms he proposed, considering his right of birth, were fair, even liberal. They were, that Kámrán should acknowledge the overlordship of his brother, and should join with him in an attempt to reconquer Hindústán. Kámrán did not altogether reject the proposal; he sent back the messenger notifying his acceptance of it in principle, provided he were allowed to keep Kábul. Humáyún replied that he was willing to admit Kámrán as his partner in empire, alike over Hindústán and Afghánistán, and that Akbar should be their viceroy in Kábul. Kámrán was much inclined to accept these terms, but Karácha Khán, who had obtained great influence over him, dissuaded him. Kábul, he said, at any cost must be kept.*

Bent on fighting, it was surely the policy of Kámrán to attack at once. All Eastern nations, except when they are behind walls of stone or of mud, fight better

and put to death. He had long previously seen that his ruin was determined upon, but he had always said, with Danton, "they dare not."

* His words were, "My head and Kábul," meaning death or Kábul—words to which the result attached a peculiar interest, his head, after Humáyún's victory, having been placed on one of the gates of Kábul.—*Vide* Erskine's "History of India," vol. ii.

when they attack. As a man who had seen many a battle-field, Kámrán must have known this. But here, at this decisive moment, superstition came to ruin him. The astrologers told him that the day was unfavourable. He resolved, therefore, not to attack, and, if possible, to avoid an action. But this resolution could not even begin to take effect without disheartening his followers. It had scarcely been announced when some of his chiefs deserted to Humáyún, carrying with them the account of the reason of the inaction. . Humáyún at once determined that the prediction of the astrologers should be true.

He advanced, but as he approached the enemy one of his generals recommended that the action should be deferred to the following day. Hamáyún, fickle and easily led, agreed; but other chiefs objected, and again he was over-ruled. He advanced again, and when within charging distance he ordered the leading division under Mirza Ibráhím to attack the height on which Kámrán was posted, he himself supporting him with the reserves. The attack was well directed and well led, and notwithstanding all Kámrán's efforts the assailants effected a lodgment and gradually gained ground. At this crisis Karácha Khán, who commanded the cavalry under Kámrán, fell with such fury upon Humáyún's left wing, commanded by Prince Hindal, that he completely broke it and drove it from the field. With the skill of a practised leader, Karácha Khán re-formed his men and led them with fury against the right wing commanded by Mirza Súlimán. The battle here was hotly contested, but victory seemed inclining to Karácha Khán, when a chance shot disabled him. He was taken prisoner and killed.

The loss of their leader so disheartened the cavalry of Kámrán, that the enemy recovering the ground they had lost, and pressing onwards, made a demonstration against the eminence on which Kámrán was still unequally struggling. The left wing too had rallied, and was coming on. It is but bare justice to Kámrán to admit that he fought with great determination, nor did he leave the field till his brother Askari had been taken prisoner and many of his foremost chiefs had fallen. Seeing then that all was lost he fled, followed by eight only of his adherents, from the field. The triumph of Humáyún was complete.

Never again was the star of Kámrán in the ascendant. Thenceforth the supremacy of Humáyún over Kábul and its subordinate provinces was never seriously endangered. Still, so long as a man possessing the unconquerable ambition and the daring energy of Kámrán was at large, he could not feel in perfect safety. It will be necessary, then, before describing the general affairs of the reign of Humáyún, to deal with that particular incident of it relating only to Kámrán.

Kámrán had fled from the field, having lost everything except hope. He fled night and day till he reached the country inhabited by the wild aboriginal Afgháns. These robbed him and his followers of all they possessed. Disguising himself then as a mendicant, he made his way to Mándráor, and discovered himself to the chief, by whom he was hospitably entertained. He then began to raise forces, and with such effect, that Humáyún sent troops to attack him, and these forced him to take refuge with the hill tribes —the Dáwézais and Mohmands. The pursuit once relaxed, Kámrán began again to intrigue with his new hosts. So great was the ascendancy he gained over them that they agreed to follow him in his enterprise, and allowed themselves to be led by him into the mountains in the vicinity of the capital. In vain were expeditions sent against him. Too weak to fight, he fled on their approach, only, however, to re-appear in another part of Afghánistán. Sometimes, when his brother pursued him in person, he retaliated by making attacks upon his camp. In one of these, his brother Hindal, fighting for Humáyún, was killed, though the attack itself was repulsed. At last Kámrán, now having a this disposal a force of fourteen thousand Afgháns, allowed his camp to be surprised. This blow was fatal. He fled across the Indus, and threw himself on the protection of Salím Sháh, the Patháu King of Dehli.

But there was no abiding place for him here. Treated with indignity by his host, he escaped from his camp in the disguise of a woman, and courted the hospitality of two Híndú princes in succession. Driven from their territories by the importunities of Salím Sháh, he then fled for protection to the Gakk'hars of the Rawal Pindi districts. It happened that the chief of that race wished to propitiate Humáyún. He sent then an embassy to him with the offer to deliver up his brother Kámrán. Kámrán, cognisant of the nature of the mission confided to the ambassador, endeavoured to secure terms for himself by sending with it a messenger, carrying a letter in which he renewed his prayers for pardon and his promises of amendment. Upon receiving the embassy and the message, Humáyún, satisfied that he could never count himself as safe so long as Kámrán should be at large, marched with an army across the Indus to receive his prisoner.

What was to be his fate? Was mercy to prevail, or was the cup of evil running over? Humáyún was, by nature, soft-hearted. His father, on his dying bed, had conjured him to be merciful to all, especially to his brothers. Hitherto he had spared them. He had welcomed back Hindal after his revolt, had twice pardoned Askari who would have slain him, had sobbed on the neck of the oft rebelling Kámrán. And now Kámrán—Kámrán who had once betrayed him, who had twice driven him from his capital, who had rejoiced over his supposed death, and who by his unceasing plots had rendered his life a burden to him—now Kámrán was in his power. Could he, in safety to himself, could he spare him once again?

Humáyún wavered. It would appear that he rather leaned to mercy. But there were men about him who saw that mercy in the shape of free pardon was impossible. These men knew too well the unforgiving nature of the prince who, if pardoned, might one day become their master. They therefore presented to Humáyún a petition, in which, after dwelling on what Kámrán had done, they prayed that capital punishment should be inflicted upon him as indispensable to the public peace. Humáyún still refused to give the order for his brother's death; but, feeling strongly how necessary it was he should be deprived of the power of action, he gave orders that his eyes should be lanced. The order was carried out. Kámrán then asked and obtained permission to proceed to Mekka,* where he died, some four years later.

It is difficult to say how Humáyún should have dealt his brother. To imprison him would have been useless. Escape sooner or later would, in those days when the sovereign was but the first noble, have been certain. No inland fortress would have held him, and Humáyún possessed no St. Helena to which to transport him. Free pardon had been tried, and tried in vain. To pardon him again would have been to ensure a further sacrifice of life.* In Europe in those days, and even at a much later period, he

* He went first to Tátta, in Sind, where his father-in-law, Shah Húsén, allotted him an estate and a residence. He persisted, however, in going on to Mekka. His wife, Chuchak Begam, insisted, in spite of her father's prohibition, on accompanying him. "You gave me," she said, "my husband when he was a king and happy, and would take him from me now that he is fallen and blind and miserable. No. I will attend and watch him faithfully wherever he goes." She carried her word and accompanied him to Mekka. She survived him only seven months.—Erskine's "History of India," vol. ii. p. 419.

† "Oh, my unkind brother, what are you doing? For every murder that is committed on either side you will have to answer at the Day of Judgment. Come and make peace, that mankind may no longer be oppressed by our quarrels." Thus wrote Humáyún to Kámrán during the siege of Tálikán, 1548.—Erskine's "History of India."

would have been tried and executed as a rebel, and it seems to me that Humáyún would have been amply justified in dealing out to him that punishment.

Kámrán was a man of considerable attainments. He was not only thoroughly well read in the poetry of that age, but he was an elegant versifier and an accomplished scholar. To have gained and kept the tender affection of such a woman as the daughter of Súltán Húsén he must have possessed some sterling qualities. His faults were, the boundless ambition which overleaps itself, undue exaltation and a continued development of a temper naturally suspicious, in times of prosperity. They were faults pertaining, in that age, almost of necessity, to one born in the purple.

The removal of Kámrán seemed to give to Humáyún the opportunity for carrying out his long-cherished wishes regarding Hindústán. He was on the borders of Káshmír. The ruler of that province, Súltán Haidar, had previously invited him, and now invited him again, to repair thither to receive its formal overlordship. Humáyún was anxious to comply. But his generals had two reasons for opposing the expedition. The first, the secret reason, was that they had left their families in Kábul; the second, and the avowed reason, was that if they were to enter Káshmír it would be in the power of Salím Sháh, King of Dehli, to cut off their retreat. For once Humáyún was obstinate. He ordered that the army should march into Káshmír by the Bímbar pass. But he found to his indignation, the next morning, that the greater part of his army had taken the road to Kábul. Vain were his remonstrances. He was forced to give into the general wish, and to fall back on Pesháwar. Here he halted a sufficient time to superintend the erection of a new fort designed to protect the town from the depredations of the hill tribes, and to serve as a *point d'appui* during his projected invasion of Hindústán. He returned at the end of the year (1554) to Kábul.

Although the general wish of the nobles had forced Humáyún to desist from his plans with regard to Káshmír, it must not be supposed that the arrangement sanctioned by him on the eve of the march from Andar-áb to Kábul in 1550 still existed. The proposer of that arrangement, Háji Mahammad, had perished by the hands of the executioner. The brother who had witnessed it, Prince Hindal, was dead. The men in fear of whom it was made, Kámrán and Karácha Khán, were no more. Other near relatives and great chiefs had also been removed. Humáyún had now neither rival to the throne nor near him a noble so distinguished by his talents and following to cause him alarm. As his prime minister he had selected Bahrám Khán, a Bádákhsháni, whose abilities as a diplomatist have been related in a previous page.* Bahrám was a man of first-rate talents and of unbounded ambition and self-assertion. It is believed that it was he who brought about the death of Háji Mahammad. But at the time of which I am writing, he had been but recently advanced to the first place

* *Vide* p. 133.

under the king. In fact he was the king's man, dependent solely upon him. The daring independence of royal authority, which in later days he was to display, had not then been developed.

Humáyún, freed then from all anxiety regarding attempts upon Kábul, resolved to invade Hindústán. Fortune singularly favoured him. Salím Sháh, the capable son of the Shír Sháh who had robbed him of his kingdom, had died in 1553. His death was the signal for disorder in Hindústán. It is true that his son, Firóz Khán, was proclaimed his successor, but three days later he was murdered by his maternal uncle. The murderer, devoid of talent, and possessing none of the qualities of a ruler, usurped the throne only to cause revolts in several portions of his dominions. Into the details of these it is not necessary to enter. It will suffice to say that in 1555 there were five rival claimants to the throne, all belonging to the Afghán family of Súr; the murderer, Mahammad Sháh, who occupied Bíhár, Jáupúr, and a great part of the country east of the Ganges; Ibráhím Súr, his brother-in-law, who after holding Agra and Dehli, had been defeated by Sikandar Sháh; Sikandar Sháh himself, now holding Dehli and Agra; Ahmad Khán Súr, who had the Pánjab; and Shújah, who had Málwa. There was besides a sixth, not related to the others, Táj Khán Keráni, who threatened Bengal.

Hindústán's distraction has always been Kábul's opportunity. Humáyún resolved to use it to his purpose. With his utmost endeavours, however, he could only raise an army of fifteen thousand men. At the head of this force he set out by way of Jalálábád and the Khaibar for Pesháwar, accompanied by his son Akbar, then twelve years old,* in December 1554, leaving his kingdom of Kábul to be administered by Múnim Khán, the son of Bahrám Khán, and governor of his second son, then about a year old. On reaching Pesháwar, Humáyún was joined by Bahrám with a body of veterans from Kandáhár. The next day the army marched for the Indus. On crossing that river Bahrám was nominated commander-in-chief of the army.

Humáyún advanced from the Indus by hurried marches to Láhor, which he occupied without a blow. Remaining at Láhor to organise fresh forces, he sent on Bahrám to the Satlaj. Meanwhile, Sikandar Sháh, the member of the house of Súr who occupied Agra and Dehli, hearing of the movements of Humáyún, had used every effort to collect an army. To check the enemy till he should form one, he despatched two of his most trusted generals with forty thousand horse to the Satlaj. At Máchhíwárah, which then lay immediately on the left bank of that river,† they were met by the Moghol force led by Bahrám. The battle that ensued was obstinately contested. One of the decisive battles of that era—a battle upon the result of which it depended whether Hindústán should be ruled by the Moghol who had planted himself in

* Akbar was born the 15th October 1542.—Blochmann's "Ain-i-Akbári."

† About seventy years ago the river took a more northerly channel, and now runs four miles from the town.

Afghánistán, or by the Afghán who had settled in Dehli —the chiefs on either side used every endeavour to conquer. The far greater number of the Indian force seemed to promise success. But Bahrám was a host in himself, and Bahrám conquered. The defeat was the more complete from the fact that the battle had been so hardly fought. Elephants, baggage, and horses fell into the hands of the conqueror. Bahrám sent parties to follow up the fugitives as far as Dehli, waiting himself at Máchhíwárah till Humáyún should join him.

It was time for Humáyún to follow, for Sikandar Sháh was advancing with an army of seventy thousand men to avenge the defeat of his lieutenants. Bahrám sent messenger after messenger to press the advance of Humáyún. Meanwhile he moved forward into Sirhind to delay as much as possible the enemy's approach. At last Humáyún joined and took command. Two days later (18th of June 1555) Sikandar Sháh offered battle. The challenge was accepted. A desperate contest terminated in the victory of Humáyún.

That victory gave him the throne of Hindústán. It is true that provinces had to be conquered and pacified in detail, but the question of supreme domination was settled. That battle—gained near the town of Sirhind—restored Kábul and its dependencies to the position of a subordinate province, subject to the Moghol who reigned in Dehli. It was difficult to manipulate all at once such immense territories into one distinct shape. Kábul, indeed, ably governed by Múnim Khán, remained stedfast, but the wily Mirza

Súlimán, the man who had always assisted Humáyún against Kámrán, renounced his vassalage, and declared Badakhshán independent. Humáyún saw the evil, and tried to remedy it. He drew up an elaborate plan for the better government of the divisions of his empire,* but before he had attempted to put it into execution he died. His death resulted from an accident. Descending one evening the narrow marble steps outside the building in which he was at the moment, his foot became entangled in the skirts of his mantle, and the steps being slippery, he lost his footing and fell headlong over the parapet. He lingered four days in a state of insensibility, and then died in the forty-eighth year of his age (24th of Jannuary 1556), two years and a half after he had blinded Kámrán, and twenty-one months before the death of that brother.

The history of the reigns of Humáyún and Kámrán has been little more than a record of the plots of the one to supplant the other, of civil wars, of intrigues, of duplicity, of treachery, and of cruelty. Of the Afgháns themselves we hear little. They are spoken of as the wild and uncivilized aboriginal inhabitants of the country, hardy, brave, inured to crime—but as

* It is doubtful, the circumstances of the times being considered, whether Humáyún's plan would have worked. He proposed to divide the empire into six provinces, each ruled by a viceroy, with a local capital and board of administration. The local capitals were to be Dehli, Agra, Kanáoj, Jánpúr, Mándú, and Láhor. Each province was to have a separate military force under its own general. Under such a system I cannot but think that the time of the emperor would have been entirely occupied in suppressing the revolts of his viceroys.

utter savages. The history of the two reigns, if they may so be spoken of, is the history, not of the Afgháns, but of the Moghol rule in Afghánistán. Not the less is it a history of the country. As it was the migration to India of the Afghán sovereigns of the house of Ghor that made the rule of the stranger a necessity for Afghánistán, so shall we find that it was the migration of the Moghol to the same more favoured land that paved the way for the uprising of a purely Afghán dynasty in the country of rocks and stones.

CHAPTER VI.

HISTORICAL.—FROM MOGHOL TO AFGHAN.

Humayun was succeeded by his son Akbar. It was a succession to a disputed inheritance. The Hindú chief Hémú, acting for the representative of the Súr dynasty, on the one side, and another member of that family, Sikandar Súr, on the other, contested the empire. But Akbar, though a boy little over thirteen, had displayed already signal promise, and he had the inestimable advantage of counting among his devoted adherents the greatest general of the age, Bahrám Khán, of Badakhshán. On this occasion Bahrám displayed his wonted daring and energy. Having driven Sikandar Súr from the Panjáb, he turned with vastly inferior forces to meet Hémú. He fought him at Pánipat, and after a fiercely contested battle completely defeated him. For the second time the fate of India was decided on that memorable field.

Kábul, meanwhile, had been left to the care of Múnim Khán, guardian of Prince Mahammad Hákim, the younger brother of Akbar, then about three years old. The real government, however, soon came to be exercised by the prince's mother, Mah Júјak Bégam, a lady of very remarkable ability—an ability which was very soon to be tested.

The news of Humáyún's death had scarcely reached the northern provinces when his cousin, Prince Súlimán of Badakhshán, clutching at the opportunity, crossed the Hindú Kush, and, for the moment, occupied Kábul. Shah Tahmasp, Shah of Persia, at the same time besieged and took Kandáhár, and gave it, with Dawar and Gaímsír, to his nephew, Súltán Húsén Mirza. The Persians retained it till 1603.* With the Badakshâni it was otherwise. It appeared to him that it would be more to his advantage to have independent possession of one province, the road to which lay through Afghánistán, than to be the ruler of two separated from each other by a lofty range, and one of them bordering on the territories of the Emperor of India. This, at least, is certain, that Prince Súlimán very shortly evacuated Kábul and returned to Badakhshán; further, that for the eight or ten years that followed he continued on terms of amity with the Bégam virtually regent of Kábul.

With the proceedings of Akbar in Hindústán this

* I must beg the reader to bear in mind that whenever, up to the occurrences of the year 1736, the city of Kandáhár is mentioned, the old city of that name is referred to. It will be related, in the course of this history, how in 1737 Nádir Shah founded a new city in the vicinity, called by him Nadirábád, to which the inhabitants of the old city migrated, taking with them also its name.

history has connection so far only as those proceedings affected Kábul and the country represented by that name. During the early part of his reign Akbar was merely the nominal overlord of Afghánistán, and was too busily occupied in settling his affairs south of the Satlaj, and in dealing with the Rájás of Rájpútáná, to be able to pay the smallest attention to Kábul.

An event which happened in that city some four years after the death of Humáyún proved this very clearly. Subsequently to the departure of Prince Súlimán, the Bégam, though she made her authority respected, had had much to suffer from the ambition and usurpations of her ministers. Múnim Khán, the son of Bahrám, had left Kábul when his father fell into disgrace. His son, whom he left behind him, was greatly wanting in tact. Intrigue followed intrigue, and crime succeeded crime. The Bégam had almost begun to despair of impressing her own will upon the turbulent nobles, when there arrived at Kábul a man who seemed at the moment born, as it were, to her hand. This was no other than Mír Shah Abúl Ma'álí, a powerful noble fleeing from revolt against Akbar. Abúl Ma'álí had been one of Humáyún's generals, and had been entrusted by that prince with the government of Láhor after by his victory at Sirhind he had established himself in Dehli. Removed—probably from his friendship with the famous Bahrám, who had rebelled—from the government of the Panjáb, Abúl Ma'álí had made a pilgrimage to Mekka. On his return he found the provinces of Western India in revolt against Akbar. He joined the rebels, at once took the lead in their councils, and defeated the royal army, commanded by Húsén Kúli Khán at Narnol, about eighty-six miles south of Hánsi. Pressing on to improve his victory, he was met by another army sent by Akbar, and totally defeated. He then fled to the Panjáb, but finding his safety menaced in every corner of the province, he pushed on to Kábul and offered his services to the Bégam regent.

It is a proof of the independence of even nominal suzerainty enjoyed by Kábul at this epoch that the Bégam at once accepted the services of a man who fled to her, a rebel to the brother of her son. He seemed just the man she wanted—a man who, devoted to herself, would yet assert her authority over the nobles who were plotting and intriguing at her court. He married her daughter, Fakhrúmissa, and she made him prime minister. Acting in the double capacity of son-in-law and vizier, he put down all opposition. Plotting ceased, intrigue was silent; there was but one will ruling everywhere. For some time the Bégam believed that that one will was her will; that Abúl Ma'álí was but the hand which put her resolves into force. But gradually it dawned upon her that his was the will as well as the hand; that he had done more cleverly that which the nobles whom he had supplanted had attempted in vain; that he had formed a party prepared to support him to the utmost. The moment this conviction forced itself upon her the Bégam struggled—but it was too late. She was not, however, powerless, and Abúl Ma'álí, certain of support, resolved to remove her from his path. He accordingly had her assassinated (1563).*

The obstacle cleared away, Abúl Ma'álí, by virtue of his relationship by marriage to Mahammad Hákim, at once assumed the regency. In Kábul his claims were allowed, and his authority was submitted to. But it was not so in Badakhshán. The subsequent conduct of the ruler of that country, Prince Súlimán, forbids the idea that in the action which he took upon this occasion he was animated by any other feeling but ambition. He had his own designs on Kábul. The young prince, the nominal ruler, was then but eleven years old; his character unformed. Súlimán could well have allowed him to continue for some time under the influence of his mother, Mah Jújak Bégam, for he and that lady were bound together by the strong ties of mutual interest. But it did not at all suit him to witness all power and authority in Kábul glide into the hands of a clever adventurer, who, moreover, had fortified his position by marrying the sister of the boy

* I have found it most difficult to trace the true account of these transactions and to reconcile the versions of different writers appearing in the same book. Let us take, for instance, the case of Mah Jújak Bégam. It is evident (Blochmann's "Ain-i-Akbari," p. 318) that this lady was the mother of Mahammad Hákim, king of Kábul. In the same page of the same book it is recorded that in the eighth year of Akbar's reign she was alive and in the very height of her power; whereas it is clear, from page 312, that she had been murdered early in that year. Ferishta's account seems to support the second story. The facts in both are, doubtless, correct, but the dates are inaccurate. It is certain, from page 322 of the same record, that Abúl Ma'álí married the daughter of Mah Jújak Bégam.

king. Prince Súlimán resolved therefore to drive, if he could, the adventurer from Kábul.

He at once, then, invaded the country, occupied Kábul after a struggle, and killed Sháh Abúl Ma'álí.* Intent on his own schemes, he then married his own daughter to Prince Mahammad Hákim, and leaving with him as vizier a Badakhsháni noble, U'méd Ali, returned to his own country. But it would seem that as the young prince grew up he resented the tutelage of the Badakhsháni vizier and dismissed him (1564). Upon this Súlimán returned to Kábul, this time with hostile intentions towards the young prince. Unable to oppose him, Mahammad Hákim implored the assistance of his brother, and fled towards the Indus. Akbar, dreading the occupation of Kábul by a possible invader of Hindústán, instructed the governor of Múltán, Mahammad Kúli Khán, to advance to the assistance of his brother should Prince Súlimán attack Kábul. But before these orders reached Múltán, Súlimán had occupied Kábul. After establishing himself there he moved on Jalálábád. It was just at this period that King Mahammad Hákim, fleeing towards the Indus, met the advanced guard of the succours sent to him by Akbar, consisting of a body of troops, detached by the Emperor from his own army, under the command of Farídún Khán, a Kábul noble.

Farídún Khán was the brother of the Mah Jújak Bégam already spoken of, and therefore maternal uncle

* Ferishta states merely that Abúl Ma'álí lost his life in the war; but in the "Ain-i-Akbarí" (Blochmann, p. 312) it is positively affirmed that Súlimán had him hanged.

to Mahammad Hákim. When he met his nephew, all seemed lost in Afghánistán—Kábul had been taken, and Jalálábád was invested. There appeared at the moment no hope of recovering it with the small *corps d'armée* at the disposal of Farídún Khán. But the uncle was a man fertile in expedients, unscrupulous, ready to grasp the attainable. The re-conquest of Afghánistán was difficult: the seizure of the Panjáb was easy. "Why not," he counselled his nephew, "take what you can get. Your brother is engaged in a life and death struggle in Bihár. He has no troops he can detach to oppose you, and I am at your disposal. Seize the Panjáb; after that, expel Súlimán from Kábul."

Mahammad Hákim jumped at the idea, and marched straight on Láhor. But his designs had transpired, and the governor of Láhor held out for the Emperor. Meanwhile, news of the invasion had been transmitted to Akbar. That great prince had just arrived at Agra after a successful campaign, the prelude, he hoped, to one which would be decisive. He at once broke up on receiving the intelligence from the Panjáb. Fortunately for his brother, the news that Akbar had reached Sirhind on his way to relieve Láhor came to him before Akbar had crossed the Satlaj. Then happened an event which would seem impossible had it not occurred. Mahammad Hákim broke up at once precipitately from before Láhor, and retreated with his cavalry in such haste on Kábul, that he arrived there and occupied the city before it was known that he had crossed the Indus! Prince

Súlimán, apprehending no attack, had gone to Bádákhshán. The news of the advance of Akbar had then been to his brother the means of regaining his lost kingdom. His invasion of the Panjáb was at once pardoned.

For the ten years that followed, Mahammad Hákim remained in undisturbed possession of the kingdom of Kábul. Nor is it probable that he would then have been molested had he remained content with what he had. But an insurrection against Akbar of the Afghán colonists in Bíhar and Bengal inspired him with the idea that he might at last realise his hopes regarding the Panjáb. That province, he was aware, had been left with but a few troops under Rájá Mán Singh, son of Rájá Bhagwán Dás, who had been appointed the preceding year to be its governor.* Mahammad Hákim, then, at the head of a considerable force, crossed the Indus. His advanced guard, consisting of about a thousand men, had but just reached the left bank, when Mán Singh fell upon it and crushed it. The Hindú Rájá was not, however, strong enough to resist the whole force, and he retreated before the invader as far as Fort Rotás on the Jailam. Reinforcing the garrison of that fortress, he fell back on Láhor, prepared to hold that till he should be relieved. Mahammad Hakím leaving Rotás, followed Mán Singh to Láhor, and sat before the place. But Akbar was not deaf to the summons despatched to him by his lieutenant. Embarrassed by his war in Bengal and

* "Ain-i-Akbari" (Blochmann), p. 333.

Bihár, he nevertheless set out without delay for the Panjáb. Again did Mahammad Hákim on the first intimation of his approach break up the siege, and, leaving only a small garrison in Pesháwar, retreat on Kábul. Arriving there he organised his defences, entrusting his advanced force to the command of his maternal uncle, Farídún Khán, whilst he himself should bring on the supports. Meanwhile, the leading divisions of Akbar's army, led by his sons, Prince Salím, afterwards the emperor Jahángir, and Prince Múrád, the fourth in order of birth, had occupied Pesháwar and Jalálábád without a blow.* Salím, or as it will be more convenient to call him, Jahángir, remained there, whilst his brother Múrád pushed on towards Kábul. He advanced without sufficient caution, for when engaged in the Shatargardan pass, some thirty miles from Kábul, he was set upon by Farídún Khan, and the whole of his baggage was cut off. It would appear that the misfortune to Prince Múrád was not very severe, for a few days later, reinforced by Mán Singh, the prince engaged Mahammad Hákim with all his forces. For the first time in the records of Afghán history, we find a battle decided by gunpowder. "Kúnwr Mán Singh and Túzak Khan Atká," writes Ferishta, "having advanced, the elephant swivels opened a fire. By mere accident an officer of Mahammad Hákim Mirza and three other persons standing near him were killed; on which he

* Jahángir could not then have numbered more than twelve summers, and Múrád one less, but Mán Singh was the real commander. Múrád died nineteen years later of *delirium tremens.*

took to flight, losing many persons of distinction in the retreat." There was no more fighting. Mahammad Hákim fled to Ghorband, whence he entreated the forgiveness of his brother. This forgiveness Akbar readily accorded, but on the condition that thenceforth the yoke of suzerainty should be enforced.* (March 1579.)

During the five years following these events, the authority of Prince Súlimán had been gradually undermined in Badakhshán. This was mainly due to the dissensions between him and his grandson, Prince Shahrúkh. The restless character of Súlimán incited the ambition of his grandson; they fought with alternate success for some years till at last they were so weakened that Uzbégs stepped in and annexed the country. The grandson then fled to Akbar, by whom he was enrolled as a grandee. Súlimán repaired to Kábul, to his son-in-law, and with him he remained till the death of the latter.

This event occurred in 1585. The transactions of the last seven years of his life are little known. It is clear that he acted simply as the viceroy of his brother, and that Kábul had been merged into the greater empire. Of the state of the people during the time of his sway I have been unable to gather any account. But the tribes of the passes leading down from the highlands of Kábul to the valley of the Indus were

* So conjectures Elphinstone, and it is a conjecture borne out by the subsequent history of Kábul during the lifetime of Mahammad Hákim. The country was formally annexed to Hindústán after his death.—"Ain-i-Akbari" (Blochmann), p. 452

to show the stuff of which they were made a very few months after his decease.

When that event happened the Emperor nominated Rájá Mán Singh to be Governor of Kábul. The Rájá at once proceeded to that capital, and possessing himself of the persons of the sons of the late ruler, the princes Afrásyab and Kaikúbád, he rejoined Akbar on the Indus, leaving his son Sakat Singh to manage affairs at Kábul.

Akbar, meanwhile, had undertaken and completed the conquest of Káshmír, and had enrolled its king amongst the nobles of Hindústán. But a more difficult task was now before him. This was to compel the submission of the wild tribes who dwelt in the mountains beyond the Indus—the Kohístanis, the Swátis, the Yúsúfzais, the Mohmands—in fact, the several large atoms of the tribes known then under the general name of Berduránis, but with whom the English are now better acquainted under the peculiar nomenclature of each.

Akbar was the greatest of all the Asiatic sovereigns of India. He had conquered and pacified Hindústán, the Panjáb, Kábul, and Káshmír. Opposed by the best generals of the age—by the renowned Hémú, by his master in the art of war, the illustrious Bahrám—he had never lost a battle. In mountain warfare, as on the plains, he had equally triumphed. Nor did it seem to him as even a chance possibility that the savages of the Afghán passes could foil his troops.

But these men were the fathers of the warriors who for thirty years have faced and warred with our own countrymen, and they were not one whit their inferiors. When they heard that Akbar had announced his intention to deal with them they made up their minds that they would deal with Akbar, but in their own manner, and in their own hills.

The first army was directed by Akbar against the Yúsúfzais, then, as now, occupying the country beyond the Mahában mountain, the Búner and Chagúrzai hills, and the country north of the former. His army was commanded by his foster-brother Zain Khán.* It would appear that this general was at first successful. It is recorded by Abúlfazl that he "moved into the district of Waijús (north of Pesháwar) and punished the Yúsúfzais. Several chiefs asked for pardon. After this he created a fort in Jakdárah, in the middle of the country, and defeated the enemy in twenty-three fights. He had at last to ask for reinforcements, and Akbar sent to him Rájá Bír Bar and Hákím Abúl Fath with some troops."† It is clear from the above recital, and from other records of the period, that however successful Zain Khán might have been in his advance into the hills, the Yúsúfzais then showed so formidable a front that he was compelled to wait for reinforcements. The reinforcements were led by Rájá

* Zain Khán was the ennobled son of one of Akbar's nurses. At the time of the expedition against the Yúsúfzais he was a commander of two thousand five hundred.—"Ain-i-Akbari" (Blochmann), p. 344.

† "Ain-i-Akbari' (Blochmann), p. 344. Rájá Bír Bar, or Bal, was a Brahman, a poet and diplomatist, and a great friend of Akbar.

Bír Bar and Abúl Fath to a point which we may suppose to have been near Jakdárah. Then there ensued, unhappily, a difference of opinion between the two chief generals. Bír Bar was in favour of a combined attack on the tribes, to be followed by a prompt retreat. Zain Khán was of opinion that the attack should not be made with the combined forces; that they should operate on two lines; that whilst one force held the position he occupied, the other should make a *détour* and attack the enemy on their flank or in their rear. But he was over-ruled, and it was decided to attack the hillmen, and, penetrating the mountains, to return by another road—by way of Karákar. Bír Bar led the advance, Hákim Abúl Fath the centre, and Zaín Khán the rear. The pass they had to traverse was long and difficult. Nevertheless, by incredible exertions, Bír Bar reached the summit by sunset. But he had scarcely arrived there, when, from flanks and from the front, the Afgháns poured down arrows and stones upon his men, and with such effect that they fled in panic, briskly pursued by the enemy. With great difficulty Bír Bar retreated to the foot of the pass, and effected there, with a portion of his force, a junction with the two other divisions, which, likewise attacked, had with difficulty repulsed the enemy.

That night and the following day the Yúsúfzais continued the attack, inflicting greater and greater loss on the imperialists. As the second night fell the generals held a council of war. Zain Khán was in favour of treating. Bír Bar would not hear of such a

13

course, but, dreading another night attack, he, without communicating with Zain Khán, drew off in the night through a defile which he believed had been left unguarded. But the Yúsúfzais had set a snare for his destruction. Hardly had he reached the gorge at the head of the defile than the mountaineers set upon him, and almost destroyed his force. The slaughter was terrific. "Nearly eight thousand men, perhaps even more," writes Badáoni, "were killed. Bír Bár also was amongst the slain." Several men of note fell with him; but, writes the same author, "His Majesty cared for the death of no grandee more than for that of Bír Bar."

Meanwhile Zain Khán and Abúl Fath had been furiously attacked. When day broke he began to retreat over the Bilandri, still followed by the enemy. All that day he managed to keep his men together, amidst enormous difficulties; but when night fell the rumour that the Afgháns were upon them produced a panic, and they dispersed in disorder. Great was the slaughter, and it was with but a few men only, and on foot, that Zain Khán and Abúl Fath reached the Emperor's camp at Atok.

The Emperor's first act was to despatch Rájá Todar Mall and Rájá Mán Singh with a force across the Indus, to prevent the advance of the Yúsúfzais into the plains. Todar Mall having taken up positions to effect this object, Mán Singh was sent to Kábul to take up his government there, and by a simultaneous attack from the west to aid Akbar in his design to punish the mountaineers.

Rájá Mán Singh reached Kábul in safety, and prepared at once to act on the instructions of his master; but before he arrived there Akbar had entrusted Zain Khán with a second army to act against the Mohmands and Ghoris, who, under their chief Jalálúdín Raushání, had committed many depredations in the Peshá-war valley. Zain Khán gained no striking victory, but his operations were so far successful that the mountaineers were driven back into their hills. But the following year Rájá Mán Singh joined in a well-concerted attack made on the hill tribes from the Indus, south of the salt range, and aided in their complete defeat. It was, however, a never-ending contest, made so, indeed, by the policy of Akbar. By rigorously confining the hill tribes to their mountain ranges, and debarring them from legal access to the plains, he forced them to become robbers for subsistence. Thus the frontier contests continued for fourteen years, until a new turn was given to them by a successful raid made by the Mohmands on the city of Ghazní. They were, it is true, quickly driven out, but they were never subdued. Indeed, it stands out as a remarkable fact the frontier tribes, under all changes of dynasties, have maintained to the present day their independence alike of Kábul and the Panjáb. They baffled even Nádir Shah.

But to return. At the end of the year 1586 Mán Singh had been appointed governor of Kábul. He was the first Hindú to whom the administration of a purely Mahomedan country had been entrusted. The result, in an administrative point of view, can hardly be pronounced satisfactory. The Kábulis complained that all the offices of state were given to foreigners (Rájpúts), and that they were neglected. That there was truth in their complaint is evident, but that Mán Singh's action was natural, even justifiable, may likewise be admitted. It is impossible to reform a state by the aid of unskilled workmen. The Kábulis were better men with the sword than with the pen, and Mán Singh was probably forced to employ his own co-religionists.

However, the complaints waxed so loud that Akbar recalled him, and sent in his place his foster-brother, Zain Khán (1588). This important viceroyalty seems to have been held in succession by many nobles. Zain Khán's first administration was principally noticeable for his incessant campaigns, with more rather than less success, against the mountain tribes. During his viceroyalty Akbar visited Kábul, spent two months there, and then replaced Zain Khán by Mahammad Kásim (1589). He was succeeded in 1594 by Kúlij Khán, of a distinguished Persian family. Of his rule of three years it is simply recorded that "it was not successful." One of the preceding governors, Zain Khán, followed him. He was governor of Kábul when the Mohmands, under their chief Jalálúdín Raushání, made the raid upon Ghazní previously alluded to. Zain Khán appears to have displayed great activity on this occasion, for not only did he expel Jalálúdín, but when shortly afterwards that leader attempted to recover the place, he fell upon him, defeated him, and, following with vigour, overtook and slew him. This was his last noticeable act as Governor of Kábul, for Akbar, regarding the pacification of the country assured by the death of Jalálúdín, recalled Zain Khán to Láhor (1601).

The name of the successor to Zain Khán I have been unable to discover, but it is of little importance. Kábul no more represented a kingdom, not even a province. After the death of Jalálúdín, Ghazní was given a separate and distinct administration, and an event was to occur which was to provide in a similar manner for a third division of the ancient kingdom.

In a previous page* I have mentioned that shortly after the accession of Akbar the Shah of Persia had taken Kandáhár, and bestowed it with other fiefs upon his nephew, Húsén Mirzá. The place was held for the Shah till the year 1603, when the disturbances which took place on the accession of Shah Abbás gave Akbar the opportunity to recover it without striking a blow. He appointed Shah Bég, a nobleman of the Arghún clan, to be its governor.

Akbar died two years later, and was succeeded in all his dominions by his son Jahángir. The change of monarchs had no effect on Afghánistán. The fate of that country indeed is more nearly connected with the career of the nobleman to whom Akbar had given Kandáhár. That career I propose briefly to follow.

Shah Bég belonged to the Bokhára Arghúni. He had been a faithful servant to Mahammad Hákim, ruler of Kábul. On the death of that prince he had

* *Vide* p. 182.

taken service under Akbar, and had greatly distinguished himself in the campaigns against the Yúsúfzais and Mahmands. In the war which ended with the conquest of Sind, he was so marked for his conduct in difficult matters, that Akbar selected him to conduct the delicate negotiations which terminated in the surrender of Kandáhár.

His administration of Kandáhár and the district represented by the town was in every respect so satisfactory, and his repression of the turbulent Kákars—then also answering to the character I have given of them in the first chapter of this book—so complete, that on the recall of Sharíf Khán from the governorship of Ghazní, that town and district were added to his charge. When Akbar died towards the end of 1605, the two most important districts in Afgánistán were held by one man—and that man distinguished alike for his character and for his conduct.

The death of a sovereign of a vast Eastern empire was in those days almost invariably the signal for disturbances. When, therefore, the news reached Persia that the great Akbar had expired, hope rose buoyant in the breast of Shah Abbás that in the convulsions which must, he thought, ensue, he might be able to recover Kandáhár. He transmitted the necessary instructions to his governor of Herát, Húsén Khán Shámlú, and that nobleman, responding, at once marched upon the place.

The siege that followed is memorable chiefly for the spirited conduct of the governor, Shah Bég. He knew that he could resist the enemy's attacks, but he was not proof against the cravings of hunger. Now, his supplies were low. A long blockade would be fatal to him. It was absolutely necessary that he should deceive the enemy.

With this view, and in order to induce the Persians to believe that his stores were plentiful, he gave feasts every evening in an open space in the castle overlooked by the enemy. Húsén Khán, partly, but only partly deceived, then demanded permission to send in an envoy, nominally to treat for terms, really to look about him. The permission was accorded. But before the gates were opened, every sack of grain in the place had been emptied into the streets the envoy must traverse. The envoy returned satisfied that the garrison was well supplied. It happened, shortly after, that Shah Abbás, finding that the disturbances he had anticipated had not arisen, disavowed his general and raised the siege.

Subsequently, in 1606, Jahángir visited Kábul, and before he left, added the city, with the district depending on it, to Shah Bég's government. Shah Bég thus became viceroy of all Afghánistán, the then Persian province of Herát excepted. When filling this high office, he was directed to prepare a financial settlement for the whole of the country. As he held power for nine years subsequently, it is to be presumed that the settlement was made. I have, however, been unable to discover any trace of a document which would be one of the most interesting of all the legacies of Moghol rule.

Shah Bég received from Jahángir in 1608 the title

of Khán Dúrán. He resigned the office he held in 1620 "on account of the fatigues incident to a residence in Kábul, horse travelling, and the drizzly state of the atmosphere of the country."* Probably the contests he was forced to wage with the hill tribes, who, growing fiercer and fiercer, at one time threatened Kábul itself, entailed upon him a more than ordinary amount of fatigue. But he was a great drinker,† and his love of liquor impaired his natural activity.

The name of the immediate successor of Shah Bég I have been unable to discover. But two years later (1622) I find Ashraf Khán governor of Kandáhár. The famous Khán Jahán Lodi was at the same time governor of Múltán. In that year Shah Abbás, Shah of Persia, resuming his old designs, marched an army against Kandáhár. Ashraf Khán implored the assistance of the Emperor. Khán Jahán was ready to march to his aid from Múltán, but was forbidden by Jahángir to stir. "Kings," wrote that monarch to him, "should be opposed by kings." The fatal effect of acting upon such a maxim was soon apparent. Shah Abbás pushed the siege with such vigour, that on the fortieth day the place fell into his hands. No attempt was made in the lifetime of Jahángir to recapture it. His son Shah Jahán was indeed ordered to the north with an army, but he did not go, the

* "Ain-i-Akbari" (Blochmann), pp. 377–8.

† "He was much given to wine drinking. He drank, in fact, wine, *cannabis*, opium, and *kúknár*, mixed together, and called his beverage of four ingredients *Chár Bhugrá*, which gave rise to his nickname *Chár Bhugrá Khur*."—"Ain-i-Akbari" (Blochmann.)

jealousies which prevailed as to the succession keeping him and his brothers in India; and for fifteen years, till 1637, Kandáhár remained in the possession of Persia.

I may here pause for a moment to refer to the condition of the Afghán tribes in the neighbourhood of Kandáhár. They were composed mainly of the great clan of the Ghilzais—now appearing once again on the scene. Naturally turbulent, and notwithstanding the fact that their clan had furnished a family the members of which had occupied the thrones of Ghazní and of Dehli, a long course of servitude had disposed the Ghilzais to obey. For many years they had been ruled from Dehli, but it is supposed that, tired of submission to that luxurious court, they had welcomed the approach of an army commanded by a man possessing the character and reputation of Abbás the Great.

Kandáhár occupied by the Persians, the Afghán tribes in the vicinity willingly, then, transferred their allegiance to the conqueror. But it would seem that the conqueror did not at first appreciate the value of the submission. Abbás himself, generally so careful to overlook none of the minor springs which so often affect the course of great events, had for the moment forgotten to reckon the vast importance to the stability of his rule of contenting the aboriginal inhabitants of a conquered country. Hence it happened that he, or rather the governor appointed by him to rule at Kandáhár, imposed upon the Afgháns vexatious imposts and exactions. These the rude mountaineers found it difficult to bear. They showed their discontent by murmurs, but as these produced no result they sent a deputation to Ispahán to represent their grievances to Shah Abbás and to request the removal of the governor and the appointment of one of their own tribe as their chief representative, recognised by the Shah and corresponding directly with Ispahán. The request opened the eyes of Shah Abbás to the mistake he had committed. He complied with it at once. Thenceforth an Afghán chief held, by letters patent, the office of Kalántar, or administrator in chief of the internal affairs of the tribes in Kandáhár.

To resume the course of events. Three years after the loss of Kandáhár (1625–6), the Emperor Jahángir visited Kábul. The occasion was a remarkable one. Originally he had intended to march thither to crush the hill tribes, then committing more than their ordinary ravages. But they were subdued long before he could approach the scene of action. He did not on that account change his destination. He pushed onwards with his force, and was crossing the river Jailam, when his person was forcibly taken possession of by Mohabbat Khán, a native of Kábul, and one of the first noblemen of the empire, but who had incurred the enmity of Núr Jahán, and who knew that his ruin had been decided upon by that famous lady.

Mohabbat Khán had been summoned to the Emperor's camp to answer charges which had been made against him, but, well aware of the enmity of Núr Jahán, he had taken care to come accompanied by five thousand Rájpúts, on whose fidelity he could depend. These men he now placed round the Emperor, and was prepared to continue the journey to Kábul, when Núr Jahán, who had employed every moment of the time that had elapsed to inspire with resolution the Mahomedan nobles with the army, suddenly attacked him, leading the attack herself.

A desperate action ended in the repulse of Núr Jahán. She had displayed great daring and energy. The elephant on which she rode—the object of the Rájpút attack—had been severely wounded, and had swum in terror to the opposite bank. The child she carried in her arms had been wounded, and her howdah was stained with blood—and after all she had failed. But she was a woman—and a very clever woman. She had not won by employing force. She determined now to try a more subtle method. She therefore joined the captive Emperor.

Mohabbat Khán now advanced towards the Indus. Schooled by Núr Jahán, Jahángir professed perfect agreement with his views; warned him against trusting Núr Jahán; and by his extreme finesse so blinded him, that long before Kábul had been reached Mohabbat Khán had the conviction that the emperor was even grateful to him for having rescued him from the thraldom of a woman he feared and of courtiers whom he detested.

Meanwhile Núr Jahán continued her plots. Now she stirred up enmity, ending in blood, between the imperial guards and the Rájpúts; now she prepared the Afgháns to seize the first opportunity to aid her. But the crowning artifice was that by which she increased her own contingent without exciting to too great an extent the suspicions of Mohabbat Khán.* When her plans were completed, she by a cunning device brought about the release of Jahángir, and restored to him his freedom of action. Mohabbat Khán being still powerful, and her son being in his hands, she made terms with him.

The Emperor did not stay long in Kábul, and the following year he died (October 28th, 1627).

Shah Jahán, his third son, succeeded, after the usual strife among the sons, to all his dominions. For the ten years following his accession the history of Kábul and Ghazní is a blank. It would seem that of that time there is nothing to record beyond the periodical intermitting risings of the hill tribes and their punishment. But in 1637 Shah Abbás of Persia, having been succeeded by Sháh Safi, and that prince showing himself a capricious and cruel tyrant, with none of the capacity of his grandfather, Shah Jahán sent an army to capture Kandáhár. The Persian

* The story is thus tersely told by Elphinstone:—"She employed agents to enlist fit men in scattered points at a distance, whence some were to straggle into camp as if in quest of service, while the others were to remain at their positions and await her further orders. She next made Jahángir suggest a muster of the troops of all the Jágírdárs; and when she was summoned to produce her contingent she affected to be indignant at being put on a level with an ordinary subject, and said she would take care that her muster should not turn out to her discredit. Accordingly she dressed out her old troops so as to make the smallness of their number conspicuous, entertained new levies as if to complete her contingent, and at the same time directed her recruits in the country to repair by twos and threes to the army."—"History of India," vol. ii.

governor of that place was a very distinguished nobleman, Ali Mardan Khán. This officer had been one of the most trusted generals of Sháh Abbás, and had ever shown himself worthy of his sovereign's confidence. But he possessed great wealth, and Shah Safi coveted it. Other nobles, in equally high position, had been summoned to court by the Shah—only to be murdered. At last the mandate came to Ali Mardan. He knew its meaning. Instead of complying he entered at once into negotiations with Shah Jahán, in virtue of which he surrendered to him Kandáhár, and repaired to the court of Dehlí. He was received with the greatest distinction, and was at once nominated by the Emperor general of the army he had formed to recover Badakhshán and to conquer Balkh.

I have shown in a previous page* how, owing to the dissensions between Mirza Súlimán and his grandson, the Uzbégs, then possessing Balkh, had conquered Badakhshán. That province they had retained. Against these Uzbégs Ali Mardan was sent. Crossing the great northern range of the Hindú Kúsh he entered Badakhshán. The Uzbégs, then engaged in a civil war, shut themselves up in their towns and their forts, offering no resistance in the field. Before Ali Mardan had had time to capture any considerable place which might have served as a *point d'appui* near the passes the winter was upon him, and he fell back on Kábul. Leaving there a portion of his troops he repaired to the Emperor's court at Dehli.

* *Vide* p. 190.

The year following (1645) the Emperor, retaining Ali Mardan at his court, despatched Jaggat Singh, a brother of Mókand Singh, Rájá of Kotá, to conquer the country. Jaggat Singh had at his disposal the troops left by Ali Mardan in Kábul, aided by a still larger number, no less than fourteen thousand, of Rájpúts.

But by this time the Uzbégs had composed their internal feuds. When, then, Jaggat Singh entered Badakhshán he met an enemy over whom, notwithstanding the prowess of his Rájpút soldiers, he could gain no advantage. He therefore sent urgent demands for aid.

A reinforcing army was at once sent, led by Ali Mardan, accompanying whom, to undergo "the baptism of fire," was Prince Múrád, the youngest son of the Emperor. The campaign was successful. Badakhshán submitted; Balkh, and with it Afghán Túrkistán, surrendered. Both provinces were united to the empire of Hindústán, and Prince Múrád was proclaimed viceroy. But he had hardly taken his seat when the invasion, the dread of which had caused Humáyún in 1549 to shrink from the occupation of Balkh, took place. The Uzbégs from Samarkand and Bokhára crossed the Oxus to plunder and destroy. There was no rest from these marauders. Múrád, fond of show and pleasure, and shrinking from the ruler's labour pressed upon him by Ali Mardan, quitted the province without orders. He was at once replaced by the third and most crafty of the sons of Shah Jahán, Prince Aurangzib, whilst Shah Jahán himself moved on Kábul to support him. Aurangzib's arrival in Badakhshán was speedily followed by a victory over the Uzbégs. But their numbers were great, their reinforcements constant, and even he, the conqueror, found himself compelled to seek refuge in Balkh.

The contest was finally terminated by an arrangement between the Emperor and the Uzbég chief, Nazar Mahammad, which amounted to a virtual renunciation by the former of his rights on Badakhshán. In pursuance of this compact Aurangzib was directed to surrender Balkh and the strong places, and to retire with his army south of the Hindú Kúsh. Aurangzib did, indeed, easily surrender Balkh and the strong places, but his retreat across the passes of the Hindú Kúsh was not accomplished without great difficulty and great loss. When entangled, in the month of November (1647) in those passes, the wild Hazáras set upon his men—not so much to destroy as to plunder. The snow, the frost, the difficult ways, the incessant and galling inroads of an invisible enemy, told their tale on the imperial troops. Aurangzib and a few horsemen did indeed reach Kábul in safety, but the survivors of the main body found their way there in small bodies, without baggage, without horses, often without arms.

Nor was this the only reverse which the Moghol arms were to suffer at this period. Shah Safi of Persia had died in 1641. He was succeeded by his son, Shah Abbás II., then only ten years old. This prince, though subsequently given to wine, was not in his youth devoid of noble instincts. One of his earliest longings was to recover the city of Kandáhár.* The details for the accomplishment of this task were overlooked by his ministers. Their preparations were made with great care, and with great secrecy. Every expense incurred was defrayed with ready money; and to prevent the chance of interruption of the siege operations by the approach of a relieving force, it was arranged that the invasion should not take place till the passes leading to India should be closed by the snow. This programme was carried out to the letter. Shah Abbas II. appeared before Kandáhár in the early days of December 1647. The siege lasted ten weeks. It had hardly begun when Shah Jahán sent pressing orders to Aurangzib, then at Láhor, to march to its relief. Then was noticed the wisdom in the choice of seasons displayed by the advisers of the Persian monarch. The passes stopped Aurangzib. He forced his way through them, indeed, but the enormous labour thus entailed on his soldiers disorganized his army. He forced them only to find that Kandáhár had just fallen, and that he with a weakened army could do no more than fall back and wait for an opportunity at Kábul.

The opportunity seemed to come the following year. The Persian sovereign had left merely a garrison in Kandáhár, and returned with his main army to his dominions. In the month of May 1649, Aurangzib appeared before the town with an army strong in men and in munitions of war. Himself a capable and

* Hanmer states that the Ghilzaí tribe sent him a pressing invitation to relieve them of their Moghol masters.

determined general, he made the capture of Kandáhár the one point from which nothing should turn him. He employed all the arts of war then known. Establishing a strict blockade, he tried mining followed by assault—and then mining again. At last Abbás II. sent an army to relieve the place. Still unshaken in his resolve, Aurangzib remained before the town to press the siege, whilst he sent a portion of his army under a capable general to drive back the enemy. The Persians were driven back, but they then took up a position in the passes, which enabled them to intercept all the supplies of the besieging army. Aurangzib was not strong enough to attack them there, and at the same time carry on the siege. At last he was starved into retreating. In September he renounced the task and fell back on Kábul.

But the idea was not abandoned. Three years later Aurangzíb led another and more perfectly equipped army against the place.* But the result was the same —repulse and raising of the siege.

Aurangzib was then sent to the Dekhan, and his eldest brother, Dárá Shekhó, a gallant soldier, an instructed prince, too liberal for his epoch, received at his own earnest request the command of a force still more strongly equipped than either of those which had preceded it in the undertaking. Nothing was omitted that could ensure success. He had, it has been stated,

* The author of the "Zabd-úl Táwárikh" was present in Kandáhár during these sieges in the double capacity of physician and astrologer. He gives full and minute details of the assaults of the Moghol army.

Europeans to point his guns.* But although skill directed, and valour carried out, the plans of the prince; although he gave an example of bravery and devotion to his men, unsurpassed and unsurpassable; although he delivered assault after assault, and in the very last of all gained the summit of the rampart, he could not take Kandáhár. The valour of the defenders equalled that of the assailants, and their fortune† was greater. After having lost the flower of his army, Prince Dárá Shekhó was forced to raise the siege. But his misfortunes did not end there. As he fell back in the direction of Kábul, the Persians attacked his rearguard, whilst the Ghilzais harassed his flanks. His losses were great, his discouragement was still greater; and it was with a force reduced in numbers and broken in spirit that he at length reached Kábul. Kandáhár was for ever lost to the Moghol.

Shah Abbás II. inaugurated the permanency of his conquest—now assured by the final repulse of the Moghols,—by the distribution of money rewards to the Ghilzai and Abdáli chiefs, and by reducing the annual tribute paid by them. These measures were successful. During his lifetime, the Afghán tribes of

* Hanmer. Hanmer indeed states that there were Europeans at the second siege, but as he speaks only of two he must mean the last. It is well known that Prince Dárá Shekhó had European engineers and artillerymen in his employ.

† The physician and astrologer previously referred to claims credit for the result. He withheld, he says, the Persian commander from making a sortie in force when the planet Mars was in the south, a circumstance which would have rendered defeat certain.

the country round Kandáhár remained content with the Persian rule.

Shah Abbas II. died in 1666, and was succeeded by Shah Sulaimán. This prince reigned twenty-nine years. Though weak, effeminate, and capricious, his relations with the Afgháns remained undisturbed. He treated them as subjects, not as slaves, and so long as they were so treated they remained faithful. It was the happy fate of their country, from the capture of Kandáhár to the death of Shah Sulaimán in 1694, that its history was a blank.

But the accession of his son, Súltán Húsén, in that year was the beginning of a new era. Húsén was one of those bigoted ascetics who care for nothing but the ease of their souls; to whom the material benefit of others is a matter of no import. The measures taken by Shah Abbás the Great, by his successors of the same name, and by Sulaimán, to ensure the contentment of the Afghán tribes, came gradually to be relaxed under the rule of Súltán Húsén, or it would be more proper to say, under the rule of the corrupt priests and eunuchs who governed in the name of Súltán Húsén. The tribes, the Ghilzais especially, were not slow to betray their discontent. Though not actually revolting, they made demonstrations so strong, that the terrified Shah and his effete advisers hesitated long as to the measures they should take to meet them. After considerable hesitation they decided upon a course, which, like all courses adopted by weak men in a panic, led to a result the very opposite of that they had hoped for.

It happened that at this time the ablest general in the Persian service was a Georgian, named Gúrghín Khán. Born a Christian, this man had endeavoured to establish independence in his native country, but his great military talents had been overborne by the numerical strength sent against him, and he had failed. So powerful was he, however, even in his defeat, that, on the sole condition of his embracing the Mahomedan religion, the Shah had taken him into his service. He had distinguished himself by two qualities—military skill and severity. He was just the man, then, in the eyes of the priestly advisers of Súltán Húsén, to deal with the Ghilzais. The Shah accordingly sent him, at the head of a considerable army, to Kandáhár, with the title of Governor, and with full powers.

Gúrghín Khán and his army reached Kandáhár. The Ghilzais were not in revolt. They had displayed simply a determination not to submit to oppression—nothing more. When Gúrghín Khán entered their country, far from opposing him, their professions of loyalty were all that could be desired; but this submissive attitude did not suit the views of Gúrghín Khán. He wished to strike terror into the tribe. He therefore treated their country as though he had conquered it, and themselves as slaves. Neither rank, nor age, nor sex, found shelter from his tyranny.

Among the Afghán tribes, however, there still lived the tradition of the beneficial results which had followed the personal appeal made to Shah Abbás the Great. Ruthless then as was the conduct of Gúrghín Khán, the Ghilzais believed that a proper representation to the Shah would be sufficient to ensure his recall and to obtain redress for themselves. They tried it; they empowered a deputation to proceed to Ispahán. The deputation reached that capital. But the Shah was not a Shah of the calibre of Abbás. For a long time he refused to see the Ghilzai chiefs; and when at last they were presented to him he gave them an answer of the character of that which, given by another king in another country, had the effect of driving five-sixths of the people in revolt to their tents.

It had not that effect on the Afgháns; their leaders were too prudent. An army of about thirty thousand men, led by the greatest captain of Persia, occupied Kandáhár and its environs. Revolt would have been an invitation to slaughter in the present, fruitless of benefit for the future. They resolved to bide their time, hopeful that events would work for them.

Prominent among the Ghilzai chiefs was Mír Vais. The head of one of the tribes, endowed with quick intelligence, attractive manners, and great liberality, he was likewise the richest and most influential man in Kandáhár. The office of Kalántar, or chief administrator, which he held, gave him a position in which he was able to make his influence felt. Mír Vais had taken a leading part in the events I have just recorded. He had signed the petition which had been sent to the Shah, had kept up the heart of his countrymen, and finally, on the unsuccessful return of the deputation, had used all his influence in favour of submission. It is scarcely to be wondered that Gúrghín

Khán should hate him. Mír Vais seemed to stand between him and the passions of a tribe stimulated to revolt, yet not revolting. He was determined to remove him from his path. He had no valid excuse for touching him, but it was easy enough to invent one. Under the pretext, then, that Mír Vais was conspiring against the Government, he arrested him and others of his influential compatriots, and sent them to Ispahán. Having ridded Kandáhár of their presence, he deemed himself secure, and allowed the greater part of his army to return to Persia.

Mír Vais arrived at Ispahán—a clever, shrewd man of the world brought suddenly into contact with bigoted priests and corrupt eunuchs, leading a weak and effeminate ruler. On the one side was the daring genius, the bold and determined nature of a leader of men; on the other, power based on corruption, and deprived of popular sympathy by the cruelty and weakness which are always the twin children of bigotry. The result of such contact was never, could never be, doubtful. Mír Vais had been sent to Ispahán, that he might be guarded, watched, tortured, if necessary removed by death; that the one living protester against the oppression of the Afghán tribes might never again cross the path of Gúrghín Khán. It was a step fatal to the Georgian governor. The intelligence of Mír Vais detected at once the weakness of the Court of Ispahán. He saw a weak king surrounded and ruled by a corrupt ministry. A trained man of the world, he disguised his contempt, and, assailing the most influential courtiers on their weak side, he bought them. He made them his men and enemies of Gúrghín Khán. When he thought the moment had arrived he demanded that the Shah himself should investigate the charges brought against him. The charges were really groundless, but so adroitly had Mír Vais managed, that had they been otherwise the result would scarcely have been different. The Shah publicly acknowledged his innocence, and Mír Vais at once assumed an influential position at the Court.

He might now have returned to Kandáhár and have bearded Gúrghín Khán. But the insight he had obtained into the character of the Shah and of his advisers, into their system of government—based actually on more than an indifference—on a contempt—for the feelings of the governed, had inspired him with wider-reaching thoughts. From this moment the independence of his country became the passion of his soul. He had in himself every quality and every qualification likely to form a basis of success. He had position, wealth, influence; he had talents, character, address. Above all, in the character of the king and his advisers, and in the position in which he stood to both, he had opportunity.*

* The condition of Persia at this period, under the rule of Shah Húsén, is thus graphically described by Hanway:—"Merit became an empty sound; all offices and dignities were given to those who paid the highest price; money decided everything; and the immense riches which were accumulated by this means seemed rather to whet than to glut the appetite of those base ministers. Every part of the State felt the effect of this disorder. The troops, discouraged by ill-discipline and worse pay, served with reluctance. Robbers infested the highways and interrupted com-

Much remained to be accomplished before he could strike his blow. It was not less an object to weaken his enemies than to inspire his friends. Of the first, Gúrghín Khán was the chief; of the second, the Afghán tribes were those who could be most easily moulded. His extraordinary tact and knowledge of character enabled him to work out both ends at the same time.

It was not difficult to arouse the suspicions of the weak monarch and his courtiers regarding the ambition of Gúrghín Khán. Mír Vais did not openly disparage that nobleman; he rather spoke respectfully of the vast power that he wielded. He took indeed fitting occasion to express his surprise that a man who had been a rebel should now hold in his hands the government of the three provinces of Georgia, Kermán, and Kandáhár. He sometimes even doubted whether a man who had been a Christian could be an orthodox Músalmán in the sense in which orthodoxy was understood by the Shah. If he praised his ability and his power, he commented on the manner in which he had once used both against his master, and on the greater means now at his disposal. In short, Mír Vais used

merce. Placemen, impoverished by the purchase of their offices, tyrannised over the people and were rapacious with impunity; in short, justice was sold in the very capital of the empire."

The same writer thus sketches Shah Húsén:—"He had a strong attachment to his religion, and might be denominated an honest man; but so excessively indolent and immoderately addicted to women and wine as to be utterly incapable of governing. Thus unworthy of being a real, he was only a nominal king."—"Hanway's Travels," vol. ii.

all his artifice to undermine, whilst seeming to praise, Gúrghín Khán.

His mysterious language fell on eager ears. The poison, distilled drop by drop, entered into the soul of the Shah. Gradually his mind began to realise the fact that Gúrghín Khán was an ambitious and too powerful subject, who had removed Mír Vais from Kandáhár as presenting the one great obstacle to his intrigues against his master.

The moment Mír Vais observed that this conviction was entering the minds of the Shah and his advisers, he proceeded to develope the course of action by which he hoped to inspire his own countrymen, the Afgháns. Influence with them he had already; but something more than influence was necessary to secure their earnest and unhesitating co-operation in a revolt. The "inspiration" needful for this purpose could be born only of religious excitement. Could he impress their minds with the belief that Persian domination was synonymous with religious persecution, he felt he could bend them entirely to his will. To induce this belief his energies were now directed.

The task was not so difficult as it might seem. The Persians were Shiahs—bigoted Shiahs: the Afgháns were Súnís. At the time of their first coming under the domination of Persia the Ghilzais had made it a condition that they should be unmolested in their belief. That condition had been fulfilled up to the time of Shah Húsén. But there had been always something galling to a Súni to be forced to serve a

Shiah; and it was upon this feeling that Mír Vais resolved to work.

No sooner had he noticed that the suspicions against Gúrghín Khán had become too deeply rooted to be effaced, that they would grow in the hearts of the Shah and his ministers by being fed upon, than he asked leave to proceed on a pilgrimage to Mekka. Such a demand at so sanctimonious a court could not be refused. It was granted at once.

Mír Vais proceeded to Mekka. The reader will have surmised that his motives for the journey were not all religious. It is true he consorted with the holy doctors at the sacred shrine, and that after ascertaining their views he continued his journey to Medina with the avowed purpose of ascertaining whether the opinions of the learned in that place coincided with those of their brethren in the other. When he had ascertained that the views were identical, he obtained from them *Fathwás*, or religious decrees, embodying the opinions, and returned with those documents to Ispahán.

What were the mysterious questions to obtain a reply to which he had made that long and difficult journey? A perusal of the two most important of them in their full length will show the reader their real bearing, and will indicate the object for which they had been propounded.

The first question was: "Is it lawful for Músalmáns, oppressed and cramped in the exercise of their religion, to take up arms to free themselves from the yoke?" The second: "In the case in which the chief men of several tribes have been forced to take the oath of allegiance to a sovereign who was a heretic, are not the members of the tribes released from that oath when the sovereign ceases to observe the convention he had sworn to?" The replies given by the learned men at Mekka and at Medina were in the affirmative.

Mír Vais, I have said, armed with these important documents, returned to Ispahán. He found there matters very much as he had left them. The pear was gradually softening, but was not yet ripe. Anxious as he was to proceed to Kandáhár to make personally the final necessary arrangements, he felt that his departure at that moment would inspire suspicion. It was necessary to wait till the still rising suspicion of Gúrghín Khán should attain its fullest development. He therefore stayed at Ispahán, maintaining his position at the court, his lavish expenditure, his intimacy with the leading ministers, whilst affecting a profound indifference to politics. In reality never had he scanned their action more narrowly. And it was whilst thus eagerly watching the atmosphere that an event occurred which gave him the opportunity for which he had been so eagerly hoping.

In the present time—the winter of 1878–9—when the European and Asiatic world seems to be convulsed by the mysterious movements of Russian agents, it is specially interesting to note that the opportunity of revolt for which Mír Vais had been so long watching came to him by the hands of a Russian ambassador.

It happened at this period that an Armenian, a native of Kapán, by name Israel Orii, in the service of

Peter the Great, Czar of Russia, had, in recompense for services rendered to the Czar in Turkey, obtained from that monarch permission to proceed, under the imperial authority, as ambassador to Ispahán. Many privileges, referring especially to the remission of export and import duties, were accorded to the ambassador and his suite. The hope of gain by this means attracted to him an unusually large number of followers, most of them his friends. Before he set out, then, his retinue counted several hundreds, men wild with hope, with excitement, and with love of adventure.

The news regarding this extraordinary embassy reached Ispahán shortly after Mír Vais had returned from Mekka. It came accompanied by many exaggerations. The story was spread that the ambassador, Israel Orii, had affirmed his descent from the ancient kings of Armenia. The idle words expressed with respect to their hopes of gain by his retinue were magnified into threats of pillage. Every day some new rumour added to the alarm.

In this conjecture the feeble bigots who surrounded the Shah turned to Mír Vais for counsel. How eagerly he seized the opportunity may be imagined. "It is true," he said to the Shah and his ministers, "it is true that the conjuncture is formidable. If the Czar had desired to send a peaceable mission into this country he would not have selected an Armenian as his agent. By sending a man, born a Persian subject, yet of his own faith, and of the ancient royal family of Armenia, his object must be to blow with effect the coals of sedition into the very heart of the kingdom. But," he added, "the efforts of Armenia, backed by Russia, would be nothing, could we be sure of Georgia. But it is only recently that the Georgians, under Gúrghín Khán, revolted against the Shah. We know that the cousin of Gúrghín Khán is now at the court of St. Petersburgh. How can we doubt that as soon as this Armenian Christian has penetrated with his following into Persia, backed by Russia, Gúrghín Khán, who was once a Christian, who is probably a Christian in heart now, who is, moreover, the lineal descendant of the ancient kings of Georgia, who can doubt but that he will turn Georgia, Kermán, and Kandáhár against us, and strike a blow at the heart of the empire."

These and similar arguments, plausible, forcibly put, and backed by rumour and probability, had their effect. The fear of provoking Russia prevailed indeed so far as to induce the Shah to authorise Israel Orii and his retinue to proceed to Ispahán. But the suspicions regarding Gúrghín Khán were strengthened and confirmed. The Shah did not indeed remove him from his commands, because he feared to provoke a refusal, and with the refusal revolt. But he did that which suited still better the plans of his astute councillor. Restoring to Mír Vais all his former appointments in Kandáhár, he directed him to proceed forthwith to that place, to watch narrowly, and to report, all the proceedings of the Georgian, and, if necessary, to take from him the command.

It is tolerably certain that Gúrghín Khán had harboured no designs whatever against the Persian Government. In his administration of Kandáhár he had really done no more than carry out the orders he had received. If his proceedings had been harsh it was because the timid and corrupt court he served recognised harshness as the one effective mode of ruling. His anger and indignation then, when he saw reinstated in more than his former authority, and armed with private instructions of which he was left ignorant, the man whom he had sent a disgraced prisoner to Ispahán, may be imagined. However, he could not help himself. His army had been very greatly diminished, and to revolt without a chance of succeeding, was not to be thought of. He received Mír Vais, then, with apparent cordiality, and reinstated him in all his appointments.

But the wound he had received rankled too much within him to allow him to remain quiet. His anger deprived him of prudence. He had been forced to reinstate Mir Vais, but he resolved to show him that he was his master, and could yet torture him in the tenderest part.

Mir Vais had a daughter to whom rumour assigned the distinction of being the most beautiful lady in the province. Very shortly after his return from Ispahán Gúrghín Khán sent him a curt message demanding this lady for his harem. The tenour of the message showed that he wanted her as a slave or as a concubine, not as a wife; and that he was resolved to have her. The position of Mir Vais was difficult. He was not ready for resistance. The governor, he knew, would give him little time for reflection. However, he was equal to the occasion. He communicated the insult he had received to the heads of the several tribes, and besought them to come and aid him with their counsel. They met secretly in his tent. Their manner and their words showed him that they were prepared to resent the affront as though it had been offered to themselves. Seeing this, Mir Vais begged them to leave the execution of the design to him, to dissemble for the moment, but to be prepared to act when he should give the signal.* (1708.)

Sure now of his countrymen, Mir Vais, to gain time, kept "the word of promise to the ear, to break it to the hope." He complied, in appearance, but only in appearance, with the governor's requisition. He caused a young and good-looking girl of his establishment to be magnificently attired, and to be then conducted as his daughter to Gúrghín Khán. The girl kept the secret well, and the governor was taken in. Mir Vais's apparent yielding in the matter greatly softened him. He admitted him to an interview, and gradually began to unbend before him and to take him into his confidence.

All this time Mir Vais was busy in preparing matters

* Hanway thus reports his concluding words :—" The interest of the nation calls on us aloud to be of one common opinion, but there are many ways to attain the same end. Let our dependence be on our courage and sagacity. The serpent that lies awake will overcome the lion when he falls asleep. Let us conceal our swords in beds cf roses; and if you think highly enough of me to leave the revenge of your cause to my care, this glorious design must be kept an inviolable secret."—" Hanway's Travels," vol. ii.

for the crisis. The one obstacle to the immediate breaking out of a revolt lay in the fact that Gúrghín Khán, when dismissing the Persian troops, had retained the Georgians, and that these guarded his palace and acted as his body-guard. It was necessary that the Georgians should be removed. To accomplish this end Mir Vais had recourse to a very ingenious stratagem.

Conspicuous among the tribes occupying the Pishin valley were then, and are now, the Taríns. Being far enough from Kandáhár for his purpose, Mir Vais incited their chiefs to refuse payment of their ordinary contributions. A man of the character of Gúrghín Khán could not for a moment tolerate conduct amounting to rebellion. He resolved to chastise the Tárins at once, and having no other troops available, he despatched the majority of the Georgians on the errand.

Mir Vais meanwhile had arranged with the members of the branch of the Ghilzai tribe, of which he was the chief, to approach within a few miles of Kandáhár, and to hold themselves in readiness for immediate action. No sooner had he seen the Georgians well on their way than he hastened to Gúrghín Khán, expressed his resentment at the conduct of the Taríns, and his admiration of the prompt action which must soon bring them to submission. When by the warmth of his outspoken zeal he had found his way to the governor's heart, he experienced no difficulty whatever in persuading him to accept his invitation to a banquet at his country seat, a short distance from the city, and at which he was anxious to present to him two chiefs of his tribe who had not before visited Kandáhár.

The banquet had been fixed for the day when the Georgians should be well out of reach, and all the approaches to the town should be occupied by Afgháns. The governor, unsuspicious of treachery, left the town attended by his friends and a small retinue. He was received with every demonstration of respect. The banquet was then served. It was perfect of its kind. The meats were succulent and varied; the wines the choicest that could be procured. Whilst Mir Vais entertained Gúrghín Khán and his personal friends, his followers feasted the retinue. Neither one nor the other spared the wine, pressed upon them with all the unction of pretended affection. After the banquet followed the siesta. The extent of the libations and the potency of the wine turned this into a heavy sleep. This was the opportunity longed for. Every outlet was guarded. Every guest slumbered. At a preconcerted signal given by Mir Vais every slumberer was murdered where he lay! (1709)

Not one escaped. On this wholesale slaughter depended the complete success of the plot. For the murderers were without the walls, and those walls were still guarded by the remnant of the Georgians. But Mir Vais had thought out every detail of the plot. No sooner had his guests been slain than he ordered them to be stripped. Arraying himself in the clothes of Gúrghín Khán, and causing the chiefs next to himself in rank to put on the clothes of his followers, and the Afgháns those of the retinue, he, an hour after

15

sunset, set out for Kandáhár, keeping the order usually observed by the governor. Naturally their appearance excited no suspicion. But, no sooner were they admitted within the gates than they turned on the guards, cut them to pieces, and admitted the undisguised Afgháns waiting in the rear. The remainder of the garrison was easily mastered. Mir Vais then issued a proclamation assuring the inhabitants of security on the sole condition of their shutting their doors to every Persian or Georgian. The compliance of the populace enabled him to dispose very shortly of every remaining follower of Gúrghín Khán.

In a previous page I have recorded how contact with the bigoted and corrupt court of Ispahán had inspired Mir Vais with the hope of achieving the independence of his country. I have added to that record an account of the truly Afghán manner by which he accomplished his hope. Kandáhár, for many years the prize alternately of the Moghol and the Persian, had now become national and Afghán.

CHAPTER VII.

HISTORICAL.—THE GHILZAI RULE.

The day following the success of the conspiracy recorded in the last chapter, Mir Vais assembled the inhabitants of Kandáhár and harangued them. He protested that his one object had been to procure their liberty; that he had no personal views. He declared that liberty was a precious possession worth conspiring for, worth fighting for; that by the death of Gúrghín Khán, Persia had lost the only soldier she possessed: that the Kandáhár which had successfully resisted the Moghol in the zenith of his power, could surely repulse troops commanded by the eunuchs of Ispahán. He concluded with these noble words, words worthy of being spoken by a patriot, of being responded to by freemen: "If there are any amongst you," he said, "who have not the courage to enjoy this precious gift of liberty now dropped down to you from Heaven, let him declare himself; no harm shall be done to him: he shall be permitted to go in search of some new tyrant beyond the frontier of this happy state."* The

* "Hanway's Travels," vol. ii.

reply of the multitude left nothing to be desired. Every soul was animated by the determination to defend the newly found liberty.

Mir Vais next assembled the leading men of the tribes, and placed before them clearly the situation. They agreed without a dissentient voice to leave the executive power in his hands, and to support him cordially in all the measures he might think necessary to defend the place and to assure the general freedom.

Thus granted unfettered liberty of action, Mir Vais entered upon his task with the energy of an intelligent statesman. He distributed such arms as he had, and set in activity workmen for the manufacture of others; he hastened the preparation of gunpowder; repaired the fortifications, and put in order the artillery. Simultaneously he sent messengers to the heads of the different tribes in the mountains, informing them of his success, and urging them to join him without delay.

His capacity as a warrior was to be tested sooner than he had anticipated. On the morning of the fourth day after the murder of Gúrghín Khán, the sentinels on the walls descried the approach of a considerable body of cavalry. These were the Georgians returning from their expedition against the Taríns. They numbered only six hundred, but they were well-disciplined soldiers inured to war. As they were evidently ignorant of the changes which had taken place during their absence, Mir Vais allowed them to approach within musket shot. He then caused the guns to open upon them, whilst he sallied out from a distant gate at the head of five thousand horse to cut off their retreat. But whether he was less skilled in war than in diplomacy, a statesman rather than a soldier, or whether his men were untrained, this at least is certain, that the six hundred Georgians charging his five thousand cut their way through them and gained the passes beyond Girishk. Mir Vais followed them for several days, and though always repulsed, he inflicted considerable loss on them as they retreated. At last, having secured the passes, he returued to Kandáhár. Here I shall leave him whilst I record the impression made by his action upon the court of Shah Húsén.

The retreating Georgians carried with them into Persia the news of the revolution at Kandáhár. The effect on a court composed as was that of Ispahán can well be imagined. The truth—that the Afgháns longed for freedom—never once dawned on their minds. Adopting the oft misapplied aphorism that history always repeats itself, they believed that because Kandáhár had once previously revolted from Persia and called in the Moghols, it would certainly, if it were attacked, follow that course now. Instead, then, of despatching an army to put down the revolt, they sent an ambassador, Jáni Khán, to assure Mir Vais that his murder of Gúrghín Khán would be forgiven if only he would admit a Persian garrison into Kandáhár. At the same time they made warlike preparations to be employed in case the embassy should fail.

The ambassador came to Kandáhár, delivered his message,—and was cast into prison. In imprisoning him Mir Vais was animated by two motives. He wished to hinder as long as possible the preparations of Persia, and therefore to delay a reply to the missive of the court; and he was desirous that she should feel that he would never voluntarily submit,—that the die was cast—for freedom.

He judged the Court of Ispahán very correctly. Hearing nothing of Jáni Khán, the ministers of the Shah, imagining everything but the actual occurrences, sent another ambassador. Their choice fell upon the governor of Herát, Mahammad Khán, a friend and fellow companion in the pilgrimage to Mekka of Mir Vais. They believed that the Ghilzai chief would be influenced by his friendship for this man. But when liberty is at stake, former friendship will never shake men resolved to be free. The new ambassador was informed that but for that former friendship he should "never again be in a position to make base proposals to men who are free;" he was told that the hour of vengeance was at hand; that the sword which had been drawn would never be sheathed till the King of Persia should be driven from his throne; that for himself, he should be detained, but detained, from old friendship's sake, as an honoured guest.

The Court of Ispahán at last realised the fact that force alone would bring Mir Vais to subjection. The Shah then directed (1710) the acting-governor of Herát to march on Kandáhár. Mir Vais, hearing that his army was composed only of Persians, and having the most supreme contempt for that nation, advanced against the invading army at the head of five thousand horse, and completely defeated it. In the course of the succeeding eighteen months, four other attempts were made against him, and invariably with the same result. In the last, when the Persians, consisting of five thousand men, were commanded by Mahammad Khán, governor of Tábriz, they were completely defeated by five hundred Afghán horsemen, and lost upwards of a thousand men in killed and wounded. Amongst the prisoners were the governor and three of his sons.

Exasperated at these defeats, the Court of Ispahán resolved to make an effort on a much larger scale. Of all the dependent portions of the Persian empire, the Georgians had the greatest reputation as warriors. Gúrghín Khán had been a Georgian. His successor in the government of his native province had been his nephew, Khúsrú Khán, a man of very considerable mental power. In the extremity to which it was reduced, the Court of Ispahán, two months after the last defeat recorded in the preceding paragraph, called this man to the head of its armies, entrusted him with the fullest powers, and directed him to march on Kandáhár, and at all costs quench the rebellion. Khúsrú Khán responded eagerly to the call. The blood of his murdered relative called on him for vengeance. Ambitious, active, skilled in the knowledge of races, he took care to place in the van of his army the tried soldiers of Georgia. Placing himself at the head of his army he advanced as far as Farrah, and there encamped while the scouts he sent out should acquaint themselves with the proceedings of the enemy. They soon returned. Mir Vais had left the passes unguarded, and had taken up a strong position not far from Girishk, on the banks of the river Helmand, the passage of which he intended to dispute.

Glad to find the passes undefended, Khúsrú Khán pushed on to attack Mír Vais. His army consisted of thirty thousand Persians and twelve hundred Georgians. The Afghán army was inferior in numbers, but it was flushed with previous success. Of the battle that followed details are wanting. It is simply recorded that the passage of the river was forced and Mír Vais defeated. With the vigour of a good general, Khúsrú Khán marched at once on Kandáhár and invested it. (1711–12.)

Mír Vais, meanwhile, though beaten, had kept the field. He believed, like Napoléon in 1814, that did the capital but hold out he would yet be able so to act on the enemy's communications that they would be glad to beat a retreat. But Kandáhár showed herself inclined to serve him as the Paris of 1814 served Napoléon. The men he had left in her to guard her, despairing of successful resistance, offered to treat. Fortunately for him the prudence that counselled the allied generals to grant terms to Marmont was wanting in the temper of Khúsrú Khán. Believing the town to be at his mercy, he refused to listen to any terms short of unconditional surrender. The garrison, believing that unconditional surrender implied death, preferred the death of the warrior—and resolved to resist.

Meanwhile Mír Vais, hastening to the south, had enlisted a large number of the Bilúchis and Taríns. Returning with these he laid waste the country about Kandáhár, cut off the enemy's supplies, and threatened his communications. Khúsrú Khán bore this as long as possible; he tried assault after assault. Baffled one day he returned to the attack the next. Nor was it until he had lost from the fire of the enemy and sickness two-thirds of his force that he was compelled to raise the siege and retire.

But it was then too late. He had hardly commenced his retreat when Mír Vais, leading sixteen thousand Afgháns, fell upon his weakened army. The *morale* was with the assailants. The Persians scarcely attempted resistance. Khúsrú Khán himself, then, seeing that all was lost, charged the Afgháns at the head of his few remaining Georgians, and found the death he sought for.* (1713.)

Another attempt made by the court of Ispahán, by an army commanded by Mahammad Rústam Khán, was rather less than more successful. That is, its operations never had the appearance of a fortunate termination. Defeated in every encounter, the Persian general owed at last the safety of his life to a precipitate abandonment of Afghán territory. (1714.)

This was the last effort of the Shah Húsén and his advisers. Opportunity then was left to Mír Vais to

* Hanway states that though Khúsrú Khán, like his uncle, had abjured Christianity for Mahomedanism, he was still at heart a Christian and a protector of missionaries, one of whom was killed by his side.

consolidate the territories he had reclaimed. These extended in the west nearly as far as Farrah, and comprehended the valleys of the Helmand and the Lora. The name he assigned to them was that of the capital, Kandáhár, and of the kingdom of Kandáhár he was the first king. All the tribes of the Afgháns —the Abdális of Herát excepted—acknowledged his supremacy, and he succeeded in welding them together in a manner that had never before been attempted. He did not long survive the last and decisive victory of his countrymen. He died at the close of the year (November 1715) following that which had witnessed it, leaving behind him the reputation of being the most able and the most wary politician of his age.

Mír Vais left two sons, Mír Mahmúd and Mír Húsén, the first eighteen, the second a year younger. They were both considered too young to bear the weight of sovereignty. Their father's brother, Mír Abdulla, was therefore nominated king of Kandáhár.

If tender years incapacitated the two sons, a weak disposition and a timid nature should have barred the brother. Far from sharing any of the large ideas of his predecessor, he was not only willing, but anxious, to retrace his steps in every particular. Persia, beaten, baffled, and humiliated, was more terrible to him than Persia victorious at the gates of Kandáhár had been to his brother. Almost his first act, then, on ascending the throne, was to lay before the heads of the tribes a proposal to invite Persia to resume her sovereignty.

In all large bodies of men there are some who are

so constitutionally timid that the smallest weight of responsibility unmans them. There were a few of this class among the chiefs—men who loved peace at any price—at the price of honour, of the country's welfare, of everything save their own ease. These men clutched at the chance of declining to support a cause which, though the cause of freedom, of justice, and of humanity, might in a very distant future bring about an invasion of their country and discomfort to themselves. These few men, then, voted for prompt submission to Persia. But the majority protested against it; they denounced a policy which would rob them of the freedom they had gained, and would place them in vassalage to those who had recoiled before them in fair fight.

Had Kandáhár rejoiced in parliamentary institutions the peace party would not have had a chance; but the voice of the king was all-powerful, and as the king found in the opinion of a few men of a mental calibre not greater than his own the support which he considered would justify his action, he determined to act. He sent, therefore, an embassy to the Court of Ispahán bearing a conditional offer of submission to Persia. The conditions were these: 1st, that the annual tribute paid before the revolt of Mír Vais should not be re-imposed; 2nd, that no foreign troops should be sent into the province; 3rd, that the government of the province should be made hereditary in the family of Abdulla.

It might be argued now, as it was argued by the Abdulla party then, that these conditions made no change in the internal life of Kandáhár; that they simply provided the province with a suzerain who would protect it against a foreign enemy. But to the great majority of the Afgháns it made the difference between freedom and servitude—a difference which no verbal conditions could efface. In their minds, too, it was alike a needless and a useless servitude, for it was a servitude to an enemy they had beaten, and to a kingdom which was decaying.

Among the Afghán chiefs, cognisant of the embassy and of its nature, was the eldest son of Mír Vais, Mir Mahmúd. Possessing many manly qualities, daring, generous, impulsive, deterred by no difficulties, Mahmúd was lost in indignation at an act which would overthrow in a moment the life-work of his father. He at once summoned the chiefs, about forty in number, whom his father had most trusted. Haranguing and taking counsel with these, and finding them of one mind with himself, he led them to the palace. Having occupied this without resistance, he entered the room occupied by his uncle, and with his own hand killed him. The perpetration of the deed was hailed with loud applause, and Mahmúd was at once proclaimed King of Kandáhár. The anti-national and peace party perished with Abdulla. (March 1716.)

Mahmúd had inherited all the aspirations of his father. Prominent amongst these was the determination to seize the earliest opportunity to strike a deadly blow at the Safi dynasty of Persia. That opportunity soon presented itself. Very shortly after his accession the Persian governor of Herát, Mahammad Zemán

Khán, behaved towards the Abdáli Afgháns in a manner that caused a large number of that tribe to rise in revolt. The Abdális north of Kandáhár had accepted the suzerainty of the Persians, on the conditions granted by Abbas the Great to the Ghilzais, that their internal affairs should be regulated by their own chiefs without pretext of interference. They were in the enjoyment of this liberty when Mahammad Zemán Khán, with the concurrence of the chief of the tribe, offered to the son of that chief an insult of the most atrocious character. The son, Azádúlla Khán, a young man of strong passions and determined will, summoned the leading men to his tent, and, with their approval, avenged himself on the father, who had consented to the insult, by depriving him of his life. He was at once proclaimed chief of the tribe. His first act was to march at the head of a few chosen men of his tribe against Zemán Khán, whom he knew to be in the district of Zamíndawár. There he surprised, attacked, and defeated him, the Persian leader falling by his hand. He then pushed on for Herát, drove out the Persian garrison, occupied it, and declared it independent of Persia. (1717.)

This was the second severe blow dealt to the Safi dynasty. But it did not come alone. The Uzbégs and the Kúrds, having ravaged with impunity the outlying provinces of the empire, waxed bolder in their designs, and penetrated almost as far as Ispahán.

Shah Husén and his advisers had witnessed, not without alarm, the gradual disruption of their empire. They had endeavoured to persuade the Persian soldiers who had fled from Herát to return to reconquer that city; but the soldiers, not possessing a leader in whom they could confide, had with one voice refused. They were still, in the haphazard manner peculiar to weak men, searching for a general, when the incursions to the vicinity of the capital quickened their action. Not finding him whom they sought in the army, they turned their inquiries into another department, and, rightly judging that a man, to be successful, must be the exact opposite of themselves, they selected for the post of commander-in-chief a nobleman who had resigned the office of lord chief justice because the rectitude with which he had discharged its duties had made him obnoxious to the court and its satellites.*

The name of this nobleman was Safi Kúlí Khán. The task assigned to him was to drive back the Uzbégs, then to reconquer Herát and Kandáhár. No expense was spared to render the army efficient. In numbers it amounted to thirty thousand men; its artillery was the newest and best appointed yet seen in the East; its enthusiasm was excited by parades attended by the Shah and his court. The prayers for its success were continuous and fervent.

At length the army marched. The Uzbégs, twelve thousand strong, were encountered near the borders. They were soon and easily disposed of. Flushed with this first success, the Persians marched against the Abdális. Azádúlla had left Herát at the head of fifteen thousand troops to meet them. Though inferior in

* "Hanway's Travels," vol. ii. p. 125.

numbers by one half, and having no guns, he felt that his only chance of success was to attack. He met them near the village of Káriz, in the province of Herát. The battle that followed was most fiercely contested. The Persians had the advantage of numbers, of discipline, of guns. The ex-lord chief justice had developed into an able general, and he had posted his men with skill. In vain did the Afgháns make charge after charge; they were always repulsed. Towards sunset their attacks slackened, and victory was about to pronounce in favour of Persia, when an untoward accident upset every calculation.

The Afgháns, slackening their attacks, had begun to give way. A body of their matchlockmen, who had occupied a rising ground which had formed during the action a prominent target for the Persian artillery, falling back, evacuated that rising ground. Instantly the Persian matchlockmen, pressing on, occupied it. The Persian gunners had not noticed this occurrence, and observing, after sunset, that the ground was more numerously occupied than before, they turned on it, without inquiry, a tremendous fire. The Persians, thus suddenly assailed, and knowing that the Afgháns had no guns, could only think of treachery. Their advance was immediately stopped, and, the artillery fire continuing, the men began to disperse in disorder. Azádúlla observed the occurrence, and resolved to turn it to good account. Collecting his cavalry, he made a charge along the whole line. It was decisive. The Persian army fled in confusion, and lost their general, their baggage, and eight thousand men in killed and wounded. The loss of the Afgháns was three thousand. (1719.)

This victory confirmed the Abdális in the possession of the province of Herát. Azadúlla added to its western limits by conquering the whole of Khorásán, excepting its capital, Meshed. He then marched south to Sabzwár, which having occupied, he proceeded to Farrah and besieged it. Leaving him engaged in this operation, I must return to Mahmúd at Kandáhár.

Mahmúd had noticed with satisfaction the blows dealt at the empire of the Safis. The defeat of Safi Kúli Khán had been followed by the loss of the dependencies of the empire in the Persian Gulf, and by attacks on its southern coast. The empire seemed distressed on every side.

Mahmúd resolved to seize the opportunity. But just at this period he heard of the march on Farrah by the Abdális, to which I have referred. Farrah was garrisoned by the Persians. But at the moment the Persians were not to be dreaded. The case would be different were that place, then a place of strength, occupied by men who, though Afgháns, were Abdálís. Before dealing his blow at Persia, he resolved then to march to the relief of Farrah.

There he met Azadúlá, killed him, and defeated his army. From Farrah he took a south-westerly route across the Sístán desert, and then moved towards Kermán. Surmounting great difficulties he reached Kermán, and caused his authority to be acknowledged in the province of which that town was the capital.

When the news of the conquest of Kermán reached

the Persian general commanding on the southern coast, Lútf Ali Khán, that officer at once directed his march northward from Bandar Abbás. Lútf Ali Khán was brother to the prime minister, Fath Ali Khán, and therefore a man of considerable influence. He would appear likewise to have possessed a good knowledge of the principles of warfare. He marched straight for the heart of the province, the town of Kermán. Mahmúd issued forth to meet him, but, whether he was too greatly outnumbered, or whether Kermán had been a Capua to his soldiers, he was completely defeated.

Lútf Ali felt that he would return. He therefore halted at Kermán till that place should be fortified, and then moved with his army to Shiráz, a place whence he could move with ease to any threatened quarter. His army was flushed with victory and eager for fresh opportunities. Affairs seemed to be looking up for Persia, when at this critical moment the corrupt clique which governed her plunged a dagger into her heart.

It happened in this wise. The fact that the brother of the prime minister had but recently gained a great victory suggested to the idea of the other members of the government that the combination of the civil and military authority in the hands of two men so related might be fatal to the interests and fortunes of the other plunderers of the State. Religion eagerly enlisted itself in a plot then and there formed for their removal. At the head of it were the chief Múllah and the chief physician to the sovereign.

These pious men, well supported from without, entered the Sháh's chamber at midnight, and persuaded the weak monarch that the safety of his crown—even of his life—depended upon the prompt execution of rigorous measures against his prime minister and his commander-in-chief.

That night the eyes of the prime minister were plucked out. He was then imprisoned, and two years later died a captive. With his brother at the head of an army it was not so easy to deal. However, the means soon presented themselves. The governor of the castle of Shiráz was devoted to the corrupt faction. He was communicated with. In consequence of this communication he invited Lútf Ali to visit him. Unsuspicious, the noble soldier unhesitatingly entered the castle scantily attended. He was at once seized and hurried off to Ispahán. His army, the sole defence of Persia, immediately disbanded itself. (1720.)

Mahmúd of Kandáhár did not immediately take advantage of the undefended state of the country he coveted. It happened that his defeat at Kermán had stirred up the governors of Farrah and of Sístán to excite disturbances in his own dominions. The conduct of his brother, Mír Húsén, had checked, and his own return finally extinguished these disturbances, but he found much to occupy him ere he could attempt a second invasion. The year following his return was a year of strict training. He had seen that he should require an army larger and better disciplined than that which had broken in his hand.

He invited, then, alike the Abdális of Herát and the Bilúchis south of his dominions to enlist in his service. The replies were enthusiastic: the wild tribes flocked in numbers to his standard. Nor did he neglect to prepare for the possibility of a reverse. He filled the magazines, repaired the fortifications, and laid in abundant supplies.

Every day, moreover, brought him news of some new misfortune befalling the empire of the Safis. Confirmed thus in his aggressive ideas he hastened his preparations. At last he was ready, and in January 1722, at the head of an army of twenty-five thousand men, he marched in the direction of Sístán.

He pursued the same route across the desert as on the previous occasion, marched on Kermán, and after a slight delay occupied the town. The citadel, however, held out. It had been well fortified by Lútf Ali, and the troops by which it was garrisoned belonged to the army which had beaten Mahmúd two years before. Every assault he made was repulsed. He was in despair. He could not retire without acknowledging himself beaten, and without discouraging his army.

He was relieved from this difficulty by the governor. This man was not enough of a soldier to see that he could keep the place by force. Trained in the principles of the corrupt clique, he believed absolutely in the purchase power of money. To money, then, rather than to arms, he chose to owe his deliverance. Full of this idea he offered Mahmúd six thousand two hundred and fifty pounds if he would go away and leave him the citadel.

Under any circumstances Mahmúd would have been forced to go away. He could not take the place. The gift then of a large sum of money to do that which under any circumstances he would have been forced to do was a gift from heaven. It not only provided him with funds. It was infinitely more valuable in furnishing him with a justification, perfectly convincing to his followers, for leaving the citadel untaken and moving towards Ispahán.

The route he adopted was the direct road by Yezd. Yezd is about two hundred and ten miles from Kermán, the country between the two places sandy and inhospitable. The town of Yezd was fortified and surrounded by a deep ditch. It boasted, too, of a citadel. The garrison being bent on resistance, Mahmúd assaulted the place, but was repulsed. Determined not to waste his time on a joint only of the empire, he determined to disregard it and push on for the heart.

Marching rapidly he soon arrived within a hundred miles of the capital. Here he found a messenger from the prime minister, Mahammad Kúli Khán, the bearer of a letter offering him thirty-seven thousand five hundred pounds if he would proceed no further. Mahammad Kúli Khán, equally with his satrap at Kermán, was a believer in the never-failing purchase power of money. But Mahmúd knew that the conquest of Ispahán meant the conquest of the Persian empire; even had he been as open to a bribe as the minister believed him, he would have put his price at a considerably higher figure than thirty-seven thousand five hundred pounds. But for the Afghán warrior, the son of Mír Vais, the Persian empire, defenceless as he then regarded it, was priceless. He did not even deign a reply, but pursued his march.

At last he reached Gúlnábád, nine miles from the capital. The panic in that city was now at its height. It was not confined to the population. The Shah, his ministers, his corrupt favourites, were still more under its influence. Ispahán, though surrounded by a wall, was not, in the proper sense of the term, fortified; neither was it provisioned to stand a siege. But while the number of troops within its walls exceeded fifty thousand, the total population amounted to six hundred thousand. The city, lying on the north bank of the river Zéndarúd, at that season not fordable, could be entered only over bridges. The only guns possessed by the invaders were a hundred small swivel guns, carried on camels. There seemed then no great reason for the panic. On the contrary, a capable leader, such as Lútf Ali, would have been thankful for the chance thus presented of annihilating the invaders.

But Lútf Ali, though in Ispahán at the time, was in disgrace. Men altogether of a different mental calibre were present at the council summoned by the Shah. One of these, the prime minister, Mahammad Kúli Khán, gave, it is true, excellent advice. He recommended that the army should be intrenched to cover the town. He pointed out that the Afgháns would not then dare to attempt to storm it; that the soldiers would become inured to fighting, and might be employed to cut off the enemy's communications.

Far different was the advice of the leader of the high nobility, Abdúlla Khan, viceroy of Arabia. He was for action, immediate action, for the extermination of dogs and rebels.

The religious party was also represented at this council. The leader of this party was one Fath Ali Khan Kajar, a soldier. This nobleman gravely assured the Shah that "he had heard from an old woman of Astrábád, who was said to be inspired, that two legs of a he-goat boiled with three hundred and twenty-five peapods in water, over which a young virgin had repeated twelve hundred times "*Lá illah, illah lá*," made a broth which would render invisible the men who drank it."*

When all had said their say, the Shah decided according to the views of the majority. He directed that broth made in the manner prescribed by Fath Ali Khan should be served out to the troops, and that they should march to meet the enemy.

The troops drank the broth, and marched (7th March 1722), more than fifty thousand, with twenty-four guns of large calibre, against twenty thousand with small swivel guns. That day was spent in skirmishing; but on the following day, the 8th, the two armies engaged. Their appearance presented a remarkable contrast. The Persians were sleek, well-fed, showily

* Ferrier's "History of the Afgháns."

dressed: — the Afgháns lean, sunburnt, clothed in rags. One spirit animated their leaders; discord and jealousy reigned amongst the Persian chiefs.

At sunrise the battle joined. The left wing of the Persians bearing down on the right wing of the Afgháns forced it back. At the same time the viceroy of Arabia, making a détour with his own troops, turned the left flank of the Afgháns, and falling upon their camp, set to work to plunder. This act, it will be seen, lost the day. When he started to engage in the turning operation, the right wing of the Persians attacked the Afgháns opposed to them, and drove them back. Mahmúd, who watched the battle from an eminence, thought that all was lost, and prepared to flee. All would have been lost had the Viceroy of Arabia not stopped to plunder. But as he did not follow up his advantage, the Afghán general, falling back, drew the enemy within range of the swivel guns fixed on the backs of the camels, kneeling in a line, and then opening out his ranks, poured in a volley. This fire not only checked the advance of the Persians, but threw them into inextricable confusion. A charge of the Afgháns converted this into a complete rout. The victors drove the enemy before them for some distance; then, wheeling round, captured their cannon, which had been left unprotected. These guns were at once turned on the Persians with decisive effect. Their centre was annihilated; their left wing forced back; the viceroy of Arabia was compelled to leave the greater part of his plunder, and flee into the town. The victory was in fact decisive. It placed Ispahán in the hands of the Afghán adventurer.

Had the Shah been a man, that result would not necessarily have followed. The proof of this is to be found in the doubts which oppressed Mahmúd after his victory. Not only did he not follow it up; he even permitted the Persians to recover some of their lost guns, nor did he rouse himself to vigorous action until intelligence of the terror and perplexity into which Ispahán had been thrown reached him.

Stunned by the defeat, Shah Husén called a council of war. After much deliberation, the council resolved to resist. The viceroy of Arabia was nominated governor of the town. Orders were at once issued to repair the walls, to throw up intrenchments, and to raise new levies. The Governor of Láristán, Ali Mardan Khán, was created generalissimo, and directed to form a camp at Khonsár, about fifteen miles north-west of Ispahán.

Mahmúd, I have said, had been astounded at his own success. He never realised its magnitude. It had been snatched for him out of the fire, first by the inaction at the critical moment of the Viceroy of Arabia; secondly, by the use made of that inaction by the commandant of his left wing. So utterly unprepared was he for so great a success, that, as already related, he allowed the Persians to steal back some of their lost guns during the night. On the morrow of the victory he remained motionless. The repulses he had experienced at Kermán and Yezd sat heavy on his soul. Nor did he fully realize his position, until the spies he had sent out returned with the information that the panic of the Persians had been so universal that he might have entered Ispahán with them.

Then he roused himself. He marched first on Farrahábád, a palace surrounded by a bastioned wall, three miles from the city. The Persians not defending, he occupied it. He then moved on Jalfá, a town a mile and a half south of Ispahán, and constituting the suburb of that city on the south bank of the Zendarúd. This place was garrisoned mainly by Armenians who, dreading the Afgháns, were ready to defend themselves to the last. The insane policy of the court of Persia deprived the Shah of the assistance of these brave men. Though they repulsed the first attack of Mahmúd, many of them were disarmed the next day, and the rest were discouraged. That night a breach was effected in the walls, and the place surrendered.*

Notwithstanding the terms of the capitulation, the Afgháns extorted enormous sums from the Armenians of Jalfá, staining their conquest with cruelty of the worst kind. Mahmúd now occupied the largest suburb

* Hanway states that the terms of capitulation were the payment to the Afghán sovereign of 175,000*l.*, and the gift of fifty of the most beautiful virgins of the town, chosen by a commission appointed for the purpose. After stating that some of them were reserved for the harem of Mahmúd, and others distributed among his principal officers, he thus records their fate. "Some of them were so shocked to see themselves abandoned to the enemies of their country that they died of excessive grief. The Afgháns, whose hearts were touched, sent home those who were most afflicted; others were ransomed by their friends: insomuch, that in a few days there remained but a small part of them in slavery."

of Ispahán, connected with that city by bridges. He lost no time now in endeavouring to carry the city. His first attack, made on the 21st of March, was repulsed. In his second—an attempt to carry the principal bridge*—he nearly succeeded. He had fought his way to the very centre of the bridge, when some guns were brought to bear upon his men, and forced them back panic stricken. The Persians pursued them, with great slaughter, as far as their intrenchments. These repulses, renewing the recollections of Kermán and Yezd, caused Mahmúd to despair of carrying the city. He sent therefore a deputation to the Shah proposing the conditions on which he was willing to retire. These were: 1st, the cession to himself in independent sovereignty of the provinces of Kandáhár, Khorásán, and Kermán; 2ndly, his marriage with a daughter of the Shah, provided with a portion of one hundred and twenty-five thousand pounds. The Shah, elated by the repulse of the Afgháns, refused the conditions.

Mahmúd then resolved to endeavour to reduce the place by famine. Better for the country had the Shah agreed to the terms, for the ruin effected by the Afgháns during the month that followed, was such, that a century later the evils of it were still felt. The

* Hanway thus describes this bridge:—"It is 360 geometrical paces in length and 13 in breadth: the two extremities of it are flanked by four round towers with a covered gallery, which ranges on both sides the length of the bridge, the whole decorated with the richest ornaments of Persian architecture. It is joined by two causeways, made with a gentle descent to a double row of trees above 3,000 paces long."

villages, the canals, the fields, the numberless works built to assist irrigation, were ruthlessly destroyed; the men were slain, the women were sent into slavery. When Mahmúd, by plunder and by devastation, had filled his own magazines and reduced the country to a desert, he began anew his attempts on the city. Learning that the Georgians posted to guard the bridge of Abbásábád had been stupified by drink, he carried that bridge. He succeeded likewise in cutting off two convoys of provisions on their way to the city. Already Ispahán appeared in his grasp, when an event occurred which filled the minds of the besieged with hope.

Three miles from Ispahán, on the declivity of a hill, stood the fortified village of Ben-Ispahán. After the battle of Gúlnábád many of the Persian soldiers had flocked thither, and from its walls they had made frequent attacks upon straggling Afghán parties. Such chances were constantly offering. At last one exceeding all its predecessors in importance presented itself. Aminúlla, an Afghán chief, returning with one of the convoys alluded to in the preceding paragraph, happened to pass near Ben-Ispahán. The men were laden with spoil, and were straggling. The temptation was too great to be resisted. The Persians sallied out and recovered the plunder, and though Mahmúd himself came to the assistance of his men, they repulsed him with heavy loss. Many prisoners were taken, amongst them an uncle, a half brother, and two cousins of the Afghán king. Dreading the fate that might be reserved for them, Mahmúd sent a messenger to the Shah to implore safety for their lives. But before the Shah could interfere, the Persians of Ben-Ispahán had massacred every prisoner they had taken!

Mahmúd retaliated by killing all the prisoners in his camp, and by ordering that, for the future, no quarter should be given. But his defeat made him despondent, and after strengthening the outpost at the bridge of Abbásábád he fell back on Farrahábád. He appears to have determined to stay there till starvation should work its effect, slowly but surely.

There was still a chance for the Safi dynasty. There were good men in Persia, but they had been persecuted and disgraced. The bad men alone had the confidence of the Shah. The man upon whom at this epoch he most depended was the very viceroy of Arabia who had lost him the battle of Gúlnábád, and who, according to the historians of the period, acted throughout the part of a traitor to his sovereign. The soldier who during the siege had rendered the best service was a eunuch named Ahmad Ali. The Arabian, dreading the popularity of this man with the populace, accused him to the Shah. The next morning the eunuch was found dead in his bed. The governor of Georgia, who might have rendered effective aid, had been treated so insolently by the corrupt clique, that he had sworn never to draw his sword for Shah Húsén. One man there was still in Ispahán, Lútf Ali Khán, he who, two years before, had driven Mahmúd from Kermán. Offered now the command of the army, he refused. The men who had blinded his brother were still the confidants of the Shah, and he himself had experienced how fatal it was, with such pilots guiding the ship, to succeed.

From his position at Farrahábád, Mahmúd had cut off the last convoy of provisions known to be on its way to the city; the eldest son of the Shah, Prince Tahmasp, who had escaped to the provinces to raise troops, had just informed his father of the failure of all his efforts for that object; the Shah, in the hope to save his dynasty, now offered to accept the terms he had previously rejected; Mahmúd spurned the offer. Ispahán was at her last gasp when, suddenly, the spirits of her princes and her people were revived by the intelligence that Malik Mahmúd, governor of Sístán, had arrived at Gúlnábád with an army of ten thousand men to relieve her.

The joy was short lived. The King of Kandáhár offered to the Malik the sovereignty of Khorásán if he would leave Ispahán to its fate. The Shah had nothing to promise as a counterpoise. So Malik Mahmúd set out for Meshed.

The end was now approaching. But Mahmúd, with deliberate cruelty, protracted the siege for two months longer. He had only twenty thousand men; and he still feared the hundred thousand of the great city. He therefore starved them into weakness, misery, and death. At last matters reached a point when further endurance was impossible. Having, on the 22nd of October, empowered his plenipotentiaries to sign a capitulation resigning the empire to his conqueror, the Shah took, on the following day, an affecting farewell of his people, and then, accompanied by the viceroy of Arabia and the principal lords of his court, and mounted on horses sent for the purpose by Mahmúd, set out for the headquarters of the Afghán king. Arrived within an easy distance of the camp, the Shah was still further humbled by an order to halt, on the pretext that Mahmúd was asleep. After the delay of half-an-hour he was permitted to proceed. A few minutes later he was ushered into the hall of the palace of Farrahábád, at the corner of which he saw his conqueror seated, leaning on a cushion of cloth of gold. He had advanced into the centre of the tent, and had pronounced the magic words "All hail!" ere Mahmúd rose to return the salute. The Shah was then conducted to a seat on the left of the Afghán: after a few words of good wishes, he resigned to his conqueror the insignia of authority. With his own hands he was forced—Mahmúd having refused to receive the emblem of sovereignty from his vizier—to attach to the turban of the still seated Afghán the royal plume. Having completed this ceremony by uttering the significant words "Reign in Peace," the Shah was allowed to resume his seat. Coffee was then served up, and Mahmúd, taking in his hand his cup of the fragrant berry, spoke for the first time. "Such," he said, addressing the fallen monarch, "Such is the instability of human grandeur. God disposes of empires as he pleases, and takes from one nation to give them to another. But I promise to consider you always as my own father; and I will undertake nothing for the future without your advice."* With these words the ceremony concluded. Practically, the dynasty of the Safis had ceased to rule.

In this manner the Ghilzai King of Kandáhár became also Shah of Persia. On the throne of the empire he had conquered I must now leave Mahmúd. It will be sufficient if I state that prosperity developed in him a ferocity and a licentiousness which prevented him from becoming the founder of a dynasty. His intellect became deranged, and he died in 1725, less than three years after the surrender of Ispahán. His cousin Ashraff, son of the Abdallá whom he had murdered, succeeded him. Ashraff was a capable man, but the disorder had become too great even for a very capable man to remedy. After nearly five years of rule, characterised by incessant warfare, he was defeated (15th January 1730) in a pitched battle by Tahmas Kúli Khán, afterwards renowned as Nádir Shah. Ashraff escaped from the field, but was killed by a Bilúchi when wandering, a fugitive, in the desert. With his death ended the Afghán rule in Persia.

* It may be convenient to note in this place the fate of the ex-Shah and his family. Confined with his sons (the eldest, Tahmasp Mirza, excepted), his uncles, his brothers, and his nephews, in the seraglio at Ispahán, the ex-King became every year a source of greater terror to the relentless Afghán. To such a pitch did that terror arrive, that on the 7th February 1725 Mahmúd caused to be murdered in cold blood all the relatives of the deposed monarch—two sons, both under five years of age, being excepted by chance rather than by design. Shah Húsén, spared for the time, was murdered four years later by the successor of Mahmúd.—"Hanway's Travels," vol. ii. pp. 222, 276.

Of the effect of that rule there can be no divided opinion. "The death and captivity of the whole of the Afgháns," writes Sir John Malcolm, referring to the consequences of the battle of the 15th January 1730, "was but a slight atonement for the great calamities which they had inflicted upon Persia. Within the short period of seven years nearly a million of her inhabitants had perished, her finest provinces had been rendered desert, and her proudest edifices levelled with the dust, and this by enemies who had neither the force nor the wisdom to maintain the conquest which they had made, and, consequently, never could repair the ruin they had effected."* Not less precise nor less condemnatory of the Afgháns is the summary drawn by Ferrier:—"During the seven years that the Afgháns held Persia that empire lost more than a third of its population; the soil remained without cultivation, the canals and watercourses for irrigation were dried up, and the greater portion of the public buildings completely destroyed. . . . The Afgháns were better qualified to fight than to govern. To appropriate, wherever they went, and without any reason or pretext whatsoever, money or money's worth, was their practice: revolts and disturbances naturally ensued, and necessitated the employment of a large army. They were in the end weakened by twenty combats, and found it impossible to recruit in Afghánistán, and were therefore obliged to admit foreign soldiers within their ranks, whose fidelity was

* Sir John Malcolm's "History of Persia," vol. ii. p. 43.

at least doubtful, and who rarely acted with vigour."*

But it is time now to return to Kandáhár. When, in 1722, King Mahmúd had set out on his expedition against Persia, he had left behind him as his vicegerent in Kandáhár his brother, Mír Húsén. This able prince governed the province with success during the lifetime of Mahmúd. On his death, in 1725, Húsén became the virtual ruler of the country, and although Herát, Sabzwár, and Farrah were successively overrun and conquered, the independence of Kandáhár was never imperilled by the wars of the successor of Mahmúd on the throne of Persia. Nor, indeed, when Tahmasp Kúli Khan overthrew the Afghán rule in that country, in 1731, was Kandáhár at the time in the slightest degree affected by the event.

But in 1736 things had changed. The five years that had elapsed since the death of Ashraff had been prolific of success for his conqueror. To understand how this success came to affect the Afgháns, it may be convenient if I place before the reader a brief sketch of the renowned Nádir Shah.

This remarkable adventurer was born in a year famous in English history, 1688, in the province of Khorásán. His father, Imám Kúli, was a Túrk of mean family. His youth was a stormy one. Sometimes attacking, sometimes attacked by, the Usbégs; now the servant, now the murderer, of a petty chieftain; a robber, and a leader of robbers, he passed,

* Ferrier's "History of the Afgháns."

when he was yet young, into the regular service of the governor of Khorásán. Fortune still smiled and frowned. Promoted and rewarded for good service, he was degraded and bastinadoed for insolence. Enraged at this punishment he fled to a place called Kalát, about ten days journey from Meshed, and threw himself upon the generosity of his uncle, who commanded there. He was received well by his uncle, but in a very short time his intrigues procured for him summary dismissal.

Again thrown upon his own resources, Tahmasp Kúli, for so he was then called, returned to his old profession of a robber. He must have been then thirty-four years old. It was just at the period when the dynasty of the Safis was being overthrown by Mahmúd, and when the disordered state of the country would be likely to render profitable robbery by profession. Gaining a reputation as a daring leader, he speedily attracted to himself a large number of men. His services were soon sought after, and when Mahmúd died he had obtained a recognised position in Khorásán as a leader of free-lances.

On the death of Mahmúd the son of the deposed Shah Húsén, Tahmasp Mirza, who had escaped from Ispahán during the siege of 1722, claimed the crown and sought adherents in every direction. Tahmasp Kúli's uncle, the man who had expelled him for intrigue, now opened negotiations with his nephew to persuade him to join the Mirza. Tahmasp Kúli agreed, provided the Mirza would grant him a free pardon for past offences. The pardon was sent to Kalát, and Tahmasp Kúli proceeded thither to fetch it. Arrived and admitted into the fort, he killed his uncle, seized the place, and having obtained a second pardon from the Mirza, now calling himself Shah Tahmasp, boldly entered his service.

The same fortune here followed him; but he was better able now than in his earlier days to bend the blind goddess to his will. Declared, for some misconduct, a rebel, he marched to the court, and made his terms. Thenceforth he was virtually master. But he still bore the nominal yoke, and he was still bearing it when he annihilated the Afgháns on the 15th January 1731, and raised Shah Tahmasp to the throne of Persia.

His reward for this victory was the government of the four finest provinces of the empire, Khorásán, Mazándarán, Sístán, and Kermán. Two years later, after a series of victories which assured his power in every part of the Persian empire, he dethroned Shah Tahmasp, and placed his infant son, Shah Abbás, as nominal sovereign on the throne.

He then left Ispahán to attack Bagdád. The Turkish army advancing to the relief of the place, he fought it and was beaten. Far from being discouraged, he stimulated and reinforced his troops, and led them again against the Turks, this time victoriously (1733). He then conquered Armenia and Georgia, and forced a peace on the Porte; then, learning that the child Shah was dead, he marched to the plain of Moghan, near the banks of the Aras, convened an assembly of the nobles, and caused himself to be elected to the vacant throne, under the name and title of Nádir Shah. He was crowned on the 26th February 1736.

After repressing the Bakhtiáris, a tribe much given to plunder, Nádir Shah marched against Kandáhár with an army consisting of from eighty thousand to one hundred thousand men. That place was held, as I have already related, by Mír Húsén, the second son of the founder of the Ghilzai dynasty. Mír Husén had been summoned by Nádir Shah to Ispahán to do homage to him as suzerain. But the Afghán chief held, with his father and his brother, that of all the gifts of God to man national liberty is the most precious, and the only reply he had vouchsafed was to strengthen the fortifications of Kandáhár.

Twenty-six years of freedom had greatly increased the prosperity of that royal city. Her commerce, her population, her wealth had increased with the security which the just rule of the princes of the indigenous tribes had procured for her. The reign of Húsén, beginning practically in 1722, had been eminently beneficial. No sooner, then, was it known that Nádir Shah was marching against the place with his hordes, than with one voice the Afghán people applauded the expressed determination of Húsén to resist him to the very last. Their hopes, indeed, were high. The city, situated at the foot of a rocky mountain which flanked it on the north and east, was surrounded by numberless stone towers connected by curtains, and following the sinuosities of the mountain, the summit of which was occupied by a fort believed to be impregnable, and commanding the citadel, half-way between it and the city.* The garrison amounted to thirty thousand men, and supplies had been laid in sufficient to enable the troops and the population to support a very long siege.

Nádir Shah advanced on Kandáhár by way of Herát and Farrah, both which places he occupied without opposition. The passage of the Helmand at or near Girishk was, however, opposed by Mir Húsén with some twenty thousand men. The Afghán chief rendered the passage difficult, but he could not make it impossible. He detained the invader on the opposite bank for some days; then, seeing that he must be turned were he to stay longer, he fell back on the capital, having lost some two thousand men.

Nádir then advanced on Kandáhár, hoping to occupy it very speedily. This hope disappeared the moment he noted its position, its strength, the zeal of its garrison. He had no heavy artillery with him. He determined, then, to blockade it and trust to the operation of famine.

Partly to house himself and his troops, partly to assure the Afgháns that he was resolved not to leave the spot till Kandáhár had been taken, Nádir, at this early period of the siege, caused to be traced out in the vicinity of his camp the lines of a new city, which he called Nádirábád—the abode of Nádir. His communications with Persia were placed on a firm and

* Ferrier. The reader must always bear in mind that this description applies to the old city of Kandáhár, abandoned in 1738.

sure basis, whilst a reinforcement of thirty thousand cavalry enabled him to scour the country in every direction. To render the blockade absolute he surrounded the city with towers connected by small batteries.

The intense determination evinced by these preparations, combined with the enormous power displayed by Nádir to humble the pride of Mir Húsén and the Afgháns. Húsén wrote to the invader, offering to submit on conditions. He offered to acknowledge the suzerainty of Nádir Shah, and to pay him homage as a tributary prince, on the sole condition that Nádir would retire to Herát.

But these terms were no longer good enough for Nádir. Ten years before, shortly after he had taken service under Tamasp Mirza, he had dreamt a dream of mighty portent. He had seen in a vision a water-fowl and a white fish with four horns; he dreamt that he shot the bird, and, after all his attendants had failed, had easily captured the fish. When he awoke the astrologers had interpreted to him the dream. The bird he had shot was the reigning dynasty of Persia; the four horns of the fish were the kingdoms of Persia, Khwárizm, Tartary, and India. The imperial symbols of the bird and the fish showed him that in his hands was to fall the sceptre over these.

Such a vision, cherished, firmly believed in, already partly accomplished, was not to be baffled by the incomplete submission of a prince who had once reigned. Kandáhár had once defied him. Conquest alone could atone for the defiance. Nádir, then, refused the offer, and continued the blockade.

For a whole year he sat before the place. Meanwhile his son and his generals conquered the country to the north-east of the place. Balkh and the country now called Afghán Túrkistán fell before their arms. His son, Rizá Kúli Khán, crossing then the Oxus, totally defeated a superior army of the Uzbégs, and would have taken Bokhára, but that Nádir recalled him, on the plea that he did not desire to extend his conquests beyond the Oxus.

Bnt Kandáhár still held out, and there were no signs of yielding. Mir Húsén and his garrison had displayed their courage and their conduct in many a sortie, and on one occasion had nearly succeeded in inflicting upon the besiegers an irretrievable defeat. Time was slipping away. Already letters from discontented nobles at the court of the Moghol whetted the longing of Nádir to possess himself of the rich heritage of Hindústán. At last his patience was exhausted; he resolved to risk an assault. The preparations for this were of the most formidable description. Relays of assaulting columns were prepared, so as to give the defenders no respite. Then the assault was delivered. It continued without cessation for two days. On the first the repulse all along the line was complete; on the second it promised to be not only complete, but decisive, when the gallantry and devotion of a body of men in his service enabled Nádir to realize his expectations.

I have mentioned that before marching from Persia, Nádir had found it necessary to repress the Bakhtiárís, a daring tribe infesting the mountains near Ispahán.

He had first chastised, then enlisted them, and they had proved to be his best troops. On the afternoon of the second day of the assault on Kandáhár, when the repulse of the assailants seemed assured, these daring soldiers succeeded, by climbing the almost perpendicular rocks to the north of the town, in reaching a little plateau, where they established themselves, and whence, making it a base of operations, they were enabled to capture several of the towers on that side of the mountain. Into these towers they managed by means of ropes to haul up from below some guns of small calibre, and by means of these they gained by nightfall possession of the remaining towers. The town was now at their mercy.

All, however, was not yet over. Mir Húsén and his gallant Afgháns had still an impregnable position in the fort on the summit of the hill. Thither they retreated, and from this place they made terms with the conqueror. The conditions were generous. Nádir had been greatly struck by the valour displayed by the Afgháns, and he knew well how useful they would be to him in his invasion of Hindústán.

He agreed therefore to recognize Mir Húsén as governor for him of Kandáhár, on condition that he should furnish him with a strong corps of his gallant following. (1738.)

It deserves here to be recorded, that almost the first act of Mir Húsén and the people of Kandáhár after the capitulation was to move into the new town, built by Nádir during the siege, of Nádirábád. It kept that name for eight years; but when, in 1747, Nádir Shah was assassinated, the old name, classical * and venerated, was restored by acclamation.

Kandáhár subjected, Nádir marched on Kábul. That city, since the date on which I last mentioned it, had undergone some vicissitudes of fortune. In common with the other provinces subject to Shah Jahán, it had after the usual period of interregnum recognized the authority of Aurangzib. In 1670, however, the Afghán tribes in the north-east part of the country completely defeated his lieutenant, and proclaimed their independence under a chief of their own nation. Little more than two years later, January 1673, Aurangzib proceeded to Afghánistán to restore his authority, but soon returned, leaving his generals to complete the work. It was not, however, until the Rájá of Jodhpur, Jaswant Singh, had taken up the office of viceroy (1675), that the Emperor's authority was completely re-established. From that period to the time of which I am now writing, it would seem that Kábul had submitted to the governors nominated by the court of Dehli.

In 1738, the Governor of eastern Afghánistán was Názir Khán; the commandant of the city of Kábul, Shir Khán. Sending a message to these noblemen that they would find it difficult to oppose the fortune and valour of Nádir Shah, and that they need expect

* "Some historians," says Hanway, "think that Kandáhár is one of the seven cities founded by Alexander, and that the name of KANDAR, which is given him by the old Persian historians, is an abridgment of that Iskandar by which this conqueror was known to the Eastern nations."

no aid from Dehli, Nádir marched from Kandáhár to Ghazní, harassed but not impeded by the mountain tribes, and thence on to Kábul. Názir Khán had fled to Pesháwar; but the commandant, Shír Khán, prepared to offer a determined resistance.

The resistance was determined but useless. The only guns Nádir had with him were the swivel guns borne on camels. Mounting these on eminences near the town, he played on the defences till he had effected a breach. He then stormed the place (June 1738), put the greater part of the defenders to the sword, and leaving a garrison there, marched for Pesháwar.

CHAPTER VIII.

HISTORICAL.—THE DURANI RULE.

THERE are two points in the invasion of Híndústán by Nádir Shah which seem, at this time, specially to deserve attention. These are, the behaviour of his Afghán troops, and the difficulties he encountered in forcing the passes.

We have already seen how, about the time of the death of Mir Vais, the Abdáli Afgháns had occupied Herát, had taken Sabzwár, and had subsequently been defeated by Mahmúd near Farrah. Their defeat had led to anarchy throughout Khorásán, nor was it until, in 1722, Malik Mahmúd concluded with the ruler of Kandáhár, then besieging Ispahán, a convention which assured to him the sovereignty of that province, that order was restored there.

The death of Mahmúd, the Ghilzai Shah of Persia; the claims to sovereignty of Ashraff and Shah Tahmasp; and the contests to support those claims, had re-introduced the elements of strife throughout Khorásán and the districts of Herát. During all this period, however, the Abdáli Afghán element had always been predominant in those districts, and when Nádir Shah, on his way to Kandáhár in 1736 conquered Herát and Sabzwár, he conquered them from the Abdáli Afgháns.

We have already noticed, too, how quick was this stern conqueror to appreciate the valour of his enemies. It was by means of his enemies of the eve that he took Kandáhár on the morrow. And now, having conquered the Abdális in Herát, the Ghilzais in Kandáhár, and a portion of both of these tribes conjoined with others in Ghazní and Kábul, he set to work to make of these whilom enemies a *corps d'armée*, sufficiently strong and sufficiently trustworthy to be launched with effect on the decisive point of the field of battle—a reserve, in a word, which should be to him what the Old Guard was, at a later time, to the great Corsican conqueror.

The contingent taken from the Afgháns amounted to about sixteen thousand men. Of these, twelve thousand were taken from the Abdális; four thousand from the Ghilzais. The former being the most numerous, it was indispensable that the chief command should be vested in one of their clan. For this high office Nádir Shah selected Núr Mahammad Khán, Alizye.

It will be sufficient to state regarding this contingent, of which Núr Mahammad Khán retained the command during the lifetime of Nádir Shah, that they behaved with a valour, a devotion, and a daring such as endeared them to their foreign master. Of all his troops he speedily learnt to trust them the most. Of all his troops they rendered him the best service. They were the men upon whose action he could always rely. Daring, they were yet obedient. To them he was a god, whose orders, no matter their nature, were to be implicitly carried out. Nádir was thus able firmly to rely upon his Afgháns — even against his own men. They participated in all his triumphs, and, at least on one occasion, saved him from destruction.

So much for the Afghán contingent. Their valour was first to be tried in forcing the passes leading to India.

"It was a favourable circumstance to Nádir," says Hanway, "that the Indian court had kept the mountaineers of the passes in arrears for their pay." In those days as in the present, it was necessary to subsidize the border tribes. Had the court of Dehli paid regularly the amounts for which they had covenanted, even Nádir Shah, leading nearly one hundred thousand men, would have found it impossible to emerge into the Pesháwar plain with a formidable and well appointed army. As it was—the Moghol power in a rapid decline, anarchy universal, and the subsidies in arrear—he found the task difficult.

Though discontented with reason with the court of Dehli, the tribes of the mountains felt but little inclined to offer a welcome to Nádir Shah. He too disdained them, refused to enter into negotiations with them, and resolved to force his way in spite of them.

He tried to force his way. The tribes baffled him. They cut down trees, blocked up the defiles,* destroyed the roads, and, crowning the heights, annoyed him with constant fire. Now they attacked his rear, now they fell upon his flanks, again they appeared to bar his progress behind the obstructions they had raised. Numbers of his men perished. For nearly a month the tribes stopped him.

They would have continued to stop him still longer had Nádir not given in. Learning wisdom from experience he came to terms with the tribes, listened to their demands, and granted them. Then they turned round, became his children, and, entering his

* What defiles were these? Hanmer thus writes:—"Passing the *Behat* and the *Cou* he advanced into the narrow defiles which cover that province. Here several Indian princes" (by princes he means chiefs of the mountain tribes) "assembled their troops, cutting down trees, &c. &c." In a note Hanmer states that the *Behat* river was known to the ancients as the *Cophene*, and the *Cou* as the *Choaspe*. It is clear that the word *Cophenes* is identical with the *Kóphín* of Arrian, and the *Kóphín* of Arrian has been accepted as the modern *Kábul* river. The *Choaspe* may perhaps be identical with the *Kúnar* or *Kámá*, a tributary of the Kábul river falling into it ten miles east of Jalálábád. If this be correct, it is clear that the defiles referred to were the defiles of the Khaibar pass.

Since writing the above my attention has been drawn by an article in the *Pall Mall Gazette* to Mr. Henry Long's "Campaign of Alexander in Afghánistán." If Mr. Long's argument, that the *Cophenes* is identical not with the Kábul river but with the Tarnak, be sound, then Nádir Shah must have followed the route he lays down for Alexander, and have invaded India by the Kojak and the Bolan.

It is a pity that a question so important, the solution of which depends on the correct rendering in modern geographical terms of Greek proper names, should still remain unsettled.

service, more than filled the gaps which they themselves had made in the ranks of his army.

It is no part of the plan of this history to follow in detail the marvellous career of Nádir Shah. It will suffice to record that, issuing from the passes, he defeated the Moghol army on the Peshâwar plain, occupied in succession Peshâwar and Láhor, crossed the Satlaj, defeated the Moghol army at Karnál (13th February 1739); received the representative of the Moghol sovereign, Mahammad Shah, in his camp; marched on Dehli and occupied it. The day after his arrival a false report of his death caused the inhabitants to attempt the massacre of his soldiers. Nádir, attempting to stop the confusion by showing himself, was himself assailed. Then, and not till then, did he give the order to retaliate. For eight hours the city ran with blood.

After a stay of fifty-eight days at Dehli, Nadir, carrying with him the far-famed peacock throne, and laden with treasure,* returned to the Indus on his return to Khorásán. But the news of the enormous wealth he was carrying with him had roused the cupidity of the wild tribes. The swollen waters of the Indus hindered his passage, near Atok, and gave them time to assemble. Nádir Shah chose rather to negotiate than to run the risk of losing the whole of his plunder. He sent for the chiefs, and induced them, by a bribe

* Computed, including coins, jewels, and cloth, at from thirty-five to seventy millions sterling. Amongst the jewels was the famous *Koh-i-núr*.

of ten lakhs of rupees (£100,000), to grant him a free passage across the Indus.*

From Pesháwar Nádir marched by way of Kábul to Kandáhár. He subsequently asserted his right of suzerainty over Sind, Bokhára, and Khwárizm, and then took up his abode at Meshed, which he made the capital of his empire. His subsequent career is full of gloom. Making an unsuccessful campaign against the Lesgís, he conceived suspicions of his son, Riza Kúli, and put out his eyes.† He then marched into Asia Minor against the Turks, and after a campaign of three years ended the war by a victory near Eriván. Every year now saw him more suspicious and cruel, and it was at Meshed, when harbouring a design to massacre every Persian in his army, that he was mercifully assassinated by the nobles of that nation. (June 1747.)

The death of Nádir Shah was the Afghán opportunity. When that conqueror, after the conquest of Afghánistán, was forming his Afghán contingent, he had sent Ahmad Khán, chief of the Sadozyes, then fourteen years old, under honourable surveillance to Mazándarán. In that province Ahmad Khán had remained until the return of Nádir from Hindústán. He was then summoned to the imperial camp, and intrusted with a high, though not the supreme, command in the Afghán contingent. The men under his orders belonging to his own tribe, his influence

* "Hanway," vol. ii. p. 392.

† "It is not my eyes you have put out, but the eyes of Persia," exclaimed, prophetically, Rizá Kuli.

over them soon made itself felt. Daring in action, firm in his resolves, true to his word, Ahmad Khán was just the man to win the confidence of the daring men who owed him hereditary homage. Nor was his influence less with Nádir Shah. His prompt execution of orders, his proved fidelity, had won the confidence and the affection of that monarch. If a service more than ordinarily dangerous were required its execution was trusted to Ahmad Khán—and Ahmad Khán never failed.

The suspicions and the cruelties which had clouded the last five years of Nádir Shah's life had not altered the dispositions of Ahmad Khán toward his person. When, therefore, Nádir was assassinated by the Persian lords whose death he himself was contemplating, the first movement of Ahmad Khán was to avenge the murder. He assembled the men of his clan, and joining the Uzbégs, who had agreed to stand by him, attacked the camp of the conspirators. Finding, however, that the whole Persian army was in the plot, and that it would be useless to contend with their vastly superior numbers, he drew off his men and rode with them for Kandáhár, all the other chiefs of the Afghán contingent and their following accompanying him. It is said that before leaving Meshed Ahmad Khán managed to take possession of the Koh-i-Núr.

Up to this period the command of the contingent had remained in the hands of Núr Mahammad Khán Alizye. But with the death of Nádir Shah, and the subsequent retreat of all the Afgháns upon Kandáhár, the position not only of the contingent but of the nation which it represented was entirely changed. A vision of independence opened before them. No longer the hirelings of a foreign prince, they constituted at the moment a national army capable of resisting the heterogeneous masses welded into consistency by the genius of Nádir, but which, his grasp over them loosened, would almost certainly dissolve.

As the contingent of a foreign prince the Abdális and Ghilzais had been not unwilling to serve under the orders of the nominee of the master who had conquered them. But that master's death had removed the reason for such obedience. Free men, they were not willing to do homage to an Alizye. Almost the first act of the chiefs of the body which from a contingent had become a national army, after their arrival at Kandáhár, was to withdraw the command from Núr Mahammad Khán.

A few days later the representatives of the wild tribes, the Abdális, the Ghilzais, the Belúchis, the Hazáras, and the Kizilbáshis, met to consider the course which ought to be followed to secure the national independence. It was universally agreed that the connection with Persia should, at any cost, be severed, and that a king should be elected from amongst themselves, wielding the executive power alike in civil and military matters. To choose the king from a number of chiefs, all deeming themselves worthy, was not so easy. It is said that eight meetings were held, and that at these the claims of every chief, excepting those of Ahmad Khán, were brought forward and discussed. At the ninth, Háji

Jamál Khán, chief of the Mahammadzyes, united a majority of suffrages, but the minority was strong, and the decision seemed as remote as ever, when a holy man who had been present at all the meetings, and had noticed the dignified reserve of Ahmad Khán, advised the chiefs to break off the conference at once, saying, "Why all this verbose talk? God has created Ahmad Khán a much greater man than any of you. He is of the most noble of all the Afghán families. Maintain, therefore, God's work, for His wrath will weigh heavily upon you if you destroy it."* Then twisting into the form of a wreath some barley straw from the adjoining field, he placed it on the head of Ahmad Khán. Háji Jámal Khán at once withdrew his pretensions in favour of the youthful chief, and his election was then and there secured.

Ahmad Khán was crowned King of the Afgháns at Kandáhár in October 1747. He was then twenty-three years old. In the midst of the rejoicings following the coronation, intelligence reached him that a convoy containing specie to the value of two millions sterling—the amount of the customs-duties of the Panjáb and Sind due to Nádir Shah—was approaching Kandáhár. No intelligence could have been more welcome. Money was the one thing wanting to give lustre to his coronation. And now money came into his hands. He seized the convoy, and immediately distributed the contents amongst the officers and men of his army, and the chief employés

* Ferrier's "History of the Afgháns."

of his government, showing, says Ferrier, a liberality "which did more for his future career than all his private virtues and noble origin."

Another circumstance attending on the coronation of Ahmad Khán deserves to be noticed in this place. Like his great predecessor, Ahmad was superstitious. Warned in a dream that if he wished to taste the full splendour of imperial glory the title of his tribe must correspond with his aspirations, he changed their name from Abdáli to Dúráni, and assumed himself the high-sounding title of Shah Dúri Dúrán. Thenceforth he was known as Ahmad Shah Dúráni.

On his accession Ahmad Shah had two great principles to settle—the organization of the Afghán tribes, and the consolidation of his kingdom.

Born an Afghán, bred among the Afgháns, possessing a clear head, and having singularly sagacious views, he was well competent to deal with the first question. He solved it in the simple manner eminently characteristic of him. Far from centralising all the springs of power in his own hands, he resolved to rule the tribes through their chiefs. War, he knew, was the natural element of the Afgháns, and believing that he could wage successful war, he determined to make it self-supporting. His principle may be briefly summed up: the independence of the tribes under their respective chiefs; the concentration in his own hands of the ruling power to be exercised in consultation with the great chiefs; the furnishing by each of those chiefs of a contingent for service in case of war; the payment to them of a certain fixed sum in acknowledgment of their service. In a word, it was the feudal system of its entirety.

The great offices of State he reserved to chiefs in his own tribe—to Dúránis, making those offices, as a rule, hereditary in the family. The privileges of his own clan, the Sadozye, he took every occasion to exalt, with the object of clothing its members with the halo which, in Oriental countries, is supposed to surround kings and royal personages.

Above all, he endeavoured to impress upon every act the stamp of nationality. He was king to extend Afghán authority, to found an Afghán nationality, to spread Afghán ideas. In all his dealings with the tribes it was to this spirit that he appealed, and it was this appeal that assured his success.

The more certainly to carry the tribes with him in these great ideas, Ahmad Shah made it from the outset a principle of his policy to gain, in the first instance, their chiefs. With this object he appointed a council of nine chiefs with whom to consult in all matters of state. In the first instance he nominated to this council the nobles who had served with him in the army of Nádir Shah. Without their consent he adopted no measure of importance. His ideas being always broad, aggressive, and essentially in the largest sense Afghán, that consent was rarely, if ever, refused. This principle of government was at once the cause of his power and of his success. It will be seen that the reversal of it ruined his grandson.

Scarcely had he been crowned than he appealed

to the national spirit. Kábul and Ghazní were yet in Persian hands—Kábul and Ghazní must be reunited to the parts of the fatherland whence they had been long severed.

The governor of Kábul at this period was the very Názir Khán who had held the province for the Moghol when it had been invaded by Nádir Shah; and who, fleeing to Peshawar, had fought and been vanquished by that monarch on the plain bearing the name of the town. Nádir Shah had pardoned and employed him, and when Nádir fell, he was governing the province of Kábul, including Ghazní and Pesháwar, in the name of that prince.

Summoned by Ahmad Shah to yield the government he held for the sovereign who had been murdered, Názir Khán replied by proclaiming the Moghol. Having little to hope for from the feeble Mahammad Shah (of Dehli), Názir Khán endeavoured to procure recruits from amongst the Hazáras and the Aimaks. But the spirit of nationality was strong within these tribes. They would not fight for the Moghol against the Afghán. Meanwhile Ahmad Shah advanced. At his approach the commandant of Ghazní fled. That fortress was occupied without a shot. Kábul cost but a few lives. After a brief resistance Názir Khán hastily retreated, and fell back, harassed and molested by the mountain tribes, on Pesháwar.

Thither Ahmad Shah followed, and thence drove him. The Indus was crossed, Láhor was gained, without resistance. Meanwhile the old Emperor awoke from his lethargy. He had witnessed the sacking of Dehli by Nádir Shah. The very thought of a repetition of the same fearful scenes quickened his dry bones into action. He sent his best army under his son Ahmad to cover the fords of the Satlaj. But Ahmad Shah outmanœuvred the young prince. Whilst the latter watched the fords, the Dúráni, hastening higher up, crossed the river in boats, and marching on Sirhind seized the enemy's baggage which had been deposited there.

Ahmad Shah had with him but twelve thousand men; the Moghols were more numerous, and their army was better appointed. It was their policy to force a battle. The prince who led them, and the vizier who guided the prince, thought so. Facing about they marched down from the Satlaj on the Afgháns. But as they approached, their courage seemed to ooze out at their fingers' ends. They marched more slowly; finally they halted. They feared to risk an action.

Seeing this Ahmad Shah attacked them. The battle must have been a series of skirmishes, for it lasted ten days. At first Ahmad Shah was hopeful, but he soon found that the Moghol soldiers were better than the vizier who led them, and when a chance shot killed the vizier, his son, Mír Manú, who was a general, handled his troops with such effect that on the tenth day Ahmad Shah was forced to retire, beaten, from the field. Why was he not followed up? Permitted to retreat, he was able to come again.

But a very short time elapsed before he attempted a second invasion. Mahammad Shah died in April of the same year, and though no internal convulsions followed that event, it seemed to offer a favourable chance to Ahmad Shah Dúráni. Turning back then from the Indus, which he had all but reached, he marched on Láhor, now governed by the Mir Manú who had defeated him in Sirhind. Mir Manú might have resisted had hopes of support from Dehli been held out to him. But the new reign had, as anticipated by Ahmad Shah, brought with it increasing distractions. Bankrupt in all save intrigue, the court of Dehli was glad to conclude a peace, by which the Panjáb was annexed to the dominions of the Afghán king. Ahmad Shah confirmed Mir Manú in the government as his viceroy. He then visited the frontier towns of the province, regulated their affairs, and returned towards the end of the year to Kandáhár.

He was yet not satisfied. Herát had been the home of the Abdális, and the home which an Abdáli had lost a Dúráni was bound to restore. He therefore began preparations to lead thither an army in the spring. But before those preparations had been far advanced, he discovered a plot to assassinate him. The head of this plot was the Núr Mahammad Alizye, who had commanded the Afghán contingent during the wars of Nádir Shah, and had been displaced after the death of that monarch. The preceding pages have teemed with instances of the invariable longing to rule again which tortures a man who has once ruled. To such a man power is a necessity of existence. Not less than the brother of Humáyún, the ill-fated Kámrán, could Núr Mahammad disregard the all-powerful impulse. He conspired, and was discovered. For such a crime, at such a period, there was in Afghánistán but one punishment possible. Núr Mahammad and his fellow conspirators suffered it. That chief, the chiefs who conspired with him, and ten men from each of the tribes most deeply compromised perished by the hands of the executioner.* The selection of ten men from each guilty tribe to suffer for the lapses of that tribe, gives a curious insight into the system of punishment for conspiracy prevalent at that period.

By the spring all the military preparations were ready, and at the head of twenty-five thousand men Ahmad Shah marched against Herát. Herát succumbed after a siege of fourteen days, and was united to the Afghán kingdom. The Dúrání then marched on and occupied Meshed, the ruler of which was the grandson of Nádir Shah. To him Ahmad Shah restored Meshed and marched against Níshápor. Níshápor shut her gates on him. He besieged it, and though the winter set in, the snow fell, and his troops suffered terribly, he still persisted in the siege. At last he attempted an assault—but was repulsed. He continued to persevere until the Kháns of Khorásán had had time to act upon his communications. They then made their presence painfully felt, the garrison aiding their efforts by a vigorous sortie.

Nothing then remained but a retreat, if retreat were yet possible. Made in terrible weather, and in the

* Ferrier's "History of the Afgháns."

presence of harassing enemies, it was accomplished, and after incredible difficulties Herát was at last gained.

The disaster was repaired in the following year by the capture af Nishápor; and in 1752 Káshmír was added to dominions of Ahmad Shah. These had now reached the fullest extent he designed for them. The next four years were comparatively tranquil. Only an occasional revolt, of slight import, and easily quelled, came to interfere with the internal administration of his dominions.

But in 1756 an event occurred in the Panjáb, which proved to be the cause of new complications with the Moghol. Mir Manú, the governor of that province for Ahmad Shah, died in that year. In accordance with the principle which ruled his policy in Afghánistán, Ahmad Shah confirmed the succession to the governorship in the family of the deceased nobleman, although, the son being an infant, that succession devolved for a time on the widow. The court of Dehli, considering the circumstances favourable for the recovery of the Panjáb, sent an army to Láhor, occupied it, and left there Adina Bég, a man famous for his power of intrigue, as governor for the Moghol.

Ahmad Shah replied to this insult by marching first on Láhor, whence he drove Adina Bég, and thence towards Dehli. Corruption and intrigue had reduced the empire of Akbar to a mere shadow of its former greatness. Its nobles were without shame, without spirit, without honour. When Ahmad Shah had arrived within twenty miles of the capital the prime vizier came to beg and to intrigue for mercy. He brought the widow of Mir Manú to plead for him. But Ahmad Shah demanded a money compensation for the insult he had received and for the expense he had incurred, and when this was refused him, he marched on and occupied Dehli. (1757.)

Again did the Moghol capital suffer the terrible misery of occupation by a barbarous enemy. Ahmad Shah wished to spare the city all needless violence; but the rough soldiers who obeyed his nod on the field slipped from his grasp in the streets and lanes of an enemy's capital. Dehli, then, suffered as much as though it had been taken by assault. Murder, pillage, and rapine went hand in hand. Those who had escaped the massacre of 1739 had cause to remember the not less terrible occupation of eighteen years later. The miseries of the people did not, however, curtail or affect the festivities of the court. The Afghán conqueror took advantage of the occupation to unite his family to that of the Moghol by marrying, and by causing his son Taimúr to marry, princesses of that house. The portions conceded were enormous. That bestowed with the bride of Taimúr consisted of the provinces of the Panjáb and Sind.

But the capital did not alone suffer. The fort of Balamgarh was taken by assault and the garrison put to the sword. Mathurá, the holy city of the Hindús, was surprised by a corps of Afgháns under Háji Jahán Khán, and its inhabitants were ruthlessly slaughtered or carried away into slavery. The same corps—their hands red with slaughter—then marched against Agra.

But the story of their bloody deeds had preceded them, and the Játs who manned the walls repulsed them with heavy loss.

The hot season was now far advanced, and as it told very severely on the northern soldiers, Ahmad Shah resolved to retrace his steps. He returned, therefore, to Kandáhár, leaving, to guard his interests in India, a brother of the deceased Mir Manú as vizier to the Moghol; and to protect his new acquisitions east of the Indus, his son Taimúr, assisted by Háji Jahán Khán.

Ahmad Shah had scarcely recrossed the Indus when the factions he had left in India renewed their contention for the decaying heritage of the Moghols. The intervention of the Maráthás from Western India, and the rise of a new sect called the Sikhs, added new elements of discord to the general turmoil.

It is no part of this history to do more than refer to the proceedings of these different nationalities, in so far as they influenced the action of Ahmad Shah. It will suffice to state that in the month of May following the return of the Dúráni to Kandáhar the Maráthás occupied Láhor, and forced the Afgháns to retire across the Indus. Taimúr lost for the moment the fairest portion of the dower of his wife.

Ahmad Shah was preparing to avenge this insult when an insurrection broke out in Bilúchistán. The chief of this province was Násir Khán—a good soldier, a chivalrous leader, but, like many men more capable than their fellows, full of ambition. Násir Khán had represented the Bilúchi tribe at Kandáhár at the time of the election of Ahmad Shah. He had given to that election his fullest consent. Subsequently he had followed his suzerain into the field, had accompanied him in his three invasions of India, and had performed his part loyally and well. Possibly all this time he was watching his opportunity. This at least is certain, that no sooner was it known in Afghánistán that the Maráthás had conquered the Panjáb than Násir Khán renounced his fidelity to Ahmad Shah, and declared his independence.

The Afghán king was at first unwilling to proceed to extremities against a man whom he regarded as a friend and esteemed as a soldier, and he used every means in his power to induce him to return to his allegiance. The result afforded another proof of the generally accepted maxim that when an Oriental chief, with an armed force at his beck and call, puts the bit between his teeth, soft words only inflate his brain. Násir Khán not only treated the advances of his late suzerain with contempt, but when the latter sent a force, under his vizier Shah Wáli Khán, against his capital, Kalát, he did not await it there, but marched forward to encounter it.

The two armies met at a village not far from Mastúng, a town sixty-nine miles north of Kalát. The battle, obstinately contested at the outset, terminated in the total defeat of the Afgháns. They fled from the field in disorder, and did not halt till they had galloped thirty miles. Násir Khán, instead of following up his victory, encamped at Mastúng, the approaches to which were guarded by a large and deep ravine and by several watercourses. Meanwhile Ahmad Shah had heard of his vizier's defeat. Dreading the effect which even a slight discomfiture might have upon the tribes, he hastened, at the head of a strong division, to reinforce him, and then moved upon Mastúng. Clearing the ravines and the watercourses, he attacked Násir Khán in his camp, completely defeated him, and followed him, retreating, to Kalát, which he at once invested.

Dashing troops, when well led, in the open field, the Afgháns have always proved indifferent soldiers when engaged in sieges. It is not the sort of work in which horsemen and mountaineers excel. It proved so on this occasion, as it had proved before and has proved since. After a protracted cannonade breaches were made in the walls, and five different assaults were delivered in succession. They all failed. It has been urged in excuse for the failure that the chiefs serving under Ahmad Shah did not desire to succeed, that Bilúchistán had ever served to them the purpose of a Cave of Adullam, to which every discontented chief could retire, and they wished it to remain so. It is probable that this reason did affect some of the chieftains, but the walls were well manned, the citadel was extremely strong, and the defenders were well commanded.

The intelligence which from time to time reached Ahmad Shah of the progress made by the Maráthás in Hindústán made him more than ordinarily anxious to bring Násir Khán to reason. But time to reduce Kalát by blockade failed him, and after the fifth unsuccessful assault he became hopeless of storming it. Násir Khán, on his part, was tired of an independence which shut him up in his capital. Terms then were proposed and were accepted. By these Násir Khán agreed to acknowledge the suzerainty of Ahmad Shah, and to furnish a contingent of troops whenever that monarch should wage war out of his own territories. On the other side, Ahmad Shah agreed to furnish a sum of money and a supply of the munitions of war whenever he should require the services of the Bilúch contingent. He further renounced his right to demand the services of the contingent for any internal quarrel, and he absolved the Bilúch chief from payment of tribute. To make the agreement more binding, Ahmad Shah married a cousin of the Bilúchi.

This important matter settled, Ahmad Shah turned his attention to Hindústán. He had, whilst engaged before Kalát, despatched a small force, under Núrúdin Khán, to observe and hold in check the enemy. This chief had crossed the Indus and advanced with but little opposition to the banks of the Chináb—the main body of the Maráthás having fallen back on Dehli. Núrúdín did not think it prudent to proceed further with his small force, but remained halted at Vazirábád, waiting the orders of his sovereign.

Those orders did not arrive so quickly as he had hoped. The revolt of Bilúchistán had entailed results which the submission of its chief did not immediately counteract, and Ahmad Shah had found it impossible to leave Kandáhár as early as he had hoped. At last, however, he set out, traversed the Bolan pass, then marched up the Indus to Pesháwar, crossed the river at Atok, picked up his lieutenant at Vazirábad; then, continuing his march through the north of the Panjáb, crossed the Jamná near Sahâranpúr, and halted there. Here he was joined by the Rohilla chiefs whom he had won to his cause.

Marching from Saharanpur towards Dehli, Ahmad Shah defeated first a detachment of the Maráthá army under Datají Sindia, and then a second under Múlhar Ráo Holkar. He then marched on Dehli, took it, and, leaving there a small detachment, cantoned his army for the rainy season at Anúpshahr, seventy-three miles from the capital.

He was at this place when, the rainy season being over, the grand army of the Maráthás, estimated at seventy thousand regular troops, aided by countless irregulars and followers, marched on Dehli, took and plundered it; then, directing their course northwards, attacked and stormed Kúnjpúrá, sixty miles from the capital, garrisoned by a small detachment of Afgháns. On learning of the taking of Dehli Ahmad Shah pushed northwards, and reached Kúnjpúra just in time to witness its fall. It had been quite possible now for a skilful general commanding a large force to reduce the Afghán to extremities, for Ahmad Shah was on the eastern bank of the river, not then fordable, and was much straitened for supplies. The pride of the Maráthás in their numbers caused, however, a fatal relaxation of vigilance, and Ahmad Shah, taking advantage of that relaxation and of a sudden fall in the river, effected a passage with but slight loss, and forced the enemy to fall back on Pánipat. There the Maráthás intrenched themselves.

Ahmad Shah, with a force estimated, inclusive of his Indian allies, at forty thousand men, took up a position which would cut off his enemy's supplies. Thus the two armies remained watching each other for more than three months, both straitened for food, but the Maráthás more so than the Afgháns. At last the former could bear it no longer. On the 6th January, 1761, they marched out to attack the invader.

The third battle of Pánipat has often been described. It fully deserves the attention which has been bestowed upon it. It was one of the decisive battles of the age. Had it been decided against the Afgháns, all India would then and there have fallen under Maráthá domination, and it is not to be expected that the English settlements in Bengal and in Madras, then just emerging from the childhood of their careers, would have escaped the unsparing hands and the overwhelming power of the marauders. The third battle of Pánipat threw back the Maráthá power for thirty years; and when towards the close of the century it had by the exertions of Mádhají Sindia recovered a great portion of its former might, the English had established themselves so firmly as not only to bear the shock of the collision but to make it recoil on their enemy.

The battle of Pánipat can be clearly described in a few words. The Maráthás tried to pierce the Afghán centre. They nearly succeeded, so nearly that many Afghán chiefs considered that the day was lost. So did not think Ahmad Shah. Occupying a position whence he could command the battle-field, Ahmad had witnessed the bold advance of the enemy, and the defeat of his front line, without losing his composure. But when he thought that the Maráthás had advanced far enough, he charged them with his reserve, whilst, at the same moment, another chosen body of horse dashed on their flank. It was a critical moment of the fight. The resistance of the Maráthás was most gallant. A little more solidity, and they had won the day,—for their left wing was victorious, and their right was maintaining an even combat with the enemy. But, at the very height of the conjuncture, whilst they were still resisting the Afghán charge, their leader, Wiswás Ráo, the son of Péshwa, fell mortally wounded. Fighting as they were for empire, the Maráthás should still have continued the struggle. But the fall of their chief unnerved them. They renounced the empire of India when it was still within their grasp.

Pánipat was a very decisive defeat. It placed Hindústán at the feet of the Afghán. But Ahmad Shah saw well what sort of a Hindústán it was—a Hindústán, whose dried-up blood must be revivified by other means than by the sword. To employ those means he had neither training nor leisure. He therefore made the settlement which appeared to him the wisest, restoring the nominal sovereignty to the Moghol, and returned to Kandáhár.

But he was not to escape the fate of founders of empires. The growing sect, the Sikhs, forced him by their pretensions to return to the Panjáb in 1762.

He drove them for refuge to the hills. He had hardly accomplished this—he was still at Sirhind, which he had taken after a desperate but decisive battle—when intelligence reached him that Kandáhár was in revolt. The rainy season had just set in, the rivers were swollen and unbridged, prompt action was necessary. Ahmad Shah saw the difficulties, and determined to overcome them. He marched down the Satlaj to Bhawalpúr; thence viâ Múltán, Déra Ishmáil Khán, and the Gomal pass to Ghazní. The heat in the early part, the cold in the later part of his march, inflicted great sufferings on his troops. Many of them died. But with the remainder he had reached Ghazní—and once there he easily stamped out the disturbances at the capital.

All these fatigues had told upon the conqueror. His constitution was shaken, when a cancer in the face gave it the final blow. He went, indeed, in 1764, into the field to crush an insurrection of the Aimaks near Herát, and again in 1767 once more to expel the still intrusive Sikhs from the plains of the Panjáb. In the following year he was forced to remain inactive whilst his son, Prince Taimúr, went to achieve, by the aid of the Shah's old enemy, Násir Khán the Bilúchi, a complete victory over the Persians. But he felt his strength waning day by day. Till 1773, however, he continued to reside at the capital. Feeling then that he had become too weak to bear the burden, he summoned the chiefs, caused them to swear fealty to Prince Taimúr as his successor; then, still directing the government, he retired to a palace he had built at

Toba Mahárúf, in the Sulaimán mountains. Here he died in June of the same year.

The chief merit to be ascribed to Ahmad Shah is undoubtedly the consolidation of the Afghán tribes. He made of them a nation. The chiefs whom he failed to conciliate he reduced. Forming, a council composed of a leading chieftain of each tribe, consulting with its members, and often adopting their advice, he was able to concert measures which commended themselves to the general body. Generous, affable, and resolute, he won the hearts of his followers, introduced and maintained order where disorder had prevailed, and justified, by his internal administration, the epitaph engraved on his tomb: "Ahmad Shah Dúráni was a great king! Such was the fear of his justice, that the lion and the hind lived peacefully together. The ears of his enemies were incessantly deafened by the noise of his conquests."

Taimúr Shah was the second of the eight sons of Ahmad Shah. Intelligent, active, and whilst conciliatory yet decided, his great fault was indolence. He had been selected by his father as, of all his offspring, the worthiest to succeed him. In the month of April, Taimúr, who governed Herát and Khorásán, as far as Nishápor, having received information that his father was dying, had set out for Toba Mahárúf to see him. Before he reached Kandáhár, however, Shah Ahmad had sent him positive orders to return at once to his government. Reluctantly Taimúr obeyed, and he was at Herát when he received the information that his father had died, nominating him as his successor, and that his eldest brother Sulaimán had proclaimed himself king at Kandáhár.

Sulaimán Mirza had neither the abilities nor the courage of his brother, but he had married the daughter of the chief vizier, Shah Wáli Khán, the same who had been defeated by the Bílúchi chief, Násir Khán, near Mastúng in 1758. It was owing to the influence of this man, and in spite of the opposition offered by a majority of the council, that Sulaimán had been proclaimed king at Kandáhár.

His triumph was very short. Taimúr, supported by the great majority of the Dúranís, the Hazáras, and the Aimaks, marched at once upon Kandáhár. The grand vizier attempted to raise an army to support his son-in-law, but, failing, resolved to make a virtue of submission. Accordingly, accompanied by his two sons, and the two Dúráni chiefs whose adherence to him had been most conspicuous, he rode into Taimúr's camp at Farrah. To Taimúr, the course of action he should adopt towards these repentant rebels—repentant only because they had recognised the impossibility of succeeding—was never for a moment doubtful. He thoroughly understood those over whom he was called to bear rule, and to inaugurate that rule by forgiveness would be an encouragement to rebellion. He determined to speak with no uncertain voice. Refusing, then, to see them, he ordered their heads to be struck off.

This act of severity had the desired effect. Taimúr Shah entered Kandáhár in triumph and was crowned King of the Afgháns. The sympathy which had been shown by the population for his brother Sulaimán had inspired him with a great dislike for the people of that city. In the vicinity too lived those Dúráni tribes upon whose support his brother had counted. He determined therefore to transfer the title of capital to Kábul, and to move with his court to that city. He carried out this arrangement without delay. Thenceforth, during his reign, he passed eight months of the year at Kábul, the remaining four at Peshâwar.

Arrived at Kábul, Taimúr's first care was to make secure the foundations of his government. A Dúráni himself, he distrusted the Dúránis. He could not indeed withdraw from the chiefs of that tribe the offices which his father had made hereditary in their families. He had recourse therefore to another process to accomplish the same end. Preserving the titles of the old offices, he created others to which he transferred their duties. As his chief councillor he selected Kázi Faizúllah of the Daolat Sháhi tribe. In this man he placed such implicit confidence that he never did anything without consulting him. This man; Payandar Khán, chief of the Barúkzye tribe; Dalâwar Khán, whom he appointed commander-in-chief; Abdúl Latif Khán, a native of Khorásán, his receiver general of taxes; Núr Mahammad Khán, president of the court of accounts; and Iltifát Khán, chief of the eunuchs, chief treasurer and custodian of the crown jewels, formed the leading members of his council. To these ministers his general instructions were to put in action towards every one the principles of justice tempered by mercy. Still dreading the effect of concentrating power in the hands of the chiefs of the tribes, he recommended them to employ in administrative positions and as public functionaries of the state men whose want of influence with their tribes would make them obedient servants of the king. His own personal guard he selected from the Isákzyes, one of the smaller Dúráni tribes, and he raised likewise a body of twelve thousand horsemen from amongst the Kizilbáshis.

In pursuance of the same line of policy he withdrew as much as possible the government of provinces from the chiefs of tribes. To compensate them he greatly increased their pay. The most formidable of them, especially of the Dúránis, he retained, as far as possible, at his court, taking care that they should be accompanied by but a small retinue.

He paid special attention to his finances, placing them upon a well ordered basis. His own expenses were small. The necessary payments were made with extreme punctuality; and the revenue was as regularly collected. The consequence was a treasury full even to overflowing.

Taimúr had not the same passion for war as his father. It is curious to observe how his peaceful inclinations prejudicially affected his power. It would seem almost to be an oriental law that the kingdom which halts in its acquisitions recedes. Taimúr Shah governed his rude country internally as few men have governed it. Yet his peaceful instincts injuriously affected its influence with the outer world. The inner kingdom indeed remained sound; but the outlying provinces, the provinces annexed from other countries

—feeling no longer the heel of the conqueror—began to think they might walk alone. The insurrections and wars of Taimúr's reign illustrate this assertion.

Khorásán was the western annexe of the Afghán kingdom. Since Ahmad Shah had taken Meshed in 1749 and restored it to Prince Shah Rokh, grandson of Nádir Shah, that city and the northern province of Khorásán had acknowledged the suzerainty of the Afghán king. Shah Rokh himself never faltered in his fidelity, but during the greater part of the reign of Taimúr the population, led by their native chiefs, had been surging against submission to the Afghán. Two armies, sent in succession, had put down the insurgents, but the return of each had been a signal for renewed rebellion. A third army went, met with determined opposition, but succeeded in asserting the Afghán authority. Nor did it leave Meshed till further insurrection had been made difficult, if not impossible.

Sind was another outlying province of the Afghán kingdom. Here, the slackening of the rein was soon felt, and as a consequence Sind revolted. About the same time Múltán was gained by the Sikhs. Against these enemies Shah Taimúr moved in person at the head of a well organized army. He defeated the Sikhs near Múltán, took that place after a few days' siege, and then marched on Baháwalpúr. Baháwalpúr with all its wealth fell into his hands. The easy capture of this place disconcerted the plans of the insurgents, and they made no stand anywhere. But the country was laid waste with fire and the sword.

Taimúr returned to Kábul. But he had not reached that place before the insurrection in Sind broke out with renewed fury. Other affairs prevented him from marching at once to quell it, and it was only five years later, 1786, that he sent his commander-in-chief Diláwar Khán with a small force to suppress it.

Diláwar Khán was not so successful as had been his master. The Tálpúri chiefs united against him, led him into an ambuscade, and forced him to fall back with loss on Shikárpúr. An accommodation was entered into, in virtue of which the chiefship of Sind was vested in a Tálpúri noble, Fath Ali Khán, on condition of his acknowledging the suzerainty of Taimúr Shah and paying him a fixed tribute. Gradually the Tálpúri strove to rid himself of both obligations, and at the end of three years he boldly severed the tie.

Afghán Túrkistán was another of the border provinces. The King of Bokhára, Shah Morád, whose dominions were separated from this province by the Oxus, had likewise noticed the lighter pressure exercised by Taimúr, and he had been, almost ever since the accession of that prince, stealthily endeavouring to attract some of the outlying districts to himself. Taimúr, made sensible by the revolt of Balkh and of Akhchah of these stealthy and persistent efforts, at first remonstrated. The remonstrance proving useless, he appealed to arms, and marched towards Kúndúz with a large army. Shah Morád crossed the Oxus to oppose him, and the two armies came in face of each other near Akhchah. Had the Afgháns then attacked the Usbégs they would almost certainly have gained the day.

Partly through his own indecision, partly through the skill of Morád, a long delay, well employed by the latter to work upon the Afghán chiefs, followed. Then Morád, having made all his preparations, offered to withdraw his forces into Bokhára, and to recognise the authority of Taimúr in Balkh and Akhchah, if he would spare the effusion of blood and agree to a peace. The too-easy Taimúr agreed. The rival armies withdrew; but Balkh and Akhchah, though still nominally subject to Kábul, became from that day virtually independent.

Another outlying province, Káshmír, feeling likewise the slackening of the rein, revolted, but was for the time brought back. Sístán, likewise, showed disaffection, but it was repressed.

But the general effect of the foreign policy of Taimúr was bad. It lost him Sind and the great towns of Túrkistán, and laid the foundation of revolt in Khorásán and Káshmír.

Nor was he entirely free from internal rebellion. The first of these revolts, made by a relative, Abdúl Hálik Khan, in 1774, was easily repressed. Nearly five years later, when Taimúr was at Pesháwar, an attempt was made to murder him, with the view of seating his brother, Sikandar, his father's sixth son, on the throne. The conspirators were nearly succeeding; they had murdered the guards of the palace, and driven Taimúr to take refuge in its upper storey, before the royal troops could assemble to attack them. But then, the conspirators were nearly all cut to pieces. In this conspiracy the chief of the Mohmand tribe, Arsalah Khán, was implicated, but he managed to flee to his tribe.

The fate of this man is remarkable, inasmuch as it illustrates the view taken by the Afgháns on the subject of revenge. Admitting, as we may, that with them revenge is a religion, this story shows that that quality indulged in by virtue of a solemn breach of faith, becomes a crime.

Arsalah Khán had tried to murder his sovereign, and, failing, had fled to the mountains. The crime he had attempted was one which Taimúr never forgave. But Arsalah Khán was beyond his power; he was in passes which his horses could not traverse. Taimúr attempted, then, to gain him by wile. He feigned to forgive him. Publicly, privately, he declared he had given him reason to rebel, and that Arsalah was almost justified in his attempt. He even went so far as to send his intended victim a Korán, on a page of which he had inscribed an oath that he would forgive his fault. Arsalah Khán was taken in. He returned to Pesháwar and gave himself up. That very same day his throat was cut by order of the king. Not even the Afgháns pardon this treatment of an enemy lured in by an oath inscribed on the Korán. They regard it as the greatest stain on the memory of Taimúr.*

In the later months of his life Taimúr became more cruel, more suspicious, and more morose than he had been before. He survived the last attempt on his life,

* I have accepted the account given by Ferrier. Other writers differ as to the mode of his death, but their version affects neither the principle of the story nor the verdict of the Afgháns.

which I have recorded, about thirteen months. Taken ill as he was journeying from Pesháwar to Kábul, he died at the latter place on the 20th May 1793. His reign had lasted twenty years. He left behind him twenty-three sons and thirteen daughters, but he died without having made any definite arrangements as to his successor.

The eldest son of the deceased monarch, Humáyún Mirza, was governor of Kandáhár; the second son, Mahmúd Mirza, was governor of Herát. These two princes had an excellent understanding with each other. Mahmúd promised to support the pretensions of Humáyún.

Of the remaining twenty-one sons, the fourth, Abbás Mirza, renowned for his Herculean strength, was the popular favourite; the fifth, Zamán Mirza, had enlisted on his behalf the all-powerful influence of the zenana.

Humayún and Mahmúd remained at their respective governments. All the other princes repaired to Kábul to urge their respective claims. Had the election taken place immediately after the death of Taimúr Shah, it is probable that Abbás Mirza would have been chosen. But the chiefs having resolved to defer the great event until after the obsequies had been performed, the zenana influence had time to work. To this influence, Payandah Khán, the great chief of the Barukzyes, added his own. The result was that at a meeting held after the interment Zamán Mirza was chosen to succeed his father.

The first act of Shah Zamán was to secure the throne to which he had been elected. Recognised as king by everyone except by his brothers, he at once placed those of the recusants who were at Kábul in confinement, and fed them for five days on an allowance of two to three ounces of bread for each individual daily. This starvation diet had its effect. On the sixth day the princes, having recognised their brother as their sovereign, were nominally freed from confinement, only however to be lodged, under careful surveillance, in the Bálá Hissar.

Like his father, Zamán Sháh wished to be served by his own men. He therefore pensioned off the old ministers, and replaced them by partisans devoted to himself. He endeavoured by various means to attach to himself those chiefs who had opposed his election. In most cases he succeeded; but those who had been violent in their opposition, and the few whom he failed to win, he put to death.

But the new king was not yet secure. He had, indeed, settled matters in Kábul, but he had yet to deal with Kandáhár and Herát, governed by brothers alike older by birth, one of them, Mahmúd, formidable from his popularity in the Herát districts.

The possession of the capital, and the adhesion of the great chief of the Barúkzyes, Payandah Khán, gave Zamán Shah at this conjuncture an advantage of which he speedily availed himself. Having to deal with two enemies, not yet united, he resolved to beat them in detail—to reach Kandáhár as an enemy before Mahmúd Mirza of Herát could reach it as a friend. As soon, then, as he had settled matters at Kábul, he marched on Kandáhár.

Humáyún Mirza played into his hands. His clearly marked out policy was to wait behind the walls—to defend the place till his brother should come from Herát. But either from self-confidence, or, as some assert, from the lukewarmness to his cause displayed by the Kandáhárís, he would not adopt this course, but went to meet Zamán Shah at Kalát-i-Ghilzai. A battle ensued, in which Humáyún was completely defeated. He fled for refuge to Bilúchistán.

It is a fact, which subsequent events have made worthy to be recorded, that the Kabúlí troops were led into action on this occasion by Shújah Mirza, the only brother alike on the maternal and paternal side of Zamán Shah.

This battle settled the fate of Kandáhár, but Mahmúd had still to be conquered, and Mahmúd was in Herát. Zamán Shah was about to continue his march in that direction—when news reached him that the outlying provinces on every side were showing symptoms of intending to test the temper of the new king's rule. Feeling then that his presence was urgently required at the capital, Zamán Shah patched up an accommodation, insincere on both sides, with his brother Mahmúd, and returned to Kábul.

Arrived here, he settled his plan of government. The revolts of the outlying provinces in his father's reign he attributed to his father's too lenient system. He resolved, unwisely, to proceed to the opposite extreme. To make himself feared he did not recoil from the risk of making himself hated. His system, in a word, was an unconscious imitation of that promulgated by Rehoboam, son of Solomon. His father had chastised his people with whips, he would chastise them with scorpions. The copy produced the same results as the original.

Beginning by taking in hand his nobles, he inaugurated a reign of terror in Kábul. Every man of influence was suspected, watched, and dealt with as occasion might demand. The great chief of the Barúkzyes himself—who had contributed more than anyone else to raise Zamán Shah to the throne—found himself suddenly deprived of all power. Other chiefs, inferior only to him, were arrested, imprisoned, and put to death, in many instances with a refinement of cruelty.

These cruelties in the capital were a prelude to others that were to follow in the provinces. The Panjáb had risen, Káshmir was in revolt, Sind had severed herself, the Uzbégs had crossed the Oxus. Zamán Shah having crushed, as he hoped, the spirit of the great feudal lords, set out with the intention of dealing, on a similar plan, with rebellion.

The first province he took in hand was the Panjáb. He had reached Pesháwar when he heard that his brother Humáyún, assisted by the Tálpúris of Sind, had seized Kandáhár. He turned back to meet him. Humáyún, betrayed by the Afgháns, fled again to Sind: but attempting to escape thence to Herát, he was taken prisoner by a body of horse sent after him by his brother. Zamán Shah ordered his eyes to be pierced.

The Afghán king, turned from his expedition against

Pesháwar, resolved to march through the Bolan pass into Sind, at once to punish the Tálpúris, and to recover the country which had glided out of Afghán power in the latter years of his father's reign. But he had scarcely entered Sind when he heard that his brother Mahmúd was marching on his rear to cut him off from Afghánistán. Foregoing, then, the pleasure of crushing Sind, then hopelessly at his mercy, he compromised the arrears of tribute due to him for one-third of their amount, and confirming the Tálpúri chief, Fath Ali Khán, in the government he hastened back to Kandáhár.

Mahmúd Mirza meanwhile was marching from Herát to Kandáhár. Suddenly the news reached him of Zamán Shah's return. He at once took up a position in the Siah-band range, with the intention of remaining there till he should receive exact intelligence regarding his brother's movements. The moment he heard that Zamán Shah had left Kandáhár and was but three marches from him, he broke up and moved into the plains. The two armies met at the village of Gúrak, not far from Giriskh. The battle that followed was most hotly contested. For a long time fortune seemed to favour Mahmúd, but towards the close of the day his men gave way. The defeat was decisive. Mahmúd fled, first to Farrah, and thence to Herát, where by timely professions of sorrow and possibly by inciting the Uzbégs to attack Túrkistán, he obtained his brother's pardon, and was allowed to continue in his government.

Whilst Zamán Shah was engaged with Mahmúd the

Uzbégs, incited by Mahmúd, had invaded Túrkistán, had defeated there the lieutenant of the Afghán king, and had taken Balkh. They renounced these conquests, however, when they heard of the victorious return of the Shah to Kábul, and, renewing the treaty made with his father, they recrossed the Oxus. About the same time, or possibly a little earlier, the rebellion in Káshmír was quelled.

The surging of the outlying provinces visible at the accession of Zamán Shah had now been quelled. He had regained Sind, but had lost the Panjáb east of the Indus. He had made more than one march to Peshá-war with the intention of expelling the Sikhs, now very formidable, but some pressing need always called him back.

The recovery of that province had now become with him a matter of paramount importance. In 1796 he once more marched to Pesháwar, crossed the Indus, and advanced some eighty miles on the road to Láhor, when he was suddenly recalled to Kábul by the intelligence that Agha Mahammad, Shah of Persia, had invaded Khorásán, and had taken and sacked Meshed.

Zamán Shah prepared an army to avenge this insult, but negotiations having taken place, and Agha Mahammad having retired into his country, the Afghán king moved again with an army to Pesháwar. He pushed on as far as Láhor, and was preparing to invade India, when the news that Mahmúd had revolted and was threatening Kandáhár forced him to return.

Zamán Shah returned, bought over one of Mahmúd's chief generals, occupied Herát, and forced his half-brother to flee for refuge to Persia. The king then resumed his plans regarding India, again reached Láḥor, conciliated the Sikhs, when intelligence that the Persians, under Fath Ali Shah, the successor of Agha Mahammad on the Persian throne, were threatening Khorásán, again called him back to Pesháwar, and thence to Herát. (1799.)

The action of Fath Ali Shah on this occasion was prompted by the British Government of India. That government had noticed with considerable alarm the preparations made by Zamán Shah to repeat the exploits of his grandfather in Hindústán. As the best mode of counteracting his designs they despatched an embassy to the court of Ispáhán. The bait of northern Khorásán was held out to Fath Ali Shah. He concluded, then, an alliance with the British, and prepared, by the invasion of that province, to divert the attention of the Afghán monarch from Hindústán.

From some cause or other the Persian invasion collapsed. Fath Ali Shah proceeded as far as Sabzwár and then returned. The demonstration, however, had, as far as British interests were concerned, been entirely successful, for it had called back Zamán Shah to Kandáhár for the winter. He was there still in the spring when the indefatigable Mahmúd disturbed his repose by invading Herát at the head of ten thousand men raised in the outlying provinces of Persia. It is possible that had Mahmúd persevered he might have succeeded. But the circumstance that he had been often betrayed weakened his confidence in his allies and followers. Of this mistrust the prime vizier of

Zamán Shah, Wafadár Khán, took advantage to insinuate such doubts of his chief supporter, the ruler of Kayn and Birján, districts of southern Khorásán, that he raised the siege, and fled to Bokhára. Driven thence by the pressing instances of Zamán Shah, he wandered first to Khiva, then to the court of Fath Ali Shah, where he remained some months, a petitioner for aid to dethrone his brother.

Zamán Shah was now at the zenith of his power. He had not, indeed, recovered the Panjáb, but he had shown that he possessed the power of overrunning the country. His only formidable brother was an exile. Apparently his system of severity had succeeded; in reality it had undermined the basis of his power. If, in a constitutional monarchy, the great aim of government is the contentment of the subjects, in a feudal country like Afghánistán security can only be assured by the contentment of the feudal chiefs. Ahmád Shah and Taimúr Shah had alike based their system of government upon this principle. They had had their council of nobles, without whose consent no important enterprise had been undertaken. The consent of the tribes naturally followed that of the chiefs. But almost from the very first, Zamán Shah had adopted a system exactly the reverse of this. He had, indeed, kept the chiefs about his court, but he had taken care that they should be without a following, and he had never consulted them. Nay, more, he had irritated them to the last degree by the steady pursuance of the system of silent persecution he had inaugurated after his first repression of Humáyún Mirza.

All his confidence Zamán Shah reserved for his prime minister, Wafadár Khan Sadozye, an intriguer with soft voice and silky manners, cringing to his superiors, overbearing and insolent to all others. Such a man was necessarily a coward, and almost necessarily avaricious and corrupt. Yet this man was the second self of the Afghán king. He encouraged his master in his design of repressing and persecuting the feudal chiefs, the confiscation of whose properties was advantageous to his private interests.

The discontent caused by this policy had long been fomenting. It came to a head at the close of the year 1799. The leading mind of the conspiracy was the head of the great clan of the Barúkzyes. Associated with him were the chiefs of the Alizyes and of the Núrzyes, the deputy Múnshí Báshi (head of the treasury), the chief of the Kizilbáshis, and the chief of the eunuchs. The *espionnage* exercised by Wafadár Khán was so rigid that it was all but impossible that five men of such consideration should meet without exciting suspicion. There was, however, one place free from the inquiring eyes of his agents. This was the house of a derwésh of renowned sanctity, accustomed to receive visits from chiefs, and to close the door when the number of his visitors had reached six. These meetings excited no suspicion. Could the derwésh be gained the conspirators could meet at his house and arrange their plans. The conspirators gained him.

At his house they met, and the door was closed upon them. They then drew up a set of articles of reform. The main articles were as follows: 1st, that Zamán

Shah should be deposed and replaced by his brother, Shújah Mirza; 2nd, that thenceforth the crown should be elective, the chiefs of the tribes alone having a right to vote at such elections; 3rd, that the sovereigns who should prove unworthy of the trust reposed in them might be deposed by the chiefs. Having fixed a day for carrying the first of these articles into execution, the conspirators separated.

Unhappily for the success of their plans the execution of them was delayed. The conspirators met again and again. The suspicions of the prime minister were excited; but he could glean nothing. But men's minds are influenced in a different way by the same events. Of the six leading conspirators five were men whose solid nerves were proof against the fear of failure and its consequences. The sixth had the heart of a hare. Safe had he remained quiet, the rustle of the hounds in the covert nearly killed him. To quiet the beatings of his timid heart he went to the minister and confessed all. The minister was equal to the occasion. He showed neither exultation nor alarm: but the following morning, inviting the conspirators, separately, to the palace, he seized and executed them. Prominent amongst his victims was Payandah Khán, the chief of the Barúkzyes.

But the vengeance of the minister and his sovereign did not stop there. They ordered that all the chiefs of the Mahomedzyes—the chief of the Barúkzye clan—should be seized. Prominent amongst these was Fathi Khán, eldest son of Payandah Khán. This chief, however, having receiving timely warning, mounted his horse and rode straight on end across the mountains to Girishk, and thence to Tebbes in Khorásán, where he joined Prince Mahmúd, who had retired thither hopeless of obtaining aid from the Persian king.

The arrival of the Barúkzye chief was of immense importance to that prince. Bold, sagacious, resolute, burning to avenge his father's death, Fathi Khán pressed upon Mahmúd the necessity, if he would win, of adopting a daring policy—of throwing himself on the Afgháns and appealing to them to shake off the tyranny under which they were groaning. Mahmúd followed his advice, and rode, attended by but eighteen mounted adherents, to Farrah, which had always been devoted to him, and made thence an appeal to the Afghán people. Painting in vivid language the tyranny and cruelties of Zamán Shah and his minister, he announced his intention of placing himself at their head and marching on Kábul. The appeal touched a very sensitive chord in the hearts of those to whom it was addressed. The Barúkzyes rose *en masse* and flocked to his standard, and, their example being followed by the other Dúrání tribes, Mahmúd marched on Kandáhár. The governor of that city, attempting to stop his progress, was driven within its walls, and the place was formally invested. For forty-two days the garrison resisted all the efforts of the besiegers, but on the forty-third day intrigue accomplished the task in which force had failed. Fathi Khán managed to gain two of the leading chiefs within the town. These, when the assault was delivered on the forty-third day, aided the assailants in such a manner that further defence became hopeless, and the place surrendered to Mahmúd.

Meanwhile Zamán Shah, considering himself the safer in consequence of the slaughter of the conspirators, was turning his thoughts to the recovery of Pesháwar and of Káshmír, both of which had revolted. With a fatal confidence in the good star which had hitherto guided him, he paid no heed to the rising disturbances in the west, to the always threatening movements of the Shah of Persia, or to the discontent of the Barúkzyes. Careless of these imports, he marched on Pesháwar, occupied it, and sent thence an army of fifteen thousand men into Káshmír, under two of his favourites. These so mismanaged the army that the men composing it dispersed before Káshmír had even been entered. Accounts of the movements of Mahmúd here reached him. They failed to disquiet him. Mahmúd had always been stirring up trouble; had always been easily put down. Mahmúd was not, therefore, to be feared. Instead, then, of marching or sending a force against his rebel brother, he left the bulk of his army, under Shújah Mirza, at Pesháwar, and returned by ordinary marches to Kábul. Arrived there, the truth burst upon him in all its gloomy nakedness. He was surrounded by pitfalls. Mahmúd was at Kandáhár; the principal tribes had declared for him. He had loved no man but his vizier, and the nerves of his vizier were shaking with fear. The very population of the city scowled upon him. The policy of "chastising with scorpions" had landed him in an abyss.

His position was indeed deplorable. All that remained to him was the native courage of his race. But not even this permitted him to remain in Kábul. Any moment might announce an outbreak there. Summoning then the chiefs who adhered to him and his and their followers he fell back in the direction of Jalálábád. It is significant of the extent to which fortune had turned, that the King of Afghánistán, the lord of north Khorásán, of Sind, of Káshmír, of Pesháwar, could muster to accompany him from his capital only two hundred cavalry and four hundred artillerymen. Only two chiefs followed him; the trembling Wafadár Khán, and Zamán Khán, chief of the Popolzyes. With these he proceeded to a small fort, not far from Jagdalak, held by Múlla Ashak, a dependent of the vizier, and, halting there, made thence an appeal to the Afgháns.

The offers of Zamán Shah were so specious, and his promises to pay were so seducing, that in the course of a few days a number of partisans flocked to his standard. Prominent amongst these was Ahmad Khán, chief of the Núrzye clan. His following amounted to not less than fifteen thousand men. The whole force was soon augmented to thirty thousand.

At the head of these, Zamán Shah marched to meet Mahmúd, who was advancing against him. Of Mahmúd's army the inspiring genius was Fathi Khán, chief of the Barúkzyes. This astute leader saw that could he but gain Ahmad Khán, Zamán Shah would be in his power. By means to which it is unnecessary to refer, he gained him. When the two armies met near Sar-i-asp, Ahmad Khán, who led the advance of Zamán Shah's army, went over with all his following to Mahmúd.

When Zamán Shah heard of this defection, he recognised the full extent of his misfortune. Attended by his vizier and three other tried adherents, he fled at once to a fort belonging to the same Múlla Ashak, still nearer than the other to Jagdalak. Here he was hospitably received. But, before he arrived, news had reached the Múlla that Mahmúd had occupied Kábul. His one thought now was to earn the favour of the conqueror. He consequently took measures to detain Zamán Shah whilst he sent to Kábul a speedy messenger to Mahmúd.

The next day Zamán Shah found that he was a prisoner. In vain did he remonstrate with his treacherous host. Recognising, after a short time, the futility of argument, he resigned himself to his fate. That night he secreted in the wall of his room the Koh-i-Núr and other jewels. The day following he was sent under a guard to Kábul. He had not proceeded far before he was met by Asád Khán, Barúkzye, a brother of Fathi Khán, accompanied by a surgeon. Had he doubted of his fate before, his doubts disappeared now. The operation of lancing the eyes was performed on the spot, and the blinded ex-king was conveyed a prisoner to the Bálá Hissar. His companions, the vizier included, were beheaded a little later.

Mahmúd now became Shah. It is strange that this prince, who had been a persistent conspirator ever since his father's death, who had declined more than once to serve under his brother—even as governor of a province—who had displayed fortitude in exile and courage on the field—who had entered Afghánistán at the head of eighteen followers to wage war—and, as it had resulted, successful war, against the king of that country—it is strange that this prince should have sunk at once, on obtaining the object of all his strivings, into indolence and carelessness of the duties attaching to royal station. Prince, he had risked everything to be king. King, he so acted as to render his fall a question only of time.

Mahmúd was generous and grateful. Proclaimed king in Kábul, he gratified the chiefs who had supported him with high office, their followers with largesses on an extraordinary scale. Fathi Khán, chief of the Barúkzyes, Akrám Khán, chief of the Alizyes, became the principal ministers. Abdúlla Khán, chief of the Alikiúzye clan, was sent to Káshmír as governor; and the king's son, Kámrán Mirza, was despatched to Pesháwar to take possession of that place, and seize, if possible, Shújah Mirza.

This young and ambitious prince had no sooner heard of his brother's capture and subsequent misfortune, than he assumed the royal title, distributed large sums amongst the tribes of the passes, and, having made all his preparations, set out for the capital.

Mahmúd, too indolent to move, despatched Fathi Khán Barúkzye at the head of three thousand men to meet his rival, whose force, though greatly superior in numbers, was composed mainly of hill men. The two armies met in a narrow plain surrounded by hills, on the banks of the brook Súrkhrúd. The battle was obstinately contested. It seemed, at first, as though the greater numbers of Shújah would prevail. They gained at the outset a decided advantage. But, having gained that advantage, their habits of plunder could not be restrained. Believing the victory secure, and bound by no ties to their leader, they fell upon the treasure which he had brought with him from Pesháwar. Fathi Khán saw their mistake, and took advantage of it. A charge along the whole line converted their incipient victory into a pronounced defeat, and they fled in disorder, carrying Shújah with them. Pesháwar was then occupied by the adherents of Mahmúd Shah.

Even before this matter had been settled Mahmúd found himself confronted by an insurrection of an import still more serious. The Ghilzais had risen in revolt.

The reader will recollect that the first purely Afghán kingdom was founded at Kandáhár by Mir Wais, chief of the Ghilzai tribe; that it was the second son of that prince who had held old Kandáhár for more than a year against the army of Nádir Shah, and in whose hands, after the capitulation of that town, the government of the district had been continued. On the election to the sovereignty of Ahmad Shah Dúráni power all over Afghánistán had passed from the hands of the Ghilzais into the hands of the Dúránis; but the respect universally felt for the ruling family of the Ghilzais had caused Ahmad Shah to settle a hereditary pension on its representative. His successors had respected that settlement, and the family had ever been treated with honour.

At the time of the accession of Mahmúd Shah, the representative of that family and chief of the Ghilzai tribe was Abdúrahím. He was not an ambitious man. But the tribe had long been disaffected, jealous of the supremacy of the Dúránis, eager to recover the sceptre passed from their hands. The substitution of Mahmúd for Zamán, of an indolent man for a tyrant, they regarded as propitious to their views. At the time of Mahmúd's accession many of the Ghilzai chiefs happened to be in Kábul. They soon detected the weak spots in the new king's character, reported that the pear was ripe, and at once began to plot to secure the crown for Abdúrahím Khán.

That chief, though not ambitious, could not refuse the proffered dignity. The tribes, prepared beforehand, broke out at once into revolt; and their leader, mastering the royal garrison at Kandáhár, started up the valley of the Tarnak for Ghazní and Kábul. (October 1801.)

Hearing of the advance of the insurgents, the governor of Ghazní left his strong position to meet them in the valley. He was defeated and driven back into the town. Attacked here, he defended himself with such skill and courage that the Ghilzais, leaving a small force to watch the garrison, directed their course by Shilgarh and Zúrmal into the Logar valley and ascended this towards Kábul.

Mahmúd Shah heard for the first time of the insurrection of the Ghilzais when he received the news of the attack on Ghazní. He had but few troops at his disposal, and the only capable general in Kábul, Shir Mahammad Khán, was in confinement under suspicion of high treason. Mahmúd might have taken the command himself, but he dared not leave the capital. Under these circumstances, forced to act, he released the suspected traitor, placed him at the head of the few Kizilbáshis who were available, and sent him to meet the enemy.

Shír Mahammad Khán set out by way of Argandi and Maidán, but learning that the Ghilzais had taken the route of the Logar valley he altered his course, crossed into that valley, and met the enemy at the foot of the Sajáon pass. Noting that the Ghilzais were coming on in tumultuous disorder, he drew up his men in three divisions, one in front, the other two supporting it in half echelon on either flank in the rear, and the whole covered by camel swivels. The Ghilzais advancing in tumultuous mass, the swivels opened fire upon them. But they pressed on, passed the swivels, and threw themselves on the leading division of the Kizilbáshis. The weight of the attack and the overpowering numbers of the assailants forced this division, and the Ghilzais, had they had a general, must have gained the day. But pressing on too far, the two flanking divisions of the Kizilbáshis wheeled inwards, and gave time to the first division to rally. Thus attacked on three sides the Ghilzais had to fall back. They retired, in good order, to a fort belonging to their tribe, six miles distant, and, receiving reinforcements during the night, they resumed the march in the morning by another road, and reached Kila Shahi, within a few miles of the capital, the same evening. Had they at once marched on the city they might have taken it.

But instead of marching on the city they set to work to plunder the villages in the neighbourhood, thus giving time to Shir Mahammad Khán, to whom they had given the slip, to make a forced march and interpose between them and Kábul. The next morning that general attacked and defeated them with great slaughter. The insurrection, though momentarily stemmed, was not finally suppressed till the month of May 1802; nor until the Ghilzais had been defeated in four pitched battles. The last of these, fought at Múlla Shahi on the 11th May 1802, was decisive. The Ghilzais, from that moment, renounced their aspirations for the supreme authority, and have ever since acknowledged, even cheerfully, the supremacy of the Dúránis.

Successful against Shújah Mirza, successful against the Ghilzais, Mahmúd was at the same time equally successful against the Uzbégs who, on his accession, had crossed the Oxus. These were completely defeated the same year (1802), near Balkh, and driven across the frontier river. To crown his good fortune, Shújah Mirza, who had again roused to revolt the tribes of the Khaibar, saw his army almost annihilated by Mahmúd's generals.

In fact, the month of June 1802, Mahmúd had the ball at his feet. He had only to aspire. The great writer who now directs the fortunes of the British empire, has, in his works as well as in his speeches, laid special emphasis on the aphorism that the man who ceases to aspire will grovel. Nothing can be more true. In private and in public life it is a guiding maxim. It is applicable to all positions, especially to the position of a man ruling a warlike, half-civilised race, divided into tribes, those tribes led by chiefs who owe to him only a feudal obedience.

On the throne of Kábul, his rivals in exile, every rebel defeated, Mahmúd would not look beyond his pleasures. Ceasing to aspire, he grovelled. The effect on his empire was magical.

That same year he lost Khorásán. Fath Ali, Shah of Persia, invaded that province, took Meshed, and held it. His successor holds it to this day. The Persians were hardly opposed. Under the lax government of Mahmúd every place was left to shift for itself. At the very time the Persians were besieging Meshed, the possession of Herát was disputed between Kámrán Mirza, the son, and Kaisar Mirza, the nephew of the Afghán king.

In Afghánistán, a king must rule as well as reign. Should he fail to rule, he will soon cease to reign. Mahmúd reigned, but did not rule. The chiefs of the Barúkzyes and the Alizyes, Fathi Khán and Akrám Khán, ruled for him, disputing with each other in the process. At last they separated, Akrám Khán remaining in Kábul, Fathi Khán taking Kandáhár and asserting his authority in Káshmír, at Pesháwar, and all along the frontier. With him the assertion of authority meant the repression of all opposition to himself. He levied money, then, from Káshmír, from Pesháwar, and along the frontier—at Kohát, at Banú, at Dámán—and, punishing the Vaziris on his way, proceeded to his government at Kandáhár. Here he was when Shújah Mirza, who had obtained three lakhs of rupees by the plunder of a caravan of the Povindahs at Quetta, made an attempt on that city, which failed.

Meanwhile, Fathi Khán's rival, the leader of the Alizyes, Akrám Khán, died. A formidable applicant for the office of vizier was Shir Mahammad Khán, son of Shah Wáli Khán, the vizier of Ahmad Shah, who had made the office hereditary in the family. This Shir Mahammad Khán was a man of ability, of boundless ambition, considerable learning, and enormous influence. He it was whom Mahmúd had taken from a prison to lead his troops against the Ghilzais. But Mahmúd Shah, far from recognising his claims, reserved the office for Fathi Khán, Barukzye, chief of the Mahammadzyes, then at Kandáhár. Meanwhile he ruled by the aid of the chief of the Kizilbáshis, who were disliked as Shiahs (heretics).

Shir Mahammad Khán, indignant at this treatment, determined to plot against his sovereign. He soon caused it to be whispered that the king was surrounding himself with heretics; that he was becoming addicted to their vices; that the ruin of the true religion had been discussed and decided upon. The whisper, penetrating every lane, gaining access to every hovel, soon developed into a cry; the cry produced a passionate movement. In the agony of the moment, the chief Syud of the mosques was appealed to by the mob. This man, venerated for his age and his learning, combined to an intense hatred to Mahmúd Shah a boundless admiration for Shir Mahammad Khán. Standing on the steps of the mosque, he listened to the people, as with tumultuous gestures and passionate words they shouted the fears for their religion that oppressed them, and then, commanding silence, pronounced the solemn sentence of extermination for all Shiahs. The effect was electric. That day and the next day the Kizilbáshis were attacked with ungovernable rage. Seeing themselves marked out to be victims, they resolved to sell their lives dearly. So vigorous a resistance did they offer, that although the Súnís from the country flocked in to aid their co-religionists; although Shir Mahammad Khán and other disaffected lords mixed with their adherents, giving them help and encouragement; although the chief Syud sprinkled the leaders of the attack with the holy waters of Mekka, and promised them the joys of paradise;—at the end of the second day both parties were so completely exhausted that they agreed to a suspension of arms.

The fact was that each party was anxious for delay; the king to give time for the arrival of Fathi Khán and his army from Kandáhár; Shir Mahammad Khán for the arrival of a prince to replace Mahmúd Shah. Of all the surviving sons of Taimúr Shah, Shújah Mirza was the only prince—the blinded Zamán excepted—who had displayed energy and capacity. A prince of the royal house was necessary for him. He had, therefore, before the disturbances had begun but when they were looming in a proximate future, sent an express to Shújah Mirza.

The disturbances had taken place on the 4th and 5th June (1803). For about a month the two parties remained in a state of veiled hostility, each watching and waiting. The truce was broken by Mahmúd Shah. The intellect of that prince had not sunk so low but that he had discerned in the insurrectionary movement the hand of Shir Mahammad Khán. He knew his talent. His military skill had been tried against the Ghilzais. He was an opponent to be feared. Could he but seize him, the conspirators would be without a head. Thus reasoning, he attempted to seize him. But Shir Mahammad, wary and watchful, detected the plot, and by a flight from Kábul to the camp of Shújah Mirza, caused it to fail. Before he left he implored the chief Syud to renew the tumults in the city, promising to support him speedily with an army.

The tumults were at once renewed. The enforced absence of their leader, far from repressing the populace, added to their fury; the knowledge that their leader would soon appear with assistance sustained them. After about a week's fighting, they drove the king and the Kizilbáshis who survived into the Bálá Hissar, and occupied the city, the heights, and all the approaches to that fortress.

Such was the state of affairs when, on the 12th July, Shújah Mirza arrived accompanied by Shir

Mahammad Khán. This astute general persuaded the prince not to enter the city—to encamp outside; and to wait there for Fathi Khán and his army, now daily expected from Kandáhár. Not on his immediate entry into Kábul, but on the issue of the battle between him and Fathi Khán, depended whether he or Mahmúd should wear the crown of Ahmad Shah.

On the third day Fathi Khán arrived and the battle joined. A daring, dashing horseman, Fathi Khán carried at first all before him. Had his men remained faithful, he would undoubtedly have gained the day. But the great chiefs had had enough of Mahmúd. In the very act of following up his success Fathi Khán found himself almost alone. The bulk of his followers had gone over to Shújah Mirza. He turned then and fled.

The next day Shújah Mirza, now become Shújah Shah, entered Kábul in triumph, amid the acclamations of the populace, Shir Mahammad Khán walking on foot by the side of his horse. They proceeded direct to the Bálá Hissar, the gates of which were thrown open as they approached. Mahmúd attempted no resistance. He anticipated the fate he had pronounced upon Zamán Shah, the brother of his conqueror. It is stated that Shah Shújah did issue the order to lance his brother's eyes, but, in consequence of the intercession of his powerful supporter, Shir Mamammad, he revoked the order, directing that Mahmúd should be placed in one of the dungeons of the Bálá Hissar.*

* On this act of clemency Mountstuart Elphinstone remarks that Shah Shújah had unfortunately sufficient reason to regret it.

The task which had now devolved upon Shah Shújah was more difficult than that which had fallen to any of his predecessors. Ahmad Shah, elected for his merit, had made the kingdom; Taimúr Shah, chosen by his father as the fittest of his sons to bear the burden of sovereignty, had, by walking in the lines laid down in the preceding reign, succeeded in maintaining his authority over the Afgháns; Zamán Shah, departing from those lines, had lost his throne. Mahmúd was welcomed as a possible restorer of the old order. Not only was he not a restorer; he allowed the guiding-reins of power to drop from his hands, to be seized by the boldest. Shújah now succeeded Mahmúd. The first necessity imposed upon him was to gather up the dropped reins, to pull them cautiously but firmly from the hands that held them. What a task! It might appal the strongest, for the hands that held those reins were the hands of feudal chiefs counting thousands of adherents! Ahmad Shah might have been equal to it. His grandson had neither the intellect to grasp the situation, the skill to use the means available to him, nor the force of will to persevere to the end.

Shújah owed his crown to Shir Mahammad Khán. Naturally that nobleman became prime minister. It was his interest to serve well the king he had made, and he showed every disposition to use his great influence to restore order and authority throughout the

The whole of this history proves that a prince who had once reigned would never be satisfied with any position short of absolute power.

kingdom. To be successful the confidence of the king alone was necessary.

Had Shah Shújah been wise he would have given that confidence. He would then have ruled through the minister, and by his means have drawn into his own hands the threads which Mahmúd had dropped. But, suspicious by nature, open to flattery, and easily influenced, he from the first withheld it. As time went on, he took even a pleasure in thwarting the measures proposed by Shir Mahammad. The natural consequences ensued. The vigour which should have been directed to a common cause—the maintenance of authority and the good of the kingdom—came to be employed by the king and the minister for their own purposes—the preparing for a struggle which each foresaw.

The first act of the king was to release from confinement his brother, Zamán Shah, and to punish by death the man who had betrayed him. Then, in concert with his minister, he prepared for an expedition to recover Kandáhár, held by Kámrán Mirza, son of Mahmúd, aided by Fathi Khán Barúkzye.

After having been abandoned by his followers when seemingly secure of victory Fathi Khán had fled to Kandáhár. Ambitious though he was, and occupying a great position as chief of the Barúkzyes, it is not probable that he entertained the idea of supplanting the Sadozyes, or that he aimed at anything beyond the securing for himself and his clan the position which was their due. His conduct at this period entirely supports this view. For when Shah Shújah, accompanied by Shir Mahammad, marched on Kandáhár, Fathi Khán persuaded Kámrán Mirza to abandon the place and flee to Herát whilst he remained to make his submission to the king.

A very favourable opportunity now offered to Shah Shújah to gain the adherence of the Barúkzyes. A few conciliatory words; reinstatement into the offices held by his father; an assurance of confidence in his fidelity for the future; and Fathi Khán would have been the Shah's man for ever. Fathi Khán wished such a reception; he even intrigued for it. It was refused him. The haughty demeanour of the Shah, the frigid tones with which he refused his demands, caused the man who had entered the hall of audience a suppliant to leave it a rebel. A few days later Fathi Khán quitted the court in disgust and retired to his fort at Girishk.

Shah Shújah entrusted the government of Kandáhár to his nephew, Kaisar Mirza, son of Zamán Shah; nominating Ahmad Khán Núrzye, the same who had deserted Zamán Shah in his contest with Mahmúd, to be prime minister. He then marched with an army, now augmented to thirty thousand men, to Pesháwar, with the intention to assert thence his suzerainty over the outlying provinces of Káshmír and Sind. But before he had marched from Pesháwar intelligence reached him that Kandáhár had revolted.

This revolt was the work of Fathi Khán—the Fathi Khán whom Shújah had failed to conciliate. It happened in this wise. I have stated that the Shah's nephew, Kaisar Mirza, had been appointed governor of Kandáhár, with Ahmad Shah Núrzye as his prime minister, and that Fathi Khán had fled in dudgeon to Girishk. Girishk is not very far from Kandáhár; Kaisar Mirza was weak, ambitious, the son of a king; Fathi Khán, then, found little difficulty in so working on his mind as to induce him to throw into prison the man who had betrayed his father, and to strike for the crown. This Kaisar Mirza did; he seized Ahmad Khán, loaded him with chains and insults, and prepared to march on Kábul with Fathi Khán. Yet, strange inconsistency! when setting out for Kábul he released the insulted prisoner from confinement, and entrusted to him the government of Kandáhár!

The natural consequences followed. Ahmad Khán, indignant at the treatment he had received, invited Kámrán Mirza, son of Mahmúd, from Farrah to Kandáhár, and made over the place to him. His son posted to Shah Shújah and induced him to return from Kandáhár to repress the revolt. Shújah returned, defeated Kaisar Mirza, and marched back towards Peshâwar, when news reached him that Kaisar Mirza and Fathi Khán had again occupied Kandáhár. Once more did he return. This time Kaisar Mirza renounced Fathi Khán, threw himself on the Shah's mercy, was pardoned, and reintrusted with the government of Kandáhár. Baulked in his projects, Fathi Khán fled to Herát, and persuaded the governor of that place, Firúz-u-dín Mirza, a younger brother, by the same mother, of Mahmúd, to rebel. Shah Shújah, however, sending an army against him, that prince, cautious by nature, accepted the terms of semi-independence offered him and returned to Herát. The whole of the western portion of the Afghán territory was at this time virtually in the hands of the adherents of Mahmúd, for whilst his own brother held Herát, his son Kámrán governed Farrah, and his adherent Fathi Khán, Barúkzye, occupied Girishk. To that place Fathi Khán had now again retired.

Matters having been settled in the manner related, Shah Shújah started on his expedition to the outlying provinces. He reduced Sind to obedience and received the arrears due to the Kábul government, of one hundred and seventy thousand pounds. Marching thence along his eastern frontier, he settled the districts through which he passed, and reached Pesháwar in April 1805. The long-deferred expedition against Káshmír was now about to be undertaken, when the intrigues of Fathi Khán again forced Shah Shújah to return to his Afghán dominions.

From his castle at Gírishk the chief of the Barúkzyes had renewed his intrigues with the weak son of Zamán Shah, Kaisar Mirza. Hesitating between the kingdom promised him by Fathi Khán, should he aid to dethrone his uncle, and the certain reward he would receive from that uncle should he possess himself of the person of Fathi Khán, Kaisar Mirza finally resolved to attempt the task which, if it promised the smaller reward, offered the least amount of risk. He resolved to seize Fathi Khán. Becoming, then, prodigal of his promises to that chieftain, he engaged, if he would only come to Kandáhár to confer with him, to place himself entirely in his hands. Fathi Khán, suspecting nothing, assented, and accompanied by his younger brother, Dost Mahammad,—a youth whose resolute character already gave promise of the future which awaited him—entered Kandáhár, and was graciously received by Kaisar. But as he was leaving the princely presence some of the attendants precipitated themselves with such violence on the chief of the Barúkzyes that he was thrown to the ground, and lost several of his front teeth. He was then gagged and placed in confinement. Dost Mahammad Khán and his followers attempted to rescue him, but failing, they forced their way into the city, summoned the few Barúkzyes who were there to join them, and attacked the citadel. They were repulsed, however, and retired to Girishk.

But Fathi Khan, though in prison, was more than a match for Kaisar Mirza. Enticing him to visit him in his bonds, he painted the delights of ruling in such glowing terms that he gained him over. He was released and sent back to Girishk to make preparations for a march on Kábul.

This was all that Fathi Khán desired. Whilst openly engaging, now with Kaisar Mirza, now with his cousin Kámrán, he was really bent on the restoration of Mahmúd. With this view he had caused to be conveyed to that captive prince tools wherewith to work out his escape, and a warning to trust only to the Kizilbáshis. But before escape could be accomplished Kaisar Mirza had returned to his pacific ideas, and Kámrán Mirza had raised the standard of revolt. It was this news which summoned Shah Shújah back from Peshávar.

His return was almost simultaneous with the invasion of the Herát districts by the Persians. This invasion necessitated the employment in the defence of the western border of the troops commanded by Firúzúdín Mirza, brother of Mahmúd Shah. This prince however, was defeated in a pitched battle by the Persians, and only saved Herát by the payment of a considerable sum of money. But this disturbance on the west enabled Shah Shujah to occupy Kandáhár unopposed. That prince was proposing to revenge the insult to the Afghán name when intelligence reached him that the prime vizier, Shir Mahammad Khan, who had with great difficulty reduced Káshmír to obedience, had returned to Kábul, having left his son, Atta Mahammad Khán, as governor of that province. Shah Shújah, who had long been jealous of that nobleman, marched at once to Kábul. There he announced to Shir Mahammad his intention to proceed once more to Sind. The vizier protested, pointing out the numberless affairs which required his attention. The discussion lasted some days, and while it was going on Mahmúd Shah succeeded in effecting his escape from the Bálá Hissar, secreted himself for several days in a tomb, and when suspicion had been diverted from Kábul he galloped off, escorted by Dost Mahammad and a band of chosen followers, and, plundering three caravans *en route*, gained Girishk.

Careless of any immediate danger from Mahmúd, Shah Shújah, despite the opposition of Shir Mahammad Khán, proceeded to Sind. Shir Mahammad, disobeying the orders he had received to follow him, remained at Kábul, and took an early opportunity of proclaiming the Shah's nephew, Kaisar Mirza, king. The conspirators then marched upon Peshâwar, and occupied it.

On learning these events Shah Shújah turned back from Sind, and marched along the border towards Pesháwar. In the plain bearing the same name he found the rebel army encamped. Negotiations were entered upon, but they were fruitless. Both parties preferred the arbitrament of the sword.

On the 3rd March 1808 the two armies joined. Shir Mahammad Khán carried at first all before him, but, attempting with too small a force to seize the king's person, he was shot dead. His death was fatal to the cause of which he was the life. The partisans of Shah Shújah rallied and gained the day.

This victory was followed up with vigour. Kaisar Mirza, vigorously pursued, submitted and was pardoned. Mahmúd, who, subsequently to his escape, had, by the aid of the Barúkzyes, raised an army and taken Kandáhár, was defeated near that city towards the end of 1808. Shah Shújah then returned to Pesháwar to receive a British mission conducted from India by Mr. Mounstuart Elphinstone.

The Shah had received the first intimation of this mission a few months earlier at Kandáhár, and he regarded it with strong prejudice and distrust. He believed that its object could not be less than to demand the cession of a province, and in this belief he was fortified by the representations of Ranjit Singh, king of the Panjáb, and of many lords of the court.

But when the real aim of the mission was explained to him, when he was told that its main object was to warn him against the machinations of France and Russia, he thought that he might derive some advantage by according it a reception. "The exaggerated reports he received," writes Mr. Elphinstone, "of the splendour of the embassy, and of the sumptuous presents by which it was accompanied, seem more than anything to have determined the king to admit the mission and to give it an honourable reception."

The embassy reached Pesháwar the 25th February 1809, and stayed there till the 14th June. Its reception was all that could be desired, and Mr. Elphinstone experienced no difficulty in concluding with Shah Shújah—whom he describes as "a handsome man, about thirty years of age, of an olive complexion, with a thick black beard"—a treaty, the main article of which stipulated that neither the French nor any other foreign Europeans should be permitted to have a footing in his dominions.

But whilst the British embassy was at Pesháwar grave events were occurring. Shah Shújah had taken advantage of his residence at Pesháwar to send his best army, commanded by the new vizier, Akrám Khán, into Káshmír, to put down the rebellion of Atta Mahammad Khán. But whilst the embassy was still there, news arrived that Akrám Khán had been defeated with great slaughter. This news was the more depressing as it had been preceded by intelligence that Mahmúd Shah and Fathi Khán had captured Kandáhár,—and the army which had been sent in to Káshmír constituted the only available force to check their progress.

Shah Shújah used every endeavour to raise troops. By degrees the remnants of the Káshmír army and their leader returned, and by the middle of June the Shah set out for Kábul. But Mahmúd Shah and Fathi Khán had been beforehand with him. They had marched on Kábul, and had set out thence towards Pesháwar. They met Shah Shújah's army advantageously posted near Gandamak. Mahmúd attacked it in front, whilst Fathi Khán took it in flank. The result was never doubtful. Akrám Khán was killed; Shah Shújah fled into the mountains, leaving all his jewels (the Koh-i-Núr excepted) and his baggage in the hands of his rival.

Thus for a second time did Mahmúd become King of Kábul and its dependencies. Shah Shújah continued the struggle for some years longer; but beaten in 1810 at Kandáhár—which he had momentarily occupied;—in the same year driven out of Pesháwar; and completely defeated in 1811 at Akóra; he was seized by the governor of Atok, and sent a prisoner to Káshmír. In 1812 he was allowed to join his family at Láhor. There he remained, under the surveillance of Ranjit Singh, till 1815, when he escaped, and after making a feeble and fruitless attempt on Káshmír, fled to the British station of Ludhiáná—then the residence of his blinded brother, Zamán Shah—and there remained till British policy drew him forth to play a dubious rôle on the scene of Afghán politics.

Mahmúd restored was still Mahmúd. He had learned nothing, and forgotten nothing. Neglecting affairs, grovelling in disreputable pleasures, he soon earned the contempt of all. He had been restored by the Barúkzyes, and he was content, for the sake of the sensual enjoyments in which he delighted, to leave power and patronage in the hands of the tried chief of that powerful clan, Vizier Fathi Khán.

That nobleman, virtual governor, commenced his administration by asserting the right of suzerainty over the outlying provinces of Sind and Bilúchistán. He then reduced the rebellious tribes to obedience; restored order in the provinces; caused the laws to be respected; reformed the various departments, and made his strong hand felt in every corner of the kingdom. The effect was most remarkable. The times of Ahmad and Taimúr Shahs returned as if by magic. Everywhere the law was enforced, and a sense of security prevailed.

He must have been a very remarkable man who could thus in a few months impress his character upon a people like the Afgháns; and Fathi Khán was a man who would in any age have commanded respect and admiration. "He united," says Ferrier, from whom I have taken these details, "to a superior genius a great aptitude for governing and for war. Not one of his predecessors had been able to reduce rebels to obedience with the same promptitude, or keep them afterwards in the path of duty. He struck hard, but he was generous after the victory had been gained, and shone by his excessive liberality. Always in the midst of combats, he still found time to direct the helm of state, and was ready for everything. In activity he had no equal."

A leading principle of this great nobleman's policy was to be sure of his subordinates. The head of his clan, he was certain of his brothers, of whom he had twenty, all of them men of mark. To these he confided the governments of Bilúchistán, of Kandáhár, of Pesháwar, of Ghazní, of Bámián—subsequently, as will be seen, of Káshmir. Of all the great governments, Herát alone remained for the moment under a ruler who was not his close kinsman. But this was a mere question of time. His other brothers assisted him in the administrative affairs of the kingdom. His younger and most capable brother, Dost Mahammad, had charge of his household, and acted as his confidential aide-de-camp.

The first great project entertained by Fathi Khán, after he had restored order throughout the kingdom, was to recover Káshmír, still held in revolt by Atta Mahammad Khán. To effect this object, he entered into an alliance * with Ranjit Singh, now recognised as King of the Panjáb. That prince, on the promise of a subsidy of nine lakhs of rupees to be taken from the revenues of Káshmír, agreed to detach a corps of ten thousand men to aid in the reconquest of that province. The allied army, commanded by Fathi Khán, entered Káshmír by the Bimbar pass, and found

* Of course in the name of Mahmúd Shah: but throughout all these transactions Mahmúd Shah was a cypher, and was treated as such.

no enemy to oppose it till Sirinagar had been reached. Nor did Sirinagar hold out more than thirteen days. The rebel governor, Atta Mahammad, preferred to make terms with Fathi Khán, rather than stand unsuccessfully a siege. The terms were liberal, and Atta Mahammad, who was a man of great force of character, united himself to the Barúkzyes. Fathi Khán, resisting the solicitations of Ranjit Singh to make over Káshmír to himself, confided the government of the province to his second brother, Mahammad Azím Khán, giving him instructions to elude the payment of the covenanted nine lakhs to Ranjít Singh. But the wily Sikh, detecting the plot, had his revenge. Withdrawing his contingent, he seized the fort of Atok with the view of intercepting the Afghâns on their return. In carrying out this design he was singularly favoured by fortune.

Fathi Khán, as soon as he had heard of the hostile action of Ranjit Singh, sent forward his brother, Dost Mahammad Khán, with two thousand horsemen to clear the way, following himself with the main body. On approaching Atok, Dost Mahammad beheld the Sikh army drawn up on some elevated ground about three miles and a half from that place, covering the Indus. Finding himself with but two thousand men in front of an army eight times as numerous, and some three miles in advance of the main body, Dost Mahammad should have waited. But he fell into the trap laid for all young and ambitious generals. Like Marmont at Salamanca, he wanted to have all the glory to himself. He would not delay so as to be joined by the forces hastening on towards him, and commanded by his superiors in rank; so without waiting for his brother, he charged the Sikh army. The charge, skilfully led, was so far successful that the enemy's guns were ridden over, and it required but the support of the main body to secure a decisive victory. But the main body was three miles distant. The Sikhs soon recovered from their first surprise, and opposing greatly superior numbers to their assailant, barred his further progress. Still hoping for victory, Dost Mahammad long maintained his ground, sending messenger after messenger to hasten his brother's advance. None of these messengers reached Fathi Khán. They had been outstripped by some recreant horsemen, who informed him that the attack had been repulsed, his brother killed, and that the Sikhs were marching against him. Instead, then, of succouring his brother, Fathi Khán at once changed his line of march, and taking ground to the right, hastened to cross the Indus. Dost Mahammad, as soon as he found his position no longer tenable, drew his men off, and made a soldierly and successful retreat in the direction taken, as he tardily learned, by the main army.

The two years which succeeded the return of Fathi Ali to Kábul were occupied by that chief in regulating the internal affairs of the country. But in 1816 the affairs of Herát imperatively demanded his interference.

I have stated in a preceding page that of all the great governorships in the country that of Herát alone had been allowed to remain in hands alien to the blood of Fathi Khán. The lord of that province was still Háji Firúzudín, Mahmúd Shah's own brother, a prince who, though he carried prudence to the limits of timidity, might properly be designated as a safe man. This prince had, for some years past, partly by force of arms, partly by the payment of a small sum of money, partly by inciting the Kháns of Khorásán to rebel, succeeded in repelling the active aggression of Fath Ali Khán, Shah of Persia. But in the year 1816 he was at his wits' end. Khorásán was at the feet of Persia, and Persia had assembled an army at Meshed, commanded by the son of her king, to take Herát. Under these circumstances Háji Firúzúdin sent to Kábul an earnest appeal for aid.

Fathi Khán responded without a moment's delay. So rapidly did he march that he reached the city of Herát before the Persians—who had delayed to wait the arrival of some heavy guns—had crossed the frontier of the province. The arrival of the most ambitious nobleman in the kingdom seemed to Háji Firúzúdin a far greater evil than would have been the arrival of the Persians. He refused, therefore, to admit his army into the city.

But Fathi Khán was not a man to be thwarted. Permitted access to the city with fifty followers only, he chose as his companions men related to the most influential families in Herát. They were well schooled in the task expected from them, and they proved themselves apt pupils. So completely did they do their work that on the fourth day the keys of the gates of the city, on the fifth the keys of the gates of the citadel, were handed to Fathi Khán.

Fathi Khán at once assumed the government of Herát; despatched Háji Firúzúdin under an honourable escort to Kábul; but no sooner had that prince left than Dost Mahammad, acting against the express directions of his brother, plundered the seraglio—in which the treasures of the late Governor had been concealed.

Having secured Herát, Fathi Khán marched against the Persians. The two armies met on the plain of Káfir Kilat near the frontier of the two states, some seventy miles from Herát. The Persians fought well, but they could not withstand the repeated charges by divisions of the Afghán horse, and about 4 o'clock in the evening, having lost, it is said, ten thousand men in killed, wounded, and missing, they left the field. An accident alone prevented the victory being decisive for the Afgháns. As he was urging on the pursuit, Fáthi Khán was struck in the mouth by a spent ball. The shock stunned him, and his followers, believing him to be dead, abandoned the pursuit. Practically, however, the victory was a substantial one, for, for some time to follow, the Persians cared not to mention the name of Herát.

Fathi Khán remained at Herát to make prparations to carry the war into Persian territory, and possibly to recover Meshed. These preparations occupied him nearly a year. They were nearly completed, when an event happened which gave a new direction to affairs in Afghánistán, and sealed the fate of the Sadozyes.

In the preceding pages I have mentioned the rivalry for the possession of Kandáhár between Kaisar Mirza, son of Zamán Shah, and Kámrán Mirza, son of Mahmúd Shah. Kaisar was weak, pliable, but generous and good-tempered. Kámrán was brutal in his instincts, cruel to the last degree of ferocity, revengeful, and perfidious. On the second accession of Mahmúd Shah the two princes had made their submission to him, and it had been the intention of Fathí Khán to confide to Kámrán, as the son of the reigning sovereign, the government of Kandáhár. But Kámrán having, to revenge an old grudge, assassinated his cousin Kaisar under circumstances of cowardly atrocity, Fathi Khán declared him to be incapable of public office, and refused him the promised government. This insult rankled in the mind of Kámrán, and he longed to avenge it.

But his own wishes could only become law when they were supported by his father's influence. Hence he played with all his skill upon the weaknesses of Mahmúd. Despicable as he was, Mahmúd was in this matter hard to move. Having Fathi Khán as vizier, Mahmúd, in his own way, enjoyed life. He had all that a grovelling mind could wish for. His sensual appetites were more than gratified. He was troubled by no cares of state. When, for a moment, he turned his eyes in a direction other than that affecting his pleasures, he saw a prosperous kingdom and a contented people. And all this, he knew, was the work of Fathi Khán. Contrasting the first period of his rule, with its tumults and its conspiracies terminating with the lancet pointed at his eyes and only withdrawn at the intercession of a man whom he had wronged, with the peaceful calm of his present hermaphrodite existence, he was too thankful that a Fathi Khán should exist to turn from him all the turmoil, to leave him the dear pleasures of royalty. For these reasons he turned a deaf ear to the solicitations of his son Kámrán.

Kámrán had almost despaired of success, when a circumstance occurred which gave vital force to his entreaties, This was the arrival at Kábul of Mahmúd's own brother, Háji Firúzúdín, late governor of Herát. It may be remembered that Fathi Khán, depriving this prince of his government, had sent him under honourable escort to Kábul; but that the day after Firúzúdín had left Herát, Dost Mahammad, brother of Fathi Khán, had broken into the viceregal harem in search of the treasures there deposited. In that process there can be no doubt that the ladies of the harem had been grievously insulted. With his heart burning with indignation at these proceedings, and longing to revenge them, Háji Firúzúdín Mirza was ushered into the presence of Mahmúd Shah.

If there is one point more than another upon which a Mahomedan is peculiarly susceptible, it is the sanctity of his harem. Even Mahmúd was kindled to anger when he heard, in general terms, of the atrocites which had been perpetrated. And when Kámrán, to rouse him to the requisite pitch, assured him that the brother of Fathi Khán had, with his own hands, stripped from Mahmúd's daughter, married to a son of Firúzúdín, the last vestment which protected her person from his gaze and from the gaze of his associates, and declared further that this insult to a royal lady was but a prelude to his own deposition, the debased monarch no longer hesitated. He gave the order that the eyes of Fathi Khán should be plucked out. The execution of this order he entrusted, at the Mirza's own request, to his son Kámrán.

Kámrán Mirza, having employed every means to keep the order as secret as possible, set out for Herát. He was there received with the greatest honour and respect by Fathi Khán. That nobleman had raised the Afghán kingdom to a level of consideration higher than any it had attained since the death of Ahmad Shah. He had no higher personal ambition. As mayor of the palace, he was really sovereign. He was, therefore, undoubtedly sincere when he begged Kámrán Mirza to join with him in consolidating the power of the Sadozye dynasty and in maintaining the glory of the Afghán nation.

Kámrán Mirza played his part well. He affected to place the most implicit confidence in the vizier; he desired to consult him upon every important public matter. Any suspicion that Fathi Khán might at the outset have felt was quickly disarmed. Since the arrival of Kámrán the vizier had waited upon him every day at his place of the Bágh Shah, outside the city, and had been received with respect, and even affection. But one morning, when he proceeded there as usual, attended by about twenty men, he was suddenly seized, disarmed, and deprived of sight.

Such was the reward bestowed, in 1818, by Mahmúd Shah Sadozye upon the man who, eight years before, had made him king, who had been the second founder of the Afghán kingdom—a man of singular ability and daring, a born ruler of men—whose failings were the failings of his country and of his education, but whose rare virtues were his own. But the malice of his enemies was not even then exhausted.

Retribution speedily followed. Of three brothers of the blinded vizier who were at Herát at the time of the cruel outrage, one, Púrdil Khán, was taken prisoner; two, Shirdil Khán and Kohandil Khán, succeeded in effecting their escape to the fortified village of Nádali, twenty-three miles from Girishk. Here, whilst rousing the Barúkzyes, they were joined by the third brother, Púrdil Khán, who some days after their departure had eluded the vigilance of Kámrán.

Revolt soon spread over the whole province. Another brother, Mahammad Azim Khán, governor of Káshmir, raised the standard, and sent a force under his brother, Dost Mahammad, to march on Kábul.

This young nobleman had been disgraced and placed in confinement by his brother, Fathi Khán, for the share he had had in the unfortunate plundering of the harem of Firúzudín at Herát. But the outrage perpetrated on the head of the family blotted out the recollection of former misdeeds. Taken from a prison to lead an army, Dost Mahammad marched by the most direct road on the capital. Mahmúd, roused from his debaucheries, fled to Ghazní, leaving the defence of the capital to his grandson, a son of Kámrán. But the grandson of Mahmúd was no match for the brother of Fathi Khán. His troops were beaten and Kábul was occupied. A few days later Dost Mahammad was joined here by his brother, Mahammad Azím Khán.

Meanwhile Kámrán, hearing of the invasion from Káshmir and of the flight to Ghazní, had marched from Herát, with all his available troops, on that fortress. Arriving there, he gave them a few days to rest, and then set out for the capital with twelve thousand men. Mahammad Azím Khán and Dost Mahammad could only command one third of that number, but they had marched towards Ghazní, and now with their small force they met Kámrán and took up a position to bar his progress. That night, however, all the troops of Kámrán passed over to the Barúkzye brothers. Kámrán fled to Ghazní, roused his debauched father, and forced him to evacuate the fortress with his valuables, a few followers, and his prisoner!

That prisoner was the blinded hero Fathi Khán. Up to this moment that noble man had borne without reply, without a sign of feeling, all the insults and all the taunts which had been freely lavished upon him. In that respect the royal Sadozyes, whom he had served so faithfully, had done their worst; whatever they might do now, they could harm him no more. But their vengeance was not yet glutted. When they saw the edifice which Fathi Khán had built, and which Fathi Khán had sustained, falling upon them to crush them, because they had rendered Fathi Khán powerless, they added the last outrage to the many which had preceded it. Halting, as they fled towards Kandáhár, at the first stage where they deemed themselves momentarily safe from pursuit, the two Sadozyes—the contemptible father and the brutal son—summoned their captive before them, and ordered him to use his influence with his brothers to stop the pursuit, and to calm the storm which they had raised. Then, for the first time, did Fathi Khán break his long silence: "I have nothing more to do," he said, "with the affairs of this world. In losing my sight I have lost my influence over others." The wretched Mahmúd then gave the signal for his death. Kámrán struck at him with his dagger; the miserable sycophants who still adhered to him followed suit. Then, still living, they flayed him, disjointed his members, and struck off his head . . . His remains, collected in a sack, were subsequently interred at Ghazní.

The king, his son, and his brother, then wandered for some time from pillar to post, abandoned by all their followers but eleven, not knowing whom to trust. At last they reached Herát, which, of all the towns in the Afghán territory, had not risen against the Sadozyes. To secure themselves there, they agreed tc acknowledge the suzerainty of the Shah of Persia. Even in the degraded position to which they were thus reduced, the members of the triumvirate were never in accord. At last Háji Firuzúdín left them and retired to Meshed. The father and son then disputed, with alternating success, the sovereignty of this corner of what was once their kingdom—now besieging, now being besieged. Herát and the Herátís suffered. These countless struggles and intrigues, and others with chieftains from Khorásán and from the mountains, and into which it is not necessary to enter, terminated in 1829 by the death of Mahmúd, caused, it was said, by his son Kámrán. The latter then proclaimed himself king of Herát, under the suzerainty of the Shah of Persia, and gave himself up to drunkenness and debauchery. The fate which befell him will be referred to in its proper place. It will suffice to record here that the murder of Fathi Khán set the seal on the fate of the dynasty of the Sadozyes.

CHAPTER IX.

THE BARUKZYE PERIOD.

The break-up of the Sadozye monarchy was as complete as it was sudden. Of the dominions so ably administered by Fathi Khán, every portion, save Herát, had revolted, and, for the moment, no master spirit had risen to weld together the scattered fragments. The next brother in order of birth to Fathi Khán, Mahammad Azim Khán, held Kábul; Dost Mahammad held Ghazní; Púrdil Khán held Kandáhár; Jabbar Khán was in Káshmír; Yár Mahammad Khán at Peshávar. The remaining thirteen brothers of the deceased vizier were in different parts of the country, all striving to restore order, but not influenced by a single and definite aim. Even at this moment the complete supersession of the Sadozyes had not been thought of. They were still regarded as the royal family. In fact, so necessary did it appear to the separated Barúkzye brothers to restore the Sadozye dynasty, that each one in his own district proclaimed one or other member of that family as the legitimate successor to the throne forfeited by Mahmúd Shah and his offspring.

But not one of the members of the Sadozyes so put forward showed sufficient force of character for the position. Each one therefore was discarded almost as soon as he had been proclaimed. Under these circumstances the condition of the country became every day more involved and more difficult. The chiefs of one clan—certainly a most important clan—separated from each other, were endeavouring to hold the different portions of the country. To attempt this, without one head and a single definite aim, was to strain the resources of that clan to a point which it could scarcely bear.

At last Púrdil Khán attempted to solve the difficulty. The brother of Zamán Shah, Shújah, was still alive, and Shújah had reigned in Kábul. Of all the surviving Sadozyes, not one equalled him in capacity. Ambitious of power, it was believed that he, more than anyone else, might be able to weld together the severed fragments. Such thoughts occurring to Púrdil Khán, he sent his brother, Kohandil Khán, to Shikárpúr, to offer Shújah the support of the Barúkzyes if he would strike for the crown.

On hearing of the revolution which had deprived Mahmúd of the crown, Shah Shújah had repaired to Shikárpúr to be ready for any opportunity which might offer. He received Kohandil Khán with unmixed pleasure. But feeling that his chances would be uncertain unless a pledge of support from all the

Barúkzye brothers were obtained, he stipulated for an assurance of that nature. The pledge was given.

No sooner had Shah Shújah received the required promise than he, too, displayed his qualification to take rank amid those princes who learn nothing and forget nothing. Before any action had been taken to restore him to the throne, he proved to the Barúkzye brothers that his intention was to use them: then to cast them away. In vain did Mahammad Azim Khán point out to him the folly of the course upon which he was entering. Like other royal personages before him he considered himself needful. He believed that they must have "a great elector" at the summit of the edifice, and he was resolved to be more than a great elector—to rule as well as to govern. He refused to give way.

The Barúkzyes then discarded him, and, after a short splutter of fireworks, Shah Shújah subsided into exiled insignificance at Lúdhiáná. The Barúkzyes then negotiated with another son of Taimúr Shah, the fourteenth in order of birth, Ayúb Mirza. This prince took a line the very opposite to that followed by his brother, Shújah. "Make me but king," he said to Mahammad Azim Khán, "and permit money to be coined in my name, and I shall be content. You can have the power." These terms were accepted; Ayúb Khán became Shah. His reign, however, was brief. Though he had promised not to reign, he had not promised to abstain from intriguing. Compromising letters written by him to his brothers having been intercepted, he was dethroned and driven out of Kábul.

About the same time another son of Taimúr Shah, Súltán Ali, was put to death at Kábul, and a third, Mahammad Murád, was killed at Kandáhár. They had intrigued and were thus punished.

Mahammad Azim Khán was now the chief administrator of the kingdom. But he was neither King nor Amír, and neither did his brothers, nor did the chiefs of the other Afghán tribes, obey him readily. He was too much on their own level.

The power of the country had receded very much since the death of Fathi Khán. Not only had Herát been alienated, but Afghán Túrkistán and Badakhshán had disappeared, whilst the great ruler of the Panjáb, Ranjit Singh, had been making successive encroachments on the Afghán border. He had conquered Káshmir, Múltán, Déra Ghází Khán, and Atok, and he was threatening Pesháwar. Mahammad Azím hoped that successful resistance to this powerful intruder would prove the most efficacious means of consolidating his power. He therefore assembled an army, and accompanied by his brother, Dost Mahammad, advanced viâ Jalálábád and the Karapa pass to Pesháwar.

The proceedings which followed have been related so differently by the native historians of the period, that it is difficult to ascertain the exact truth. One fact is certain, that in the campaign against Ranjit Singh the Afgháns were beaten at Naoshíra. By some the defeat is attributed to the treachery or connivance of some of the Barúkzye brothers, by others to the bad generalship of Mahammad Azim. I am inclined to believe that both causes contributed to the result. That a battle took place at Naoshíra is certain, and that the Afghán army was badly handled is equally clear. It is not necessary, perhaps, to seek for more recondite causes.

Of the battle there were two main consequences. The one—the possession by Ranjit Singh of the right banks of the Indus, and the assertion of his suzerainty over Peshâwar. One of Mahammad Azim's brothers, Súltán Mahammad, remained, indeed, governor of that city, but on condition of paying a tribute to Ranjit Singh. The other result was the death of Mahammad Azim. In weak health previously, the defeat broke his heart. Confiding the command of the army to Dost Mahammad, he took the road to Kábul. But at Látáband his strength failed him, and he died (1823), leaving his wealth, and, could he maintain it, his position, to his son, Hábib Ulla Khán.

Hábib Ulla Khán had more than the failings, none of the good qualities, of his father. The sceptre, unhallowed by legality, could not long remain in his feeble grasp. Urged by his father, on his death-bed, to wage war against the Sikhs, he neglected this advice to devote himself to the bottle. His power lasted as long as the treasures bequeathed by his father remained undissipated, but no longer.

Never was the kingdom founded by Ahmad Shah in a more perilous position. It was evident that the rule would be to the strongest of the Barúkzye brothers. But the problem, "who was that strongest," had neither been solved nor even definitely indicated.

Dost Mahammad was still at Ghazní, Súltán Mahammad at Pesháwar, Púrdil Khán and two of his brothers were at Kandáhár. They were all jealous of each other, all watching with anxiety the decline and fall of Hábib Ulla Khán, each dreading to make the first move himself or to see another take it.

Dost Mahammad was the first to strike. Learning that Hábib Ulla was in his last extremities for money, he marched on Kábul, took the city, and invested the citadel. At the first symptom of his movements Hábib Ulla had sent a swift messenger to Kandáhár to warn the three brothers residing there. The eldest of the three at once despatched a force under Shirdil Khán, a younger brother, to Kábul. Dost Mahammad, beaten, fell back on Jalálábád, and thence retreated into Kohistán. Shirdil Khán then took possession of Kábul, and deposed the chief who had implored his assistance.

Then ensued a civil war between the Barúkzye brothers, into the details of which it does not seem necessary to enter. It will suffice to state that after many attempts to settle matters by the assassination of rival chiefs, a compromise was finally arrived at. In virtue of this, whilst Kandáhár should remain with the three brothers who had till then held it, Súltán Mahammad was to have Kábul, and Dost Mahammad Ghazní and Kohistán.

This arrangement was so little acceptable to Dost Mahammad that he took the very earliest opportunity to modify it. Appearing suddenly with an army before Kábul, he summoned his brother to resign the place to him and return to Pesháwar. Súltán Mahammad was forced to comply.

Dost Mahammad was now lord of Kábul and of Ghazní. To these he subsequently added Jalálábád. From this time to the year 1834 nothing beyond the repression of an occasional rebellion called him into the field. But in that year an event happened which had a marked effect on his subsequent fortunes.

This event was the reappearance in the field of Shah Shújah. The anticipations of that prince that the very strength of the Barúkzyes would prove their weakness, and that the disunion of the brothers would pave the way for his restoration, had not been realised. With growing dismay he had noticed the gradual ascension to a preponderating position of one amongst them, and that one the ablest, the most prescient, the most daring of the family. But, ascending though he still was, Dost Mahammad had not yet reached the summit. That point attained, and he would be unassailable. Kandáhár and western Afghánistán obeyed brothers older than he; but, though older, those brothers did not possess a tithe of the ability of Dost Mahammad. To gain them, or strike them before they should be swallowed up by their brother, became then an article of faith with the exiled Sadozye. He resolved to try both methods.

One brother, Jabbar Khán, he gained. The negotiations he entered into with the others being responded to less promptly than he had hoped, Shah Shújah quitted his asylum at Lúdhiána in the month of January 1834, raised a small force, crossed the Indus, and seized upon Shikárpúr, a fief of the Dúrání empire. Completing, then, his forces to twenty-two thousand men, composed mostly of Hindústánis drilled after the European fashion, and of a few Afgháns, he first engaged and beat at Rori the Amírs of Sind, and then, turning westward, traversed the Bolan pass and entered Afghánistán.

The three Barúkzye brothers at Kandáhár had been no inattentive spectators of Shah Shújah's preparations. They had levied troops, and as soon as they heard that Shah Shújah had left Shikárpúr they despatched those troops under one of the trio, Kohandil Khán, to stop him at the Khojak Kotal pass. This pass is strong, but it can be turned. It is probable that Shah Shújah, knowing the ways of his countrymen, amused them in front whilst a turning force went to take them in rear. It is probable—for on no other ground is the sudden retreat of Kohandil Khán to be accounted for. He hastily retreated on Kandáhár: Shah Shújah followed him and laid siege to the city.

The Kandáhár Barúkzyes at once sent pressing messengers to their younger brother at Kábul, urging him to come to their assistance. In the invasion of Shah Shújah Dost Mahammad had seen his opportunity. Anxious, however, to ascertain the exact position of the Sadozye prince, he sent a messenger to the British political agent at Lúdhiáná to inquire whether Shah Shújah was supported by the British Government. The reply was weak and ambiguous. It was to the effect that the Government of India had taken no part in the expedition, but that Shah Shújah had their best wishes.

Asiatics always place a correct interpretation upon ambiguous phrases. Dost Mahammad saw that Shújah would not be supported by the British. He therefore hastened down to Kandáhár and attacked him. The battle which ensued would seem to have been most obstinately contested. The Hindústáni troops in Shújah's army, commanded by an Englishman named Campbell, repulsed every charge, and drove back the enemy in disorder. The phrase, rendered historical from its use on a previous memorable occasion, might now have been spoken to Shújah, "One more charge and the day is your own." Whether it was spoken may be doubted. Shújah, instead of leading his troops on horseback, was mounted on an elephant. From that elevation he watched the doubtful battle, the repeated repulses of the enemy. Then he saw that Dost Mahammad, far from being disconcerted at these repulses, was preparing to renew the attack. But he did not notice that in preparing to renew the attack Dost Mahammad was employing his last reserves. The sight that should have gladdened his heart paralysed his nerves. He might have trusted Campbell to repulse that last attack as he had repulsed the others: and then ——. But the "then" was not to be. The preparations for the last charge unmanned him. He turned and fled, carrying the bulk of his army with him. It was but one new experience. He had previously proved that he did not know how to govern; he showed most completely now that he could not command an army. The Englishman, Campbell, covered with wounds, and resisting to the last, was taken prisoner where he had fought. The unnerved king fled, first to Farrah, whence he opened out negotiations with Kámrán at Herát. But finding that Kámrán intended treachery he again fled by way of Jawain and Kalát to Shikarpúr, and thence to his home at Lúdhiáná. The "best wishes" of the British Government had profited him little.

Whilst Dost Mahammad was thus engaged at Kandáhár, Ranjit Singh, ruler of the Panjáb, profiting by the occasion, had pounced upon Pesháwar, and annexing it, had made the Sikh frontier that which it is at the present day. One intrigue leads to another. The Afghán governor of Pesháwar, Súltán Mahammad, dispossessed by Ranjít Singh, fled to Jalálábád. Learning there that Dost Mahammad was at Kandáhár, engaged in a contest which might well seem doubtful, Súltán Mahammad, associating with him two of his brothers, resolved to make an attempt on the capital. Before, however, their preparations had been quite completed, the news reached them of the great victory obtained by their brother over Sháh Shújah. This news caused them to abandon the plot and to prepare to receive Dost Mahammad with every demonstration of joy. But the Dost was not the less acquainted with all that had been intended.

The victory achieved at Kandáhár by Dost Mahammad had assured him of that predominance over his brothers which Shújah had so dreaded. Out of the many fragments of the Dúrání empire he had consolidated one small remnant—small, yet compact—having as its centres the towns of Kábul, of Ghazní, of Jalálábád, of Kandáhár—for though Kandáhár was still governed by his brothers events had bound them to him by the closest ties of interest. To establish this fact in the eyes of the Afgháns and of the world, he resolved formally to assume a sovereign title. The Dúránís had called themselves kings—but then they had a kingdom. A practical man, Dost Mahammad contemned titles indicative of a state of affairs which did not exist. When it was urged upon him to follow the example of the Dúránís and to call himself Shah, "I am too poor," he replied, "to support my dignity as a Sirdar; it would be absurd for me to call myself a king." At last, after much consideration, he decided, in consultation with the chiefs adhering to him, to assume the modest title of Amír-ul-Momerín, Commander of the Faithful. With this title he was invested by the chief priest of Kábul, at a solemn darbár attended by all the grandees, early in 1835. This is the title now borne by his son and successor, Shir Ali. Dost Mahammad announced his elevation to the governments of the states bordering his own, the Sikh and the British governments excepted.

The first act of the Amír was to remove the various governors and functionaries of whose loyalty he was not absolutely sure, and to replace them by his sons. He ordered likewise that thenceforth the public money should be coined in his name. With a view to inaugurate his new authority by some striking success, he directed the levying of taxes, in order to pay the expenses of an army destined for the recovery of Pesháwar.

The taxes were raised—it has been stated, somewhat arbitrarily; the army was levied; and it marched on Pesháwar. Though Ranjit Singh was alarmed, he was still equal to the occasion. He knew the military capacity of the Amír, and he believed that the result of a contest was at least uncertain; but he had money. This money he used. He sent negotiators to the camp of the Amír, nominally to treat, really to bribe. He succeeded. In a few days the army of the Amír melted away, and Dost Mahammad was forced to return to Kábul with the loss of his camp and his prestige. Such are the Afgháns! One of the Amír's brothers, Súltán Mahammad, who had been bought by Ranjit Singh, was made by that prince governor of the fortress of Rotás.

The loss of Pesháwar continued to fret the Amír. It has been asserted that he even entered into negotiations with Persia and Russia to help him to recover it. But though aid from those powers was asked for by Barúkyzes, it was not asked for that purpose, neither was it demanded by the Amír. The history of the transaction is as follows.

During 1836 Persia and the Amír were alike making warlike preparations: the former against Herát, the latter against Pesháwar. The Amír was first ready, and in the spring of 1837 he detached a force under his son, Akbar Khán, with directions to proceed viâ the Khaibar pass to the Pesháwar plain. Issuing from the Khaibar Akbar Khán found Jamrúd strongly occupied by the Sikhs. He laid siege to it. The commander of the Sikh forces at Peshâwar, Hari Singh, marched at once to its relief, and offered battle to Akbar. Akbar accepted it, defeated the enemy with the loss of their general, and drove him under the walls of Jamrúd. The arrival of large reinforcements to the Sikhs prevented him from pursuing his advantages, and he was forced to return to Kábul, his mission unaccomplished. The recovery of Peshâwar was as distant as ever.

Later in the year the Persians entered the Herát territory, captured Ghorian, and laid siege to Herát.

Such was the state of affairs when the Amír heard that a new Governor-General, Lord Auckland, had arrived in India. The opportunity was too favourable to be lost. By means of a British alliance he might check Persia and recover Peshâwar. He accordingly despatched to Lord Auckland a complimentary letter in which, after the compliments, he referred to his grievances against the Sikhs.

But the very alliance which he thought would be propitious was regarded by his brothers at Kandáhár as fraught with evil to themselves. They sought at once to protect themselves against the consequences to themselves of a great increase of power to their brother. They did this by sending an embassy to Persia asking for the protection due from a suzerain to a vassal; and they even sent a letter to the Czar of Russia through the Russian embassy at Teherán.

The reply from both was favourable. Persia

promised aid. Russia sent an ambassador, in the person of Captain Vikovitch, to Kandáhár.

I must now refer, briefly, to the answer sent by the Government of India.

In reply to the Amír's complimentary letter to Lord Auckland, and to the scarcely veiled request for British aid against the Sikhs, that nobleman replied by reciprocating the compliments, by curtly informing the Amír that it was not the practice of the British Government to interfere with the affairs of other independent states, and by notifying his intention shortly to depute some gentlemen to the Amír's court to discuss commercial topics. Shortly afterwards the gentlemen to be so deputed were selected. They were Captain Alexander Burnes, of the Bombay Infantry—a daring officer and accomplished diplomatist; Lieutenant Leech of the Bombay Engineers; Lieutenant Wood, of the Indian Navy; and Dr. Percival Lord, of the Indian Medical Service. In this place I have to do only with the mission of Burnes, for Leech was deputed to Kandáhár, and Wood and Lord were sent further on to Kúndúz.

Burnes entered the Khaibar pass the 30th August 1837, and after an easy journey reached Kábul on the 20th September. "We were received," he writes, "with great pomp and splendour by a fine body of Afghán cavalry, led by the Amír's son, Akbar Khán. He did me the honour to place me on the same elephant upon which he himself rode, and conducted us to his father's court, whose reception of us was most cordial." The next day he was admitted by the Amír to a formal audience and was most graciously received.

Three days later, at a private conference, the Amír opened his heart to Burnes. The real purport of his request, veiled as it was by many phrases, was aid against Ranjit Singh. The Sikhs, he said, robbed me of Pesháwar when I was engaged in combating Shah Shújah, and they have not, nor had they ever, a right to it. Burnes had no authority to offer any tangible aid; he could not even promise the "good wishes" of the British Government. He could only express a hope that Ranjit Singh might restore Pesháwar, not to the Amír, but to his brother, Súltán Mahammad, to be held in vassalage to Láhor.

In vain did the Amír, subsequently, by professions of humility, by offering to express contrition to Ranjit Singh, and by engaging, if he would restore Pesháwar, to hold it as his vassal, endeavour to engage, through Burnes, the British Government on his behalf; Burnes could promise nothing. He could only write and wait for an answer. He wrote; but before the answer could arrive, the Russian agent, Captain Vikovitch, appeared upon the scene.

This agent had proceeded in the first instance to Kandáhár. Detecting that that city was but a limb whilst Kábul was the heart of the Afghán territory, he pushed on, armed with a letter from the Czar, to that place. The letter, to the address of the Amír, professed to treat only of commercial matters, but that phrase veiled other and more important affairs.

Vikovitch had not been many days in Kábul when Burnes received the replies to his first communications to India. In these Lord Auckland recommended the Amír to waive his claims, and be content with such arrangements as Ranjit Singh might make with Súltán Mahammad. The purport of the Amír's reply was that he would sooner see the Sikhs at Pesháwar than his brother, and that, though fully sensible of the good offices of the British Government, he must decline to renounce his claims to that place.

At this time, 26th January, and for nearly a month later, the Amír continued to hope that the representations made by Burnes to the Governor-General might elicit a more favourable reply. Unwilling to compromise his chances of success by coquetting with the Russian envoy, he throughout this period kept Captain Vikovitch at a distance, conversing with him rarely, and then coldly. But on the 21st February, Burnes received despatches from India, which contained a very plain though a very courteous refusal of the Amír's demands. The negotiations which followed could not affect this decision. The Amír was grievously disappointed. "I have often written," he said, "to the British Government about my affairs, and they reply to me about their own." He had wished earnestly for the alliance, and when Burnes, on the 28th April, quitted Kábul, he carried with him a letter from the Amír to Lord Auckland, imploring him in touching language "to remedy the grievances of the Afgháns, and give them a little encouragement and power."

From the date, 21st February, on which Burnes had received a final refusal from Lord Auckland, the treatment of the Russian envoy underwent a change. Profuse in his offers of money and assistance he was now, without a rival, master of the situation. He promised to provide the Amír with money, and to negotiate with Ranjit Singh. Returning then with the Amír's sanction to Herát and Kandáhár he brought to conclusion the contemplated alliance between the Kandáhár Barúkzye brothers and Persia, by virtue of which that power agreed to aid the Afgháns with troops. The treaty containing the Shah's signature was sent to Kábul for the approval of the Amír.

The first consequences of the new alliance quickly showed themselves. Assuming to himself the power of a suzerain over Afghánistán, the Shah commanded Kámrán of Herát to make reparation to himself and to the Barúkzye chiefs his subjects. This close connection between Afghánistán and Persia, with the shadow of Russia in the background; the avowed determination of the Amír to recover Pesháwar by the aid of his new allies; the cessation of friendship with the Amír, caused partly by the failure of Burnes's mission, partly by the success of that of Vikovitch, determined the English Government to reconsider the principles of policy which had up to that time guided its relations with the country of the Amír.

It may be worth while, at the present moment, to inquire briefly what the dangers were which it apprehended; what modes were available to avert them.

The danger that the Government of the day saw

was Russia—Russia using Persia and Afghánistán as its pawns, warring with them, encroaching by their means upon the preserves of England. This idea was translated into a certainty by the fact of the credit obtained by the Russian envoy at Kábul, and that it was he who had negotiated the treaty which seemed to bind the Barúkzyes to Russia.

How should the danger have been averted? By any way certainly rather than by that which was adopted. Granting that Russia was in the background pulling the strings, she was in those days too distant from the scene of action to act with effect, nor was the most powerful of her satellites, Persia, sufficiently strong to strike a blow that the British power would feel. The result showed that Persia could not even take Herát. But granting that she had been strong enough to take Herát, there were means more efficacious and less costly to force her to relax her hold. Grown wiser by experience, we tried those means in 1856. An attack on her seaboard then brought her on her knees. The very threat of such an attack in 1837 would have had a result not less satisfactory.

The idea of any danger at that time from the Afgháns was too absurd for serious consideration. British India was separated from Afghánistán by the Panjáb, occupied by the martial Sikhs, the hereditary enemies of the Afgháns. The chief grievance of Dost Mahammad lay in the fact that he could not retake Pesháwar from the Sikhs. How could a power so weak be in any sense dangerous to the British?

The whole question was so simple, that with time it would have settled itself. The facts, brought into a small compass, were simply these. The Amír of Kábul had requested the British Government to aid him in the recovery of Pesháwar, taken from him by the allies of the British, and the British Government had refused. The Amír had made the same request to the Russian envoy, and that envoy had promised him, on the part of the Czar, money, the restoration of Herát, and the propitiation of the ruler of the Sikhs. As an earnest of the fulfilment of his promises, the Persian army was marching on Ghorian and Herát.

This was the question, fraught, in the opinion of the ministers of Great Britain, with danger to our Indian possessions. "The welfare of our possessions in the East," they announced by their agent, the Governor-General, "requires that we should have on our western frontier an ally who is interested in resisting aggression and establishing tranquillity, in the place of chiefs ranging themselves in subservience to a hostile power and seeking to promote schemes of conquest and aggrandisement."

The mode they proposed to adopt to bring about this result had the merit or the demerit of being remarkable. They proposed to depose the ruler who, out of the chaos resulting from the expulsion of the Sadozyes, had evoked at least a semblance of order, a form of good government, and, most certainly, a respect for authority; who had gained, more than any other Afghán since the death of his father, Fathi Khán, the confidence of the people, and to replace him by a prince belonging to the expelled family—a prince who had already enjoyed, under—for Afghánistán—favourable circumstances, the opportunity of ruling, and who had failed; who, when subsequently treated with as to the conditions of his return by the Barúkzye chiefs, had acted in a manner which plainly showed that he had learned nothing and forgotten nothing; who had twice attempted to force his return, and had twice been driven back; and who—when at one time, by the aid of foreign mercenaries, victory was in his grasp—had preferred flight to making the effort requisite to gain it.

The ministers of England who adopted this remarkable solution of a very slight difficulty were Liberals. Certainly, to dethrone by arms a popular sovereign in order to force upon an unwilling people a prince proved to be incompetent and known to be distasteful, is not a cardinal point of Liberal principles. No sane man will question the immense benefits which the great Liberal party have rendered to the cause of freedom and good government. Those benefits are visible, palpable; we feel them every hour of our lives. But there have been periods in our history when that great party has been struck with a blind fatuity. It would seem as though some malignant spirit sometimes inspired them not only to deviate from their principles, but to appropriate doctrines of an opposite character so extreme that even their political opponents reject them. We have seen something of the same sort within the last three years. On each occasion the result has been traceable to a similar cause. On each the great Liberal party has delivered itself bound hand and foot to the prejudices of a man. In 1838 it allowed itself to be led astray by the exaggerated fears of Lord Palmerston. In 1876 it followed blindly the course dictated by the rancorous jealousy of Mr. Gladstone. Will it recover its reason in 1879?

The siege of Herát by the Persians, in whose ranks were Russian, French, and Italian officers, had begun on the 23rd November 1837, had been continued all the winter of that year, and the spring, summer and autumn of the year succeeding. Owing mainly to the exertions of one English officer within its walls, Eldred Pottinger, of the Bombay artillery, the efforts of the Persians had been entirely baffled. It was Eldred Pottinger who repaired the fortifications, who inspired the garrison, who forced even Shah Kámrán and his minister, Yár Mahammad, to play the warriors. It was Eldred Pottinger who, on the 24th June 1838, repulsed the enemy's attack led by the Russian general, Borowski, and a battalion formed of Russian volunteers. Finally it was mainly through Eldred Pottinger's exertions and example that, on the 8th September 1838, the Persian army raised the siege and retired, beaten, baffled, and humiliated, within its own borders.

With the raising of the siege of Herát the main reason for British intervention in the affairs of Afghánistán disappeared. But before the news of this event reached the Governor-General, Lord Auckland had pledged himself to a policy of interference. In a manifesto, dated the 1st October 1838, that nobleman announced the principles upon which the Liberal ministry he served had based the action he had been directed to carry out. Declaring that the Barúkzyes, "from their dissensions and unpopularity, were unfitted under any circumstances to be useful allies to the British Government," he announced the resolve to replace them by a member of the expelled Sadozye clan, Shah Shújah úl Múlk, "a monarch who, when in power, had cordially acceded to the measures of united resistance to external enmity, which were at that time judged necessary by the British Government, and who, on its empire being usurped by its present rulers, had found an honourable asylum in the British dominions."* The manifesto further announced that in this work of the restoration of Shah Shújah, Ranjit Singh, the ruler of the Panjáb, having been guaranteed in his then existing possessions, had bound himself to co-operate.

This manifesto had not been published five weeks when the Government of India learned that the basis upon which their policy had been built had disappeared. The Persian army, with its forty thousand native troops, its Russian battalion, its foreign officers,

* The manifesto did not add that Shah Shújah had twice quitted that honourable asylum to attempt, mainly with the aid of mercenaries raised within British limits, to recover the throne from which his brother had driven him, and had been twice beaten by the family whose members, despite their "dissensions and unpopularity," had gained the good wishes of the greater portion of their Afghán subjects.

and its Shah at the head of them all, had been repulsed from Herát, and had retreated across the frontier. The Russo-Persian-Afghán alliance had collapsed. The dangers with which it was supposed to be fraught had been proved to be non-existent; their very shadows had disappeared! A lieutenant of artillery had made the political situation in western Asia more favourable to England than it had been at the time of Burnes's mission, for he had caused the Russo-Persian bubble to burst under the very nose of the Amír of Kábul and his brothers!

Surely if ever reason existed for putting a stop to military preparations it existed then. What was there to do? To replace a Barúkzye by a Sadozye—a man loved by a man hated—a man respected by a man despised—a brave man by a nerveless man. Yet, notwithstanding the cessation of all real cause for war, the preparations were not abated; the war was not abandoned. The exile of Ludhiáná was, at any cost, to be restored. Such was the mud through which Liberal principles were dragged by the Liberal party in 1838!

But one change was made by the Government in consequence of the bursting of the Russo-Persian bubble, and that in a point of detail. The strength of the invading army was slightly diminished. But there was another change, not the action of the Government. The Commander-in-Chief in India, Sir Henry Fane, had been appointed to command the expeditionary army when it was believed that that army would have to deal with the Russo-Persian force; but when Persia and its Russian battalion disappeared, and it only remained to replace a Barúkzye by a Sadozye on the Kábul throne, Sir Henry Fane withdrew from the personal command of the expedition. Sir John Keane, Commander-in-Chief of the Bombay Army, was nominated in his place.

The army collected to invade Afghánistán consisted of three distinct bodies. The Bengal force under Sir Willoughby Cotton, numbering seven thousand five hundred men of all arms, assembled at Firozpúr; a contingent of Hindústánís, raised for Shah Shújah, numbering six thousand men, officered by British officers, was to start from a place well known by past experience to the Shah, Shikarpúr; and a third force, called the Bombay column, composed of five thousand five hundred men, under the personal command of Sir John Keane, was to march through Sind and proceed by the Bolan and Khojak Kotal passes. A fourth body of about two thousand five hundred men was likewise formed to keep open the communications with the Bombay Presidency by the occupation of Sind. The whole force to be employed thus amounted in round numbers to twenty-one thousand five hundred men.

It must always be remembered that this war for the replacement of a Barúkzye by a Sadozye was undertaken in alliance with Ranjit Singh, whose dominions we guaranteed. It seems remarkable, under these circumstances, that our ally should refuse our troops a passage across his territories. But he did refuse. The consequence was that the Bengal column, instead of marching across the Panjáb and entering Afghánistán by the Khaibar pass, was forced to follow the river Satlaj to its junction with the Indus, to follow that river to Rori, and there cross it.

A glance at a map of India will show the extreme unsoundness, the danger, of the military position of the invading army. Invading one foreign country, Afghánistán, from the basis of another foreign country, Sind, and with a third and very powerful foreign country, the Panjáb, on its flank, the very existence of the British army really depended on the good will of the Amírs of Sind and the ruler of the Panjáb. If it be affirmed that we could command the loyalty of the Amírs of Sind, a similar statement cannot be made regarding the ruler of the Panjáb. It cannot be denied that we marched into Afghánistán by the sufferance of Ranjit Singh, then old, worn out, and unadventurous. He died in June 1839. After his death we were in Afghánistán by the sufferance of his successors, who, fortunately, were not ambitious.

CHAPTER X.

HISTORICAL.—THE BRITISH INVASION.

THE plan of my history will not allow me to give more than an outline of the first British invasion of Afghánistán and its consequences. The graphic records of the late Sir Henry Havelock, and the detailed story of the late Sir John Kaye, are available to readers who require more than I have space to give them. Sir John Kaye's detailed story occupies alone three volumes. I can afford but one chapter.

Yet within that chapter can be compressed, I would fain believe, all that is necessary for the information of the historical, in contrast with the military, reader. The details which the latter yearns for might prove uninteresting and tedious to the former.

Shah Shújah, with his force of six thousand men, left Firozpúr for Shikarpúr, by the Satlaj and Indus, early in December 1838. He was accompanied by Mr. Macnaghten, of the Bengal Civil Service, who, in anticipation of success, had been appointed envoy to his court. A week later, the 10th December, the Bengal column, under Sir Willoughby Cotton, pursued the same route for the same destination. Sir John Keane on his side had entered Sind by the Hajámri mouth of the Indus early in the same month, with the Bombay contingent, and encamped at Vikkar.

Leaving the Bengal column and the Shah's contingent, I propose first to march with Sir John Keane from the mouth of the Indus to Gandawa. It was a very difficult undertaking. Sir John Keane found himself with a small number of camels, and with but few supplies. The agents of the Amírs of Sind professed unbounded friendship and devotion, but threw every possible objection in the way of the movement of the troops. Day followed day, week succeeded week, and still the force could not move. Sir John Keane was naturally an irascible man, and the treatment he received certainly did not improve his temper. The Amírs promised everything and did nothing.

At last, by incredible exertion, Sir John Keane moved on his force to Tátta, forty-eight miles from Haidarabad. The Amírs now changed their system. From professions combined with obstruction they proceeded to something approaching open hostility. Sir John Keane continuing his march, they cut off his supplies, harassed his communications, intercepted his letters, and imprisoned the followers of his camp. This sort of treatment was more to the mind of the English general than the other. He knew now exactly what to do. Sending then a message to Sir Willoughby Cotton, then at Rori, to support him, he prepared, in the last days of January 1839, to assault the capital. The Amírs observing this, yielded, and promised the Political Agent to agree to all the demands the British Government had made upon them. Thenceforth all difficulties disappeared, and, on the 10th February, Sir John Keane resumed his march northwards.

On the 23rd of that month one brigade of the Bengal column traversed the Bolan pass and reached Quetta on the 5th March. There a month later it was joined by the Commander-in-Chief and by Shah Shújah and his levies. The Bombay force entered the Bolan pass on the 9th and 11th April, and pushed on for the same destination.

Anxious to secure the Khojak Kotal pass Sir John Keane moved forward from Quetta on the 7th April. This pass presents a succession of steep ascents and descents with narrow gorges where no draught cattle can work with effect. The general was not apparently aware that a path existed by which it could be turned, for he made no attempt to use it. In the manner of the British he marched straight on. Fortunately, perhaps, no attempt was made to utilize the great natural advantages offered by the pass. A handful of the enemy's horsemen indeed appeared but a few shots sufficed to disperse them.

From this point the march to Kandáhár was easy and unopposed. The army appeared before that city on the 25th April and at once entered it. "The Kandáhár chiefs," writes a distinguished soldier, then a young artillery officer of promise, since realized, "had fled for refuge to Persia without striking a blow, and the inhabitants tendered their reluctant homage to the old monarch who was thus unceremoniously thrust upon them by foreign bayonets."*

The army stayed at Kandáhár till its component parts should be re-united and rested, nor was it till the 27th June—the very day on which Ranjit Singh died—that Sir John Keane, leaving a strong garrison in Kandáhár, pursued his way up the valley of the Tarnak towards Ghazní.

Judging from the reception he had till then encountered that the opposition would be slight, and knowing from his experience of the Bolan and the Khojak the enormous difficulty of dragging a siege-train over rocks and precipices, Sir John left at Kandáhár the heavy guns with which he had been provided to batter Ghazní. This was a mistake which might have cost him dear.

Ghazní was reached on the 21st July. The British force consisted of eight thousand men; the Shah's contingent of four thousand; they had in all forty field guns. They found the fortress occupied by Prince Haidar, a son of the Amír, with a garrison of three thousand five hundred men.

In the earlier portion of this volume† I have given a slight description of Ghazní. It was in many respects a strong place; proof, if well commanded, against a *coup de main;* but not capable of sustaining a siege.

* A retrospect of the Afghán war by Maj.-General Sir V. Eyre, K.C.S.I., C.B.

† Pages 15 and 16.

For a siege Sir John Keane had neither the time nor the guns. But he had good troops and skilled engineers, so he resolved on the 23rd to attempt a *coup de main*.

He succeeded. Four officers of the engineers, prominent, amongst whom was Lieutenant, afterwards Sir Henry, Durand, were told off to blow open the Kábul gate, the weakest gate of the fortress, and storming parties were held in readiness to profit by the explosion. The daring scheme succeeded—Ghazní was carried, and her governor was taken prisoner.

The sudden fall of Ghazní spread consternation amongst the Barúkzyes. Sir John Keane took advantage of this feeling by pressing on at once towards the capital. Leaving Ghazní on the 30th July, he reached Kábul without opposition on the 6th August. The same evening Shah Shújah made his triumphal entrance into the capital, and took up his residence in the Bála Hissar.

Where, in the meanwhile, was the Amír, Dost Mahammad, and what had he been doing?

The Amír had been stunned by the first rumours of a British invasion. He had not desired hostility with the British. He had regretted the Russo-Persian alliance brought about by his Kandáhár brothers almost in spite of him. That alliance was unpopular with the Afgháns, and unpalatable to himself.

But what could he do to conjure away the invasion? He could do nothing. He had shown courtesy to the one British envoy, and he would have given a reception as friendly to any other whom the Government of India might send. But these foreigners wanted only the one thing he could not give them. They wanted his crown, not indeed for themselves, but to bestow it on the brother of the man by whose orders his father had been blinded and murdered. And now they were going to invade his country to pluck that crown from his brow. Unable to avert the invasion, he resolved, with the spirit of a true Barúkzye, to resist it. He accordingly repaired the fortifications of the Bálá Hissar; strengthened those of Ghazní; sent his son Haidar to command the latter fortress; his son Afzúl with a force to lie in its neighbourhood and fall upon the English when Haidar should repulse them; his son Akbar to guard the Khaibar, whilst he himself would be prepared to take up a position between Ghazní and Kábul to act according to circumstances.

We have seen how matters went against him; how Ghazní fell, almost without a blow. Then Afzúl, paralysed by the fall of the fortress which was to have given him his opportunity, abandoned his elephants and his camp equipage, and fled to Kábul. What now was the Amír to do?

He still resolved to make the best of it—to treat, yielding all that he could yield. Holding a council of his chiefs, he told them his determination. They approved it. He then despatched his brother, Jabbar Khán, to the British camp, offering to resign everything to Shah Shújah, provided that the Shah would confirm him in the office of vizier—an office made hereditary in his family by the founder of the Sadozye dynasty, the grandfather of Shuját, Ahmad Shah.

Jabbar Khán had always been well disposed towards Shah Shújah, and in the selection of him as envoy lay, the Amír hoped, the best chance for a peaceful and satisfactory solution of the question. But the proposition was refused—more than refused; it was received with mockery. In reply he was offered the "honourable asylum" at Lúdhiáná which Shújah had quitted to assail him.

The Amír declined the offer, and resolved, as a last resource, to try the supreme appeal. Not, indeed, that he cherished any hope of victory; he knew that he was overmatched. But he would at least die with his face to the enemy, fighting for his right.

But even this last consolation was denied him. The fall of the strong fortress of Ghazní, and the prompt following up of that success by an immediate march on the capital, had produced on the Afghán chiefs and their followers, on the Kizilbáshis, and on the tribes about Kábul, an effect identical with that which had paralysed the courage of Afzúl Khán. In the success and its consequences they detected a power greater than that of Shújah. With him they might have dealt; but how were they to oppose these foreigners, whom precipitous mountain passes could not stop, before whom their strongest fortresses were as packs of cards, their soldiers as mountain sheep? The attitude, the demeanour, the very language of the Afghán lords, showed plainly to their chief that imagination had quenched their courage; that they were beaten before they had fought!

Vainly did the Amír attempt to rouse them to a

truer conception of the actual state of affairs; in vain did he assure them that these English were, after all, but men like themselves, neither stronger nor braver; that their force could be met by force; and that, even if they were beaten, it would be nobler to die fighting than to submit to a prince brought in by the foreigner. Fruitlessly did he point to the position he had taken up near Maidán, naturally strong, and made almost impregnable by art. The spark of patriotism had been completely extinguished, and he could not re-kindle the saturated tinder.

Then, and then only, rather than fall into the hands of the invaders, he resolved to flee. He had barely time to get away, for his chiefs and courtiers were fast falling off to pay their obeisance to the rising sun. Deserted by his nobles, left with scarcely two thousand followers, the Amír mounted his horse and galloped off in the direction of Bámián.

Twelve hours had not elapsed before the Shah and his allies reached the spot he had quitted. It was soon ascertained from the numerous deserters that the Amír had fled. Amongst the English officers present was Captain James Outram, then in the full promise of a glorious career. He at once volunteered to command any party that might be placed at his disposal to pursue the Amír. Some ten or twelve other officers* volunteered to accompany him. Had the general placed at their disposal a body of English cavalry the

* Amongst the survivors of these is General Sir George Lawrence, K.C.S.I.

Amír must inevitably have been captured. But it was unfortunately decided to employ a body of Afghán horse, commanded by one Háji Khán Khákar, a deserter from the Barúkzyes, in the pursuit. This decision was fatal. Hájí Khán Khákar, though a deserter, was a trimmer. The one aim of his life was to be always on the winning side. Though the star of the Sadozyes was in the ascendant, there was no reason why he should incur the undying resentment of the Barúkzyes by capturing their leader. He accepted, then, the commission to pursue Dost Mahammad, with the intention of saving him from capture.

He did save him. He knew the country, the route, the passes. The English officers did not know them. He thus managed to insure that the Amír should be thirty miles beyond Bámián when the pursuers reached that place. Outram had orders not to proceed further than Bámián. The Amír was then able to make his escape to Bokhára.

I have now accounted for all the troops and the leaders of troops detailed by the Amír to oppose the invasion of his country, with the exception of one—the division under the command of Akbar Khán detached to the Khaibar pass.

It had been decided that whilst two limbs of the triple alliance, the British and Shah Shújah, should invade Afghánistán by the Bolan pass, the third, the Sikhs, accompanied by Taimúr Mirza, a son of the Shah, should penetrate into it by the Khaibar.

The contingent provided by Ranjit Singh amounted to about five thousand troops, mostly Patháns.

Accompanying them as political agent, was Captain Wade, who had as escort a small detachment of native soldiers of the Indian army; but the man whose rank gave to the expedition its importance was the Taimúr Mirza just referred to.

The illness of Ranjit Singh, his death, the break in the administration which followed it, delayed this small force an unusually long time at Pesháwar, nor was it till the beginning of the fourth week of July that it set out.

Naturally, and notwithstanding the presence of the Sadozye prince, the chief direction of the expedition devolved upon the senior English officer present, Captain Wade. Wade entered the Khaibar, and marched cautiously on Ali Masjid. He encountered a fitful but ineffective opposition, and with a loss of 180 in killed and wounded he occupied that fortress on the fifth day (26th July) after leaving Pesháwar.

All this time Akbar Khán was at the further end of the pass, at Dáká. Why did he not come to the relief of Ali Masjid? Why, when Ali Masjid had fallen, did he retreat, without firing a shot, beyond Kábul? These are questions which are more easily asked than answered. Ghazní fell on the 24th July. Bad news travels quickly, and it is quite possible that the fall of this fortress, which influenced so many other things in the campaign, influenced likewise Akbar Khán. This is certain, that he offered no opposition to Wade's advance. That officer, accompanied by Prince Taimúr and his following, reached Kábul on the 8th September.

The object of the expedition was, apparently, now accomplished. The British Government had redeemed one part of their pledge. They had—to use the words employed subsequently by Lord Ellenborough—they had "expelled from Afghánistán a chief believed to be hostile to British interests, to place upon his throne a sovereign represented to be friendly to those interests and popular with his subjects." But another part of the programme still remained to be accomplished. In his memorable manifesto of the 1st October 1858, Lord Auckland had promised that "when once he (Shah Shújah) shall be secured in power, and the independence and integrity of Afgánistán established, the British army will be withdrawn." It would seem that the time had arrived to fulfil this pledge. Dost Mahammad and his two sons, Afzúl and Akbar, had fled to Bokhára, and had been at once placed there under a *surveillance* amounting almost to close custody. The submission of the tribes appeared sincere. Indeed the British resident, Mr. Macnaghten, who had accompanied the Shah during his progress to Kábul, had been so struck by the manner in which he had been received, that he recorded his testimony that "the Afgháns have received the Shah with feelings nearly amounting to adoration."

Under these circumstances, why was not the pledge redeemed? Every argument seemed to speak loudly in favour of such a course. The Shah's contingent—consisting of troops of the three arms, with the *matériel* belonging to each—could have garrisoned the towns. A conciliatory demeanour towards the chiefs, and the bestowal upon them of the offices within the gift of the Shah, would have, under ordinary circumstances, secured their loyalty. The halo of success would be certain to secure to that prince at least some months of peace, and these might be well employed in arranging the internal administration of the country. More than all, the withdrawal of the British troops would have tested, truly and honestly, the soundness of British policy. An opportunity would have been afforded of ascertaining, under circumstances very favourable to Shah Shújah, whether the Sadozyes were better fitted than their rivals for the control of a warlike, mercenary, contentious, and faithless people.

The decision as to the proper time for the redemption of this pledge had been left by Lord Auckland to Mr. Macnaghten and Sir John Keane. The Governor-General had merely stipulated, and prudently stipulated, that if troops were to be retained, their number should not be too few.

The decision really rested with Mr. Macnaghten. A ripe scholar and a skilful diplomatist, Mr. Macnaghten was deficient in that rare audacity which fits a man to face a revolution. Like so many men who have risen in a graded service, he feared responsibility. Then again, though possessing unquestioned ability he never gave it fair play. He allowed sentiment—or perhaps, to put it more correctly, the secret impulses of the heart—to override his judgment. The type is not an uncommon one.

Thus it happened that though he believed in Shah

Shújah's popularity, though his judgment told him that if the British were to remain occupying the high places of the State, the people would come to regard them as intruders, that true policy required that the Shah should be left face to face with his people;—various minor causes combined to make him wish for an excuse to evade the obligation. His position at Kábul, supported by English troops, the all-powerful representative of England in Central Asia, the visible symbol of the check given to Russian intrigue—these were matters tangible, and their disappearance might, the secret voice told him, act adversely to the policy of the Governor-General. Then the Shah too whispered his secret fear lest the departure of the British should be the signal for the re-appearance of Dost Mahammad. What other causes there may have been, I know not. This at least is certain, that whilst policy and calm judgment combined to counsel the immediate withdrawal of the army, the secret impulses of Mr. Macnaghten prompted him to long for an excuse to keep at least a portion of it.

The excuse came. The Amír of Bokhára was at this time retaining in confinement Colonel Stoddart, an officer of the British army, who in 1838 had been despatched from Teherán to Bokhára to attempt to obtain the liberation of the Russians pining in captivity in that town. It was known likewise that a Russian force, destined for Khiva, was assembling at Orenberg. Moreover, there had been rumours that Jabbar Khán, the brother of Dost Mahammad, who was at Kúlúm with the family of the Amír, was restless—and his restlessness foreboded no good to Shah Shújah. With a view, then, of making a demonstration which should produce some effect on all these parties, the envoy, soon after the installation of the Shah despatched a small force, consisting of a regiment of Gúrkhás and a troop of Horse Artillery, by the Kúlú and Irák passes to Bámián. Dr. Percival Lord was instructed to accompany the force as political agent, and to use it as occasion might require.

Dr. Lord has been described as "a medical officer of rare accomplishments," but he was an undoubted alarmist. Whilst the force traversed the passes mentioned, Dr. Lord was allowed to use his discretion as to the route he should pursue. The force took a month to accomplish the short but most difficult journey. Dr. Lord set out later to join it, but he had not ridden thirty-six miles from Kábul when he returned, open-mouthed, to announce that the whole country, within forty miles of the capital, was in open rebellion; that Dost Mahammad, escaped from Bokhára, had established himself at Kúndúz, and that the thanes and the people from all sides were flocking to him!

This intelligence responded to the inner instincts—it might almost be said, to the secret but unwhispered wishes—of Mr. Macnaghten. It gave him the opportunity he wanted. Instantly he wrote to Sir John Keane, telling him that half the army might go, but that the other half must remain.

In a few days it turned out that Lord had been duped by his Afghán escort. Unwilling to cross the

Hindú Kúsh at that season, and unable to stop Lord's progress by any other means, they had invented the story of the rebellion and of the evasion of Dost Mahammad. The credulous doctor, too easily believing them, had ridden back to give the alarm.

But the story had done its work. The envoy had committed himself to Sir John Keane and the Governor-General, and he had no mind to draw back.

One half of the army, lead by Sir John Keane, returned then to India, punishing on their way, by an assault on his fortress, the Khán of Kalát,* for conduct called refractory—but which was really the conduct of an honest, outspoken man—towards the army during its advance. The other moiety, under Sir Willoughby Cotton, remained behind.

Shah Shújah had by no means shared the confidence of the envoy as to the stability of his position. Fear of the great chiefs of the tribes haunted him; he dreaded their vigour, their relentless daring, their boundless ambition. He had never forgotten how they had driven him from power in 1812. His pride would not allow him to court them. Alone he could not crush them, but with the aid of the British garrison he might grind them to powder. For this reason he had used all his arts with Mr. Macnaghten to induce him to retain a considerable force. He had succeeded. What was his position? The most miserable that could fall to the lot of any man—a position restricting

* The brave old chief died in defending his household gods; his fort was taken from his son and given to another.

the exercise of those qualities dear to the heart of a free man. He was a king supported by foreign bayonets!

Nor was the position of the envoy much better. The master of the foreign bayonets, he became thus a second power in the State; a power which must draw to itself the hatred of everybody—the hatred of the king who owed to it his crown, the hatred of the people who saw in it alike the support and instrument of a monarch whom they loathed. It was inevitable there should be a clash!

The clash came sooner even than might have been expected. The envoy wanted to house his troops. His engineer reported that in a military point of view it was incumbent that they should occupy the Bálá Hissar, the citadel of Kábul. The Shah objected. Macnaghten yielded at first, but upon the urgent representations of the engineer, Lieutenant (afterwards Sir Henry) Durand, he again addressed the Shah on the subject, and wrung from him a reluctant assent that the citadel should be prepared for occupation as a strong military post. The pioneers were at once detailed for the work, and began it. But no sooner did the Shah hear that the work had been begun than he renewed his objections — which were extremely frivolous—with so much pertinacity that Macnaghten yielded. Fatal weakness! Striking example of the absence of the audacity which knows when to brave a weak nature! Macnaghten's yielding on this occasion caused the Kábul disaster of 1841. For a brief period, indeed, certain rooms in the Bálá Hissar were given up to be occupied by our troops; but eventually, at the request of the Shah, Macnaghten made over those rooms for the use of the royal harem.

I have said that Shah Shújah had wished to retain the British in order that by their aid he might crush rather than conciliate the great Afghán chiefs. Unhappily Macnaghten allowed himself to be swayed to support this policy. He placed virtually at the Shah's disposal British officers detailed to drill and command corps of Khaibaris, of Jazailchis, of Kohistánis, of Jánbáz. These corps became really the janissaries of Shah Shújah. They held the detached forts, collected revenue; and, quartered often in commanding positions, superseded the authority of the tribal chieftains. The measure was in every sense unsound. Whilst it alienated the chiefs it did not even conciliate the savage mountaineers who received the pay of the Shah. An Afghán will do a great deal for money; but he abhors discipline, and except in the excitement of battle he does not care to be commanded by one whom he regards as an infidel. It was evident that the organisation produced no such tie between the levies and their commanders as that which attaches the native soldier of India to his officer; that the men regarded it simply as a tie of interest to be broken when convenient.

In another point of view it was not less objectionable. In an earlier chapter I have detailed the measures adopted by Ahmad Shah and continued by his successors for the levy and maintenance of a national army. It was the feudal system in its integrity—each tribe obeying the call of its chief summoned by the overlord. But this new system of levies under European officers required monthly payments, and monthly payments to a sort of regular army necessitated increased taxation or increased oppression.

But although Macnaghten had weakly yielded to the Shah on these two important points, his conduct with reference to the administration of the Government was at least as blameworthy. "The envoy deemed it possible"—I quote from an admirable essay written nearly thirty years ago upon this subject*—"to reconcile the assumption by himself of the main powers of sovereignty with the treatment of Shah Shújah as an independent monarch, and sought to effect this by leaving the administration of civil and criminal justice, the settlement and collection of the revenue, and its irresponsible appropriation, entirely in the hands of Shah Shújah, precluding him however from any control in measures concerning the external relations of his government, or those having reference to independent or revolting tribes. Although allowed to make grants to his favourites, and to authorise aggressions and usurpations, when these could be effected without troops, the Shah had no voice in the deciding on the employment of force in support of his own or the envoy's measures. The Shah had thus much power for evil, and could commit the Government to measures, the odium of supporting which must fall on Macnaghten, who alone ordered expeditions, settled the strength of detachments, gave instructions to their commanders, and pointed out the objects to be at-

* "Calcutta Review," December 1850.

tained and the mode of accomplishment. It was a vain hope, by thus incurring the opprobrium of all harsh and violent measures, and by leaving to the misrule of the Shah's greedy favourites the credit of evoking them, to dream of blinding the nobles and the people to the really servile condition of their king. The farce was too broad and too cuttingly insulting. From the first it was pregnant with danger."

Such, in brief, is an outline of the military and political system adopted and pursued for two years by the British envoy at the court of Shah Shújah. The policy which sanctioned this system had, it must be remembered, nothing in common with the policy advocated in later years, of establishing British agents at certain Afghán centres. Those agents were to be prohibited from interfering with the administration. The policy of 1839 was essentially a policy of interference with everybody and everything. It superseded local rule and local customs. It devolves upon me now to relate as concisely as possible the results of that policy.

In a preceding chapter I have told how under all dynasties and under all circumstances the tribes of the mountains and the passes had maintained their independence. The great Akbar had tried to subdue them, but in vain. His successors had bought them. Nádir Shah and Ahmad Shah had been reduced to the same course; and the annual subsidy, fixed by the latter sovereign and continued by his successors of the Sadozye dynasty, is understood to have amounted to not less than eighty thousand rupees per annum.

But with the expulsion of Mahmúd Shah in 1818, the relations with the Khaibarís changed. For a long time there was no king in Afghánistán, and when at length Dost Mahammad had felt himself sufficiently secure to assume the title of Amír he reduced the annual subsidy to twelve thousand rupees, and though he raised it subsequently to twenty thousand, this amount fell far short of the expectation of the tribes.

In the interval, and even prior to the expulsion of Mahmúd Shah, the tribes of the passes had been devoted to the cause of Shújah. They had fought for him; they had concealed him; they had secured his escape. These good offices were not forgotten by the Shah when he was restored by British intervention to his throne. He had authorised his son Taimúr to promise the tribes the restoration of their ancient privileges; and on the safe arrival of his son at Kábul, he had confirmed this promise on the condition that the passes should remain open to the British convoys.

Shah Shújah had made this promise without consulting the British envoy. Mr. Macnaghten, when he heard of it, took the matter into his own hands to be dealt with after the manner of a modern diplomatist. He offered, then, the tribes an annual subsidy, larger indeed than that bestowed upon them by Dost Mahammad, but falling considerably short of the amount which the promises of the Shah had led them to expect. He coupled this offer, moreover, with conditions which neither the Moghols, nor Nádir Shah, nor Ahmad Shah had been so unwise as to propose —for they had for their object entirely to supersede the authority of the tribes in the passes which they regarded as their own. The result may be anticipated. The tribes refused the subsidy—the proposal to supersede their authority heated their blood to boiling pitch. An opportunity to show their power was soon afforded them. Sir John Keane returned indeed with his small army through the Khaibar. But he had hardly quitted the defile when the Khaibaris invested Ali Masjid, and though the British general succeeded in throwing into this fort a sufficient amount of ammunition and provisions, the Khaibaris cut off a battalion of Najibs and captured from four to five hundred camels from the relieving party as it returned to Pesháwar. Then, only, were serious negotiations opened with them,—that is to say, negotiations which had some chance of arriving at a satisfactory conclusion. It is unnecessary to enter into these in detail. It will suffice to state that the Khaibaris extorted from the necessities of the British agent the subsidy (eighty thousand rupees) which when promised by Shah Shújah they had gratefully accepted, and they showed their knowledge of their position by attempting to plunder, after the treaty had been signed, every successive detachment of the returning army of Sir John Keane.

If the fears of Macnaghten had been roused by the revolt of the Khaibaris, the general aspect of affairs on the conclusion of the agreement just referred to did much to re-establish his composure. He was now indeed, or he seemed to himself to be, master of the situation. And what a situation! One agent, Dr.

Percival Lord, who had, after the scare already referred to, succeeded in reaching Bámián, was engaged in disseminating British principles, and spreading, as he believed, British influence, up to the banks of the Oxus, even beyond the banks of the Oxus. Another agent, Captain d'Arcy Todd, deputed to Herát, had uot only succeeded, he had reason to feel confident, in finally establishing British influence in that city, but had given the most substantial proof of the reality of that influence, by deputing, without credentials, an officer—Captain James Abbott—to Khiva with the avowed object of inducing the Khán of that country to release from the captivity in which he held them the subjects of that nation whose designs upon Central Asia were even then a cause of nightmare to Macnaghten—the subjects of Russia.

To any man less influenced by the secret wishes of his heart than was Macnaghten, the very circumstances I have referred to would have been a cause of anxiety and dread. The fussy interference by Dr. Percival Lord, backed by a British force, in the affairs of the petty chieftains north of the Hindú Kúsh, had raised a feeling of alarm and insecurity throughout the country south of the Oxus. Nor had it stopped there. Crossing that river it had penetrated to Bokhára, had filled the mind of the Amír with alarm, and had induced him to connive at the escape of three men whom he had till then kept under close surveillance—Dost Mahammad, and his sons Akbar and Afzúl.

Nor, in reality, did the presence of d'Arcy Todd in

Herát spread less real alarm. It is true that d'Arcy Todd himself was a type of the chivalrous soldier, subordinating all to duty; high-minded, pure hearted; in the highest sense of the term, noble. It is true that James Abbott was the most loveable, the most estimable, the most unselfish of men. It is true that by a considerable expenditure of money, d'Arcy Todd had saved the people of Herát from starvation and misery; that he had made secure the throne of the infamous Kámrán. What was his reward? The dread of Persia gave place to the dread of the British infidel; and Kámrán, in January 1840, wrote to the Shah—the Shah who had lately threatened his throne and had caused the misery from which d'Arcy Todd had relieved him—to the effect that he merely tolerated the English envoy from motives of expediency, but that his hopes centred in the favour of the Shah!

The mission of James Abbott, inspired by the noblest motives, and its consequences, deserves more than the passing notice I am able to bestow upon it. I have already stated the nature of the task he had undertaken. This task, which in the hands of one less true to the purpose he had in view, less patient, and less single-minded, must have failed, was, despite of extraordinary obstacles, carried out by him and by his successor, Captain Shakespear, to a successful conclusion. It was, indeed, the only real success attaching, from first to last, to the attempt made by the British nation to foist upon an unwilling people a sovereign for whom they had no sympathy.

Enough has been shown of the real working of

the missions upon whose success Macnaghten was pluming himself, to demonstrate the rottenness of the ground on which he stood. Nevertheless, confident, hopeful, even exulting, he accompanied the Shah in November to spend the winter at Jalálábád. Whilst there, he gave other and more striking examples of the erroneous view he had conceived, not only of his own functions, but of the proper duties of a king of the Afgháns.

Macnaghten's negotiations with the Khaibaris, already noticed, are a type of the general system he had conceived. Backed by the British force, he resolved to rule with a high hand—to force submission with the sword. How and with what untoward results he had failed with the Khaibaris, we have seen. We have to see now how even more decidedly, and with what more fatal results, he failed with others.

When the British force entered Afghánistán, its strength, its prestige, the marvellous conquest it made of Ghazní, produced a striking effect throughout the country. Dost Mahammad and his sons disappeared at once. Chieftains who had carefully cherished their independence bowed their head. One alone refused—the chief of Kúner. True to his principle of ruling, Macnaghten determined that the chief of Kúner should be deposed, and his place taken by another. A British force was accordingly sent against him.

But native chiefs, occupying castles descended to them through a long line of ancestors, object, as a rule, to being deposed. Certainly the chief of Kúner was one of these. He repulsed the English, and successfully defied the enemy. The chief of Bájor followed his example, and with like success, forcing his assailants to abandon a gun.

Nor were these the only misfortunes. The Ghilzai tribe—the men who in earlier days had given so many rulers to the country, occupied in central and western Afghánistán a position somewhat analogous to that of the Khaibaris. Jealous of their independence they lived on transit fees and plunder. To such men civilisation was death—such civilisation more especially as would organise the great caravan routes independently of their authority. At such civilisation it seemed to them that the foreign infidels, who had made no arrangements with them, were aiming. They accordingly took the law into their own hands, and exercised a guerilla warfare on the convoys and detachments of the invaders. To such a length did their exactions proceed, that Colonel Nott sent a force under Major Anderson against them. Anderson beat the Ghilzais; but it became evident that a tribe which could command forty thousand warriors must be dealt with in another way. Naturally that way was to buy them. Macnaghten yielded. The annual subsidy was thirty thousand rupees.

Further south, in Bilúchístán, the more than grave error, the crime, the British had committed in attacking and slaying the noble-hearted Khán of Kalát, and in disinheriting his son, was slowly producing its legitimate fruits. These ripened in May.

The result was on the whole most unfortunate for the British. They were forced to atone for the crime of their assault on Kalát, by renouncing the *protégé* they had imposed upon it, and by having to witness the temporary restoration of the son of the murdered chieftain. They were compelled, too, to hear of the murder of the agents of the British power, of the defeat of detachments, of the interruption of communications, caused by the justly infuriated Bilúchis before they could be brought under subjection by detachments sent from Kandáhár.

It is now time to return to Dr. Lord. The officious activity of this officer had contrived, before the spring of 1840 had set in, to embroil the British with the Hazáras and other tribes north of the great range. Disdaining any attempt to conciliate the hardy mountaineers, Lord relied solely upon force. To anyone less self-confident, the spirit that had been evinced by the people of the country upon more than one occasion would have seemed to necessitate at least caution in dealing with them. But Lord was eager to press onwards, and his eagerness so ran away with his judgment that he succeeded in compromising—he almost succeeded in ruining—the British interests in the districts under his charge.

When Dost Mahammad and his two sons had taken refuge in Bokhára, a third son, Jabbar Khán, of whom mention has already been made in these pages, had proceeded with the famlly of the Amír to Kúlúm. The chief of this place, certainly out of no regard for the Amír, but probably because the escorting party under Jabbar Khán was considerable, had extended to them his hospitality. Acting strictly under the orders of the envoy, Dr. Lord had entered into negotiations with Jabbar Khán, with the view of inducing him to submit himself and his charge to British generosity, and, to quicken his decision, had intimated to him pretty plainly that Kúlúm was within reach of the British detachment at Bámián. To prove that these were not words only, Lord ordered a small party of troops to march northwards. When the intelligence that British troops were about to move in the direction of Kúlúm reached the chief of that district, he, to square himself with the agent, offered to place at his disposal the little fort of Bájgah, a place of some repute in the estimation of the natives, situated at the mouth of the defile beyond Kámúnd. A cautious man would have hesitated ere he consented to lock up a portion of his small force in a little fort at a considerable distance from his base, the occupation of which could not fail to excite in the minds of the native chiefs suspicions of ulterior proceedings. But Lord was the reverse of a cautious man. He wrote to Kábul, to which place the envoy had now returned, to ask sanction to his proposals, and, having obtained it, pushed forward five companies of Gúrkhas to Bajgah, left two at Syghán, and retained one, and three hundred Afghán levies, at Bámián.

The first result of this experiment corresponded entirely to the wishes of Lord and Macnaghten. Jabhar Khán brought his charge to Bámián, and surrendered. But the occupation of the frontier post made an enemy of every Uzbég chief in the vicinity. Even the Wáli of Kúlúm, who up to that time had shown a jealous dislike of Dost Mahammad and his family, began to long for the sound of his war-cry.

Suddenly it came. In the month of July 1840 Dost Mahammad and his two sons succeeded—probably with the connivance of the king of Bokhára, whose alarm had been greatly stimulated by the advance of the English—in escaping from the veiled captivity in which he had been held. After many adventures they reached Kúlúm. They found prevailing there a feeling of hatred to the British—a desire at any cost to rid the country of the infidels. The Uzbégs flocked to his standard, and in a few weeks the Amír found himself at the head of five to six thousand fighting men.

Space will not permit me to give more than a mere outline of the military events which followed. It will suffice to say that on the 30th August a small detachment of Gúrkhas, under Sergeant Douglas, on its way from Syghán to Bajgah, was attacked by Afzúl Khan, and though the Gúrkhas, well commanded, fought splendidly, they were saved only from destruction by the prompt appearance on the field of Lieut. Sturt, of the Engineers, with two companies of their comrades. The result, though full of honour for the Gúrkhas, was regarded by the tribes as a triumph. They hastened, the Amír at their head, seriously to threaten Bájgah. The fort, weak as a military position, could not be held. Our men fell back on Syghán. But on their way to that place, the Afghán levies, trained and led by British officers, deserted and went over to Dost Mahammad. The remainder of the British force retreated on Bámián.

Meanwhile, the envoy, on hearing of the escape of the Amír from Bokhára, had reinforced the garrison at Bámián by a regiment of native infantry under Colonel Dennie, a very capable officer. Dennie, on learning the misfortune near Syghán, marched towards that place to meet the Amír, who was pressing on, flushed with anticipations of victory, towards Bámián. The rival forces joined battle on the 18th September. Dennie had only two guns, but they were sufficient to win the battle. Such was the effect of their fire, and so firm was the countenance of the sepoys, that the hill men fairly turned and fled, carrying the Amír and his two sons with them, and leaving their camp equipage, their kettledrums, their ammunition, and their only gun on the field.

Dost Mahammad fled into the Kohistán, there, as will presently be seen, to excite new troubles. For the moment, however, the country north of the Hindú Kúsh had been quieted. Some valuable experience, too, had been gained—the most important, and in the eyes of the envoy the most alarming, being, that the Afghán levies were not to be trusted.

The desertion of the Afghán levies must indeed have been a very rude awakening to Mr. Macnaghten. It would seem that for the first time the extreme falseness of the position of the British presented itself to him in its real light. His communications with India depended upon the fidelity of the mountain tribes: Between the Afghán frontier and the Indian frontier—the Indus and the Satlaj—lay the warlike nation of the Sikhs, no longer restrained by the firm hand of Ranjit

Singh, but boastful and aggressive. But Mr. Macnaghten, though he recognised the danger of his position, was far from divining either the real evil or the true remedy. The policy which at this period he pressed upon Lord Auckland proves clearly how little he comprehended the real situation. To send him more troops—to declare war against the Sikhs; this was his policy—a policy which, if carried out, would probably have lost India.

Some allowance ought perhaps to be made for a man in the position Macnaghten then found himself. Desperate situations require desperate remedies; and certainly Macnaghten's situation might well have appeared desperate. On the one side Dost Mahammad was in the Kohistán; the chiefs in that mountainous district had given him a cordial reception and assured him of their sympathy and support. Expressions of goodwill and affection were sent to the Amír from the city of Kábul itself. These matters were hidden neither from the envoy nor from the Shah. On the other side, the Sikhs, always jealous of the British, perfectly cognisant of the utterly false military position of their rivals, were doing their utmost to raise the country between Peshǽwar and Kábul, so as to sever them from their supports.

Keenly sensitive now to the fact that the popularity he had hitherto ascribed to the Shah had been unreal, Macnaghten saw that he had only British bayonets to rely upon. He therefore recalled Dennie from Bámián, and sent a force under Sale into the Kohistán to make head against Dost Mahammad and his turbulent sympathisers. Dost Mahammad led Sale a dance. During the entire month of October he flitted about from one place to another, appearing now in the Ghorband valley, now at Nijráo, now in the vicinity of the capital. At last, on the 2nd November, the British force came in sight of him at Parwandarrah. So certain was Sale that he had him, that he lined the hills to prevent his escape. The battle joined. It is needless here to enter into details. Suffice it to say that the swarthy troopers of the 2nd Bengal Cavalry, failing their officers at a critical moment, permitted the Amír to gain a victory so decisive that Sir Alexander Burnes, who was present, wrote from the field of battle to Macnaghten to the effect that there was nothing left for the British force but to fall back on Kábul, and that it was absolutely necessary to concentrate there all the troops that were available!

What Macnaghten would have done had Dost Mahammad used his victory to the utmost can be conjectured from the manner in which at a later date he met the crisis caused by Akbar Khán. This time he was spared the pain of arriving at a decision. The reasons which prompted Dost Mahammad to yield on the morrow of his victory can only be conjectured. It may have been, as Sir John Kaye believes, that, foreseeing his ultimate defeat, he preferred to fall victorious. Possibly, knowing well the nature of the Afgháns, and aware that the country, though seething, was not yet wound up to the pitch of revolt, he preferred to await in captivity the summons which he saw looming in the future. The fact remains, that on the evening of the day after the battle, as Mr. Macnaghten was returning from his evening ride, an Afghán approached him and told him abruptly that the Amír was at hand. "What Amir?" asked Macnaghten. "Dost Mahammad Khán," was the reply, and immediately afterwards Dost Mahammad, who had ridden from the field of battle with this one attendant, stood before him.

The surrender was complete. Dost Mahammad, courteously received, wrote to his sons exhorting them to follow his example. A week later he was conducted under a strong escort to honourable exile in India.

Again were the hopes of Macnaghten in the ascendant. Once more was the choice offered him of pursuing the course which policy demanded. The Sadozye prince was on the throne; the Barúkzye leader was an exile. What need was there of British bayonets unless to support on the throne a prince unacceptable to the people?

Unhappily the system adopted by Macnaghten—the system of concentrating in his own hands all the power of the state—had alienated from the government of Shah Shújah all the great feudal chiefs of the land. Even the Dúranis, the kinsfolk and tribesmen of the Shah, had revolted against a policy which excluded them from power and influence. That power, that influence, and all the patronage belonging thereto, were virtually exercised by the infidel strangers. Not for this had the great clans asserted their freedom under Ahmad Shah. Not for this had they blinded Zamán and expelled Mahmúd—not, that under the nominal rule of a puppet they might become the servants of the infidel.

The surrender and deportation of Dost Mahammad did not then really affect the vital points at issue. The fact that, subsequent to the surrender and the deportation, the discontent spread more widely and rooted itself more deeply in the hearts of the people, ought to have satisfied Macnaghten that something more than a dynastic question was involved. To fairly test the original British policy the British should have left Afghánistán with Dost Mahammad. It was the last chance afforded them of leaving it with honour.

The first event to disturb the tranquillity which, it was fondly hoped, had been secured by the deportation of Dost Mahammad, was a rising in Zamindáwar, headed by one Aktar Khán, and secretly fomented, it was said, by the Shah, with the view of shaking himself free from the British yoke. This, after a first show of success, was only suppressed by a detachment of British troops sent from Kandáhár.

It happened that at this time there was a man at Kandáhár whose great abilities and keen insight into character had enabled him to form a just view of the situation. This was Captain (now Sir Henry) Rawlinson. The duties which devolved upon him had satisfied him as to the false position occupied by the British. Evidence was in his hands that the disturbance referred to in the preceding paragraph had been fomented by Shah Shújah himself. He wrote his convictions, and he enclosed the evidence, to Macnaghten. Macnaghten showed them to the Shah. Shah Shújah feigned indignation and hoodwinked Macnaghten. The only consequence of the remonstrance was the removal of certain officials, and a promise made by the Shah that he would visit Kandáhár in the autumn.

The year 1841 dawned ominously for the British. The Khaibaris were murmuring, and the Ghilzais showed symptoms that they were tired of infidel rule. An expedition to repress the former was actually being organized by Colonel Shelton. Macnaghten knew this, yet so blinded was his judgment by the minor instincts to which I have more than once referred, that he actually wrote at this period (February 1841), "All things considered, the present tranquillity of the country is, to my mind, perfectly marvellous."

I must hurry over the proofs which time was to give of the existence of this marvellous tranquillity. Shelton suppressed the revolt in the Názián valley. But the rising of the Ghilzais was more serious. Embittered by the capture, for an alleged insult to a British officer, of a small fort belonging to them within two miles of Kalát-i-Ghilzai, and of the slaughter of its chief and fifteen of his followers, they rose *en masse*, attacked the British force sent against them under Colonel Wymer, and only gave way at 10 p.m. after a very severe contest. Defeated, they were far from being subdued, and to aid them, Aktar Khán—the former rebel of Zamindáwar—again rose with a following of six thousand men, in the neighbourhood of Girishk.

Thanks to the energy of Nott and his lieutenants, both these rebellions were suppressed; and on the

2nd August following, Macnaghten, cheery and confident, recorded his opinion that the British "prospects are most cheering; and, with the materials we have, there ought to be little or no difficulty in the management of the country." This opinion, concurred in by many of his subordinates, was not shared by the wiser portion. Rawlinson opposed it; Nott even denounced it; D'Arcy Todd, perceiving that British protection was more dreaded by the rulers of Herát than Persian domination, had withdrawn his mission from Herát rather than continue to pay large sums which he knew to be diverted to aims subversive of the views of his Government.*

Cheering as the prospects were, in the eyes of Macnaghten, yet even Macnaghten must have been conscious that in dealing with a country like Afghánistán, and with a people like the Afgháns, a very small matter suffices to produce a storm. Disregarding, if not forgetting, the symptoms displayed by the tribes of the passes in 1839–40, the envoy, in the autumn of 1841, determined, in deference to the urgent calls made upon him by the Home Government and the Government of India to retrench his expenditure, to curtail the annual subsidies guaranteed to the tribes, guardians of the passes. For this purpose he summoned the chiefs of those tribes to Kábul, and informed them that the necessities of the state required that their annual stipends should be reduced.

* For thus withdrawing his mission Todd was disavowed and removed from political employment.

The chiefs received the announcement without a murmur, but they did not the less act as though they regarded it as an infringement of a solemn compact. They immediately passed the word to their adherents that the communications with India were to be interrupted.

It is impossible to palliate or even to explain the fatuity which directed so costly an economy. D'Arcy Tod had been removed from political employ, because he had protested against the payment to the infamous Kámrán of a sum used mainly by him to subsidize our enemies. Economy being necessary, it would have been far wiser to withdraw that annual payment, than to endanger our communications at a very time when the maintenance of our position in Afghánistán depended on our army, and on our army alone.

Yet at the very moment when the tribes of the passes were alienated, the northern parts of Afghánistán were again in commotion. Akbar Khán was on the Bámián frontier; disaffection was rife in the Kohistán, in Zúrmut, in Kábul itself. And now to these hostile indications were added the gathering of the Ghilzais on the Kábul river.

An incident which occurred at this period, less than a month before the outbreak of the storm, ought to have warned the envoy and his assistants of the fate they had prepared for themselves. On the 3rd October, Burnes, knowing that the passes were blocked up, wrote to an officer, Captain Gray, who was about to return with a small detachment to India, and advised him to join himself to a chief who, with four hundred men, was about to march to Laghmán. Gray marched with the chief, Mahammad Uzín Khán, and he owed it to his chivalrous assistance that he made his journey in safety. Mahammad Uzín saved Gray and his detachment, but, in the frankness of friendship, he informed his English comrade that "all Afghánistán was determined to get rid of the Feringhis, and that the whole country was ready to break out." Gray sent the information to Burnes, and Burnes received it.

Still, matters were allowed to go on as if the situation were secure. But there soon came warnings of the storm. On the night of the 9th October the 35th Native Infantry, commanded by Colonel Monteath, and encamped at Bútkak, nine miles from Kábul, was suddenly attacked in force. The attack was repulsed, and Sale, marching from Kábul, cleared the passes. The 35th Native Infantry, remaining encamped and isolated at Bútkak, was again attacked, and again repulsed the enemy, on the 17th. Sale, aware now of the error he had committed in leaving that regiment isolated, joined it on the 20th with the rest of his brigade, and began his march for the Tazín valley.

On entering the valley on the 22nd there ensued with the Ghilzais a skirmish, which, though badly managed by the British general, who was non-efficient from a wound, impressed the Afghán leaders with the idea of their enemy's power. They therefore determined to avoid by a ruse the punishment they had evoked, and they actually succeeded in beguiling the political officer with Sale's force, Captain Macgregor, to persuade the general to accept their submission, on condition that their fort should be spared. The opportunity of inflicting a blow where it was most necessary to strike was thus lost by the political officer. When it offered again it was lost by the commander.

Sale, though one of the most gallant of men, was no general. In the march from the Tazin valley to Gandamak more than one splendid opportunity was offered him to strike a deadly blow at the Ghilzais—a blow which would annihilate them. He missed them all, not because he did not wish to strike—for since the transaction related in the preceding paragraph he had become convinced of the perfidy of the Afgháns—but because the opportunities were invisible to him. He reached Gandamak on the 30th October.

On the 2nd November the storm burst in its full fury on Macnaghten and the English. The tale has often been told, and I can find no space for it here. It found its victims totally unprepared. The envoy had denuded Kábul of his best troops. The remainder were commanded by a worn-out invalid, incapable of forming a firm resolution, equally incapable of acting upon one formed for him by another. What sort of a man the envoy was these pages have shown. Possessing considerable ability, he had, nevertheless, trained his intellect to believe that to be true which he wished to be true; and he persisted to the last, despite of the most glaring evidence of bad faith, in trusting the Afgháns.

The natural results followed. With division everywhere and self-reliance nowhere, it was impossible to effect great things. There was, in fact, no command.

The measures which had been resolved upon one moment were cancelled an hour later; and this indecision, commencing in the tent of the general, had a fatal effect upon the officers and men. Credulity continued to the very last. The most open marks of hostility on the part of the Afgháns served but to induce the British leaders to pretend a greater confidence in their good faith. This confidence was disturbed neither by the murder of Burnes within the city, nor by the assassination of the envoy at a conference by Akbar Khán. Notwithstanding these undoubted proofs, and others scarcely less significant, of determined hostility, the leaders of the British force —a force numbering, all told, nearly five thousand* men—suffered themselves to be beguiled to trusting to the promises of the Afgháns rather than to the bayonets of their soldiers. To use the emphatic language of an officer who, young then, had already displayed signs of the ability which he brought to such ripe results in later years—the late Sir Henry Havelock, himself one of those who had accompanied Sale to Gandamak,—"they credulously confided in Afghán faith, moved in the power and at the dictation of Akbar Khán, took up the positions he pointed out, forbore to fire on the partisans he had arrayed to destroy them; and, as much to the last the dupes of intrigue and treachery as the victims of the sword, cold, hunger and fatigue, were engulfed in the eastern Ghilzai moun-

* The force consisted of 4,500 fighting men, of whom 700 were Europeans. There were besides the wives and children of the officers and men, and 12,000 native camp followers.

tains." In the first month of 1842 there survived of the entire British force only the prisoners and hostages taken by Akbár Khán, and one man, Dr. Brydon, who had escaped to Jalálábád.

Thus ended, practically, the attempt of the British Government to foist upon an independent people a king previously rejected by that people, governing by means of British agents, and supported on his throne by British bayonets. It is true that the British did not lose entire hold of the country. They kept Jalálábád and Kandáhár against all the forces which the Afgháns could bring against them. A few months later Kábul was reoccupied, and the captives and hostages were recovered by the avenging armies of Nott and Pollock. It would be foreign to my purpose to enter into the military details of these events. The British soldiers met with no real difficulty in reoccupying the country, but they evacuated it after they had vindicated their prestige and shown their power.

The unhappy Shah Shújah did not long survive the destruction of the supports upon which he had so long rested. Enticed out of his palace, on the 4th April, by the fierce feudal chiefs raised by the successful insurrection to the summit of affairs, he was waylaid and shot dead. Until the 15th September following—the date on which Kábul was reoccupied by the avenging army of Pollock—anarchy was so far rampant that the supreme authority was held in abeyance. Accompanying General Pollock's force was the second son of Shah Shújah, Fathi Jang—a young man who, escaping from Kábul at the time of his father's assassination, had deemed himself happy in being able to join, clothed in tatters, the British force at Gandamak, on the 1st September. This unhappy prince was now placed by the British authorities on the throne of Kábul, but he was, at the same time, emphatically warned that he was to expect no assistance, neither in money, nor in men, nor in arms, from the British Government. On these terms Fathi Jang accepted his father's throne. A little later he shared his father's fate.

Meanwhile Dost Mahammad, awarded an annual income of two lakhs of rupees, had lionised India. He had been shown our arsenals, our ships, our industries, our courts of justice, and our troops. He had witnessed the order, the contentment, the just administration, prevailing throughout Hindústán. He had lived in Calcutta, but, the climate not agreeing with him, he had proceeded to the hill station of Misúri. Thence he was summoned, 25th October 1842, by the order of Lord Ellenborough, to return, so soon as the armies of Pollock and Nott should have recrossed the Indus, to his native country.

He returned; was received by Shir Singh, King of Láhor, with respect; then prosecuting his journey to Kábul, entered that city, and quietly and unostentatiously resumed the office of which, nearly three years previously, the British had deprived him. No attempt had been made, during his absence, to occupy his seat. It had been reserved specially for him. He returned the elect of the people, the chosen leader, to whom alone they were prepared to tender homage.

Such was the closing scene of the premature and ill-conducted attempt of the British upon Afghánistán. It failed, and it deserved to fail. It failed because, first, it had for its principle the foisting upon the Afghán people of a king whom they did not want; secondly, because the English agents sent with that king concentrated in their own hands the government of the country, making him appear a cypher to his subjects; and, thirdly, though to a less degree, because the danger to combat which the expedition was undertaken, was distant, intangible, and imaginary. Time has changed many things since that stirring period. Extreme caution has taken the place of recklessness in our councils; the danger which was then distant, intangible, and imaginary, is now close at hand, real, threatening. That that danger must be met all are agreed. I am much mistaken if an application of the sounder portion of our past policy to the improved territorial position we have acquired since 1842 fail to indicate clearly the method by which we may influence the Afghán people to become, in very deed, "the friends of our friends and the enemies of our enemies."

CHAPTER XI.

HISTORICAL.—AFGHANISTAN FROM 1842 TO 1869.

THE first seven years following the return of the Amír may be described as politically uneventful. His brothers resumed their rule at Kandáhár. His father's murderer, the infamous Kámrán of Herát, was himself murdered that same year (1842), by his not less infamous minister, Yár Mahammad. The territories now known as Afghán Túrkistán and Badakhshán were virtually independent. The Amír had returned only to the position which he had left, the sovereignty over Kabúl up to the Hindú Kúsh, and of Ghazní. The natural tendency of the rulers of Kandáhár and Herát was still to place their dependence upon Persia.

The conquest of Sindh by the British in 1843, by bringing that people near his frontier, very much weakened the power for intrigue possessed till then by Kohandil Khán, the representative Barúkzye at Kandáhár; and the annexation by the same people of the Panjáb in 1849, had upon him a not less sobering influence.

That annexation Dost Mahammad had striven his utmost to prevent. During the life and death struggle between the British and the Sikhs in 1848–49, he had, at the head of a body of troops, traversed the Khaibar pass, occupied the Pesháwar valley, and had detached two thousand of his best horsemen, commanded by one of his sons, to aid the Sikh chieftains, then hoping much in consequence of the indecisive battle they had fought at Chilianwála. Those horsemen took part in the battle of Gújrát, but though, it is said, they attempted to imitate a manœuvre they had learned from the English, by making a détour, and then dashing down with a swoop on the English general and his staff, their plans were detected and foiled by the British cavalry, notably by the Sindh horse, and they were driven from the field. Pursued without intermission by Sir Walter Gilbert, they did not halt even at Jamrúd, but galloped helter-skelter into the Khaibar, whither the Amír had preceded them, beaten, baffled, and humiliated. The annexation of the Panjáb, in spite of himself and his horsemen, the exchange of a neighbour falling to pieces, for one united, powerful, and civilised, by no means tended to decrease the enmity of the Amír towards the British. Neighbours as they had become for some years, he avoided all intercourse with his former enemy, and throughout that period he never ceased to incite the tribes of the passes to annoy the British by perpetual hostilities.

The year following the annexation of the Panjáb by the British, the Amír crossed the Hindú Kúsh to re-assert Afghán authority in the provinces south of the

Oxus. In this expedition he entirely succeeded, and thenceforth he could reckon Afghán Túrkistán and Badakhshán as integral portions of his dominions.

Herát and Kandáhár still continued, however, to give him annoyance. The intrigues of Persia were constantly directed to the recovery of the important district represented by the former, and in these intrigues she was well served by the nobles, who seemed to live only to struggle there for supremacy. Yár Mahammad, the assassin of Kámrán, was in his turn murdered. His son, Syud Mahammad Khán, succeeded him, but shortly went mad. The nominal successor of this prince was Mahammad Yúsúf; but having selected as his vizier a man, Esau Khán, cleverer than himself, he was soon dethroned. His place was naturally occupied by Esau Khán, and under the sway of this astute intriguer the suzerainty of Persia would have become almost an accomplished fact, but for the warnings which the British Government of the day caused to be communicated and repeated to that power.

But though the warnings of the British Government checked the actual movements, they failed to stop the intrigues of Persia alike with Herát and Kandáhár. These in the end so affected Dost Mahammad that they caused him to forget his enmity to the British, and opening negotiations with them, he agreed, in 1854, to detach his son, Gholám Haidar Khán, to Peshávar, to conclude a treaty of alliance with his ancient enemies.

Gholám Haidar came to Peshávar. The Government of India was represented by the Chief Commissioner of the Panjáb, Mr., now Lord, Lawrence. The articles of this treaty were but three in number. The first provided for "perpetual peace and friendship" between the Amír of Kábul and his heirs on one side and the East India Company on the other. By the second, the said Company engaged to respect the Afghán territory, and never to interfere therein. By the third, the Amír entered into a like engagement with respect to the territory of the Company, and promised in addition "to be the friend of the friends and enemy of the enemies of the Honourable East India Company."

This treaty marks a sensible departure from the position of isolation maintained up to that time by the Amír of Kábul. It shows that he felt, and felt acutely, that which all the Moghol rulers of Kábul had felt before him, that Afghánistán and Hindústán had need of each other. On this occasion the need was felt by Afghánistán, or rather by the northern and eastern parts of Afghánistán, and the need was felt in consequence of the stealthy endeavours of a neighbour to attract to herself the really fertile and valuable portions of the rocky country.

If the Amír had hoped that his alliance with England would put an immediate stop to Persian intrigues he was disappointed. Those intrigues continued, and culminated in the march of a Persian army to Herát, and by the surrender of the city to that army in October 1856.

But the British alliance was not useless. On the

1st November following, the English Government declared war against Persia, and followed up that declaration by the despatch of a fleet and army to the Persian gulf.

Into the operations of that fleet and of that army it is not necessary to enter. It will suffice to state that they were successful; that Persia, beaten on her own territory, was humiliated; and that on the 4th March 1857 the representative of the Shah signed, at Paris, an agreement by which the Shah pledged himself to renounce all claim of sovereignty over Herát and over Afghánistán.

Before that agreement had been signed, but not before the issue of the war with Persia had been made certain, the Chief Commissioner of the Panjáb, Sir John Lawrence, and Colonel Herbert Edwardes, had met the Amír, Dost Mahammad, at Pesháwar, and had conferred with him regarding the most practicable method of cementing a strong alliance and a good understanding between British India and Afghánistán. Lord Lawrence has since stated that the Amír objected very strongly to the idea which had been mooted of sending a British officer to Kábul to act there as agent for his government. But by the fourth article of the treaty the Amír agreed, under the actual circumstances, to the deputation of British officers, with suitable native establishments, to Kábul, or Kandáhár, or Balkh, or all three places, or wherever an Afghán army might be assembled to act against the Persians. The fourth article then proceeded as follows: "It will be their duty to see generally that the subsidy granted to the Amír be devoted to the military purposes for which it is given, and to keep their own government informed of all affairs. They will have nothing to do with the payment of the troops, or advising the Kábul government; and they will not interfere in anyway in the internal administration of the country. The Amír will be responsible for their safety and honourable treatment while in his country, and for keeping them acquainted with all military and political matters connected with the war."

The first of the articles of the treaty, thirteen in number, provided that as the Shah of Persia had, contrary to his engagement with the British Government, taken Herát, and had manifested an intention to interfere with the other possessions of the Amír, therefore, the British Government, being at war with Persia, would aid the Amír to defend his possessions, and would grant him for that purpose a monthly allowance of ten thousand pounds.

The second and third articles related to mere details. The fourth I have already quoted. The fifth provided for the appointment by the Amír of a vakil to reside at Pesháwar. The sixth and seventh provided that the monthly allowance should cease with the war, or at the pleasure of the Indian Government; that on its cessation the British officers should be withdrawn from Afghánistán; but that a native vakil, not a British officer, might remain at Kábul. The remaining six articles related to matters in no way material.

In consequence of the fourth article of this treaty a

mission composed of three British officers was deputed to Kandáhár early in 1857. These officers were in Kandáhár when the news that a mutiny had broken out in India reached that place. Gholám Haidar Khán the governor of the city, sent a message, then, to the Amír, telling him that news had arrived that all the English in India had been murdered, adding: "Had I not better cut the throats of these three?" The reply of the Amír showed that his exile in Hindústán had not been without some advantage to him. "It is useless," he answered; "I know these English well. It may be true that all those in India have been murdered, but they will come in thousands from beyond the sea, and reconquer the country. Better leave these three alone." They were accordingly permitted to remain and to return in safety.

The city and districts of Herát had devolved after the Persian war on Ahmad Khán, a nephew of the Amír, nominally as an independent holding. But Persia, though beaten in 1857, had not renounced her love of intrigue; and Ahmad Khán, to protect himself against the Amír, had virtually agreed to recognise the Shah of Persia as his suzerain. The Amír was not at all inclined to tolerate this intrusion, and he finally settled matters by marching with an army against Herát and storming it, thus re-uniting western and eastern Afghánistán—for Kandáhár and Girishk had previously acknowledged him—under the rule of one man. Nine days after the Amír had entered Herát as a conqueror—9th June 1863—he died.

Of the sons who survived Dost Mahammad, the five

eldest, ranking in the order in which I have placed them, were Afzúl Khán, Azim Khán, sons of one mother, and Shir Ali Khán, Shárif Khán, and Amín Khán, likewise maternally related. Besides these were Aslam Khán and Húsén Khán, to be presently referred to. Gholám Haidar, who had been designated as heir of the Amír, had died in 1858, and the Amír had then notified to the Government of India that he had nominated Shir Ali to be his successor. This notification was received and the nomination was recognised by the government of Lord Canning.

The reasons for the selection of Shir Ali, in preference to Afzúl and Azím, were patent. What Afzúl Khán was, preceding pages of this history have indicated.* Dost Mahammad had judged him from his behaviour after the fall of Ghazní and in the country round Bámián in 1839–40. Azim Khán stood, certainly not higher, in his opinion. Morally he was regarded as vile, even in Afghánistán. Neither possessed the force of character necessary to keep together, to control, a people like the Afgháns. Shir Ali, though possibly not equal to either Akbar Khán or Gholám Haidar, as they had been, was still superior to the elder survivors. Though cruel, ungrateful, and self-seeking, he possessed tenacity of purpose and cool courage. If, therefore, a son of Dost Mahammad were to succeed his father, it was inevitable that that son should be Shir Ali.

Shir Ali at once notified his accession to the office of

* *Vide* pp. 377 to 400.

Amír to the government of India, expressing his intention of "following the laudable example of his father in maintaining the strong ties of amity and friendship subsisting between the British Government and the Afghán state." Lord Elgin was then Governor-General. Simultaneously with Shir Ali's notification came rumours—but only rumours—that the discarded brothers were preparing to contest his claims. These rumours, which had but slight foundation at the time, caused Lord Elgin to hesitate. He determined "to wait further information before taking a formal step in acknowledgment of Shir Ali."

Taking into consideration the fact that Shir Ali was then *de facto* ruler; that no outbreak had actually occurred, and that any such outbreak would have been rebellion; that the message of Shir Ali was courteous and friendly; the reticence of the Indian Government cannot be too greatly deplored. We have seen how, step by step, Dost Mahammad had shaken off his mistrust of the British government until at last a cordial friendship had been cemented. The first advances of his successor were met by a rebuff. The silence of Lord Elgin could only have been regarded by Shir Ali as a warning that the British did not intend to continue to him the cordial friendship they had promised to his father.

Lord Elgin died in the autumn of 1863, and his place was temporarily taken by Sir William Denison. Meanwhile no disturbance amounting to rebellion had broken out in Afghánistán. Sir William Denison, then, six months after the receipt of Shir Ali's letter, acknowledged it—not in the warm and friendly terms employed by Shir Ali, but in the stilted language of cold officialism.

On receiving the acknowledgment the Amír once again evinced the importance he attached to the friendship of the British by requesting the Viceroy, in a friendly way, to supply him with six thousand muskets of which he had need. He asked likewise that his eldest son, Mahammad Ali, might receive in official correspondence his title of heir apparent; and he further solicited pardon for the brother of one of the chief functionaries at the Court of Kábul—that brother having been sentenced in Calcutta to seven years' transportation for receiving stolen property.

At the time that these requests were received, Sir John, now Lord, Lawrence had taken up the office of Viceroy. Lord Lawrence granted pardon to the offending brother; agreed to recognise Mahammad Ali as heir apparent; but refused the muskets.

When, three months later, April 1864, the two brothers, Afzúl Khán and Azím Khán, broke out into rebellion, the government of India refused to regard their outbreak in any other light than as civil war—to be fought to the bitter end between the brothers. They announced in fact that they were prepared to recognise, and to treat with, as ruler of Afghánistán, any one of the brothers who should establish himself on the throne of that country. This was the policy to which was accorded the name of masterly inactivity.

In pursuing this policy, Lord Lawrence had the support of the able men by whom he was surrounded in

India. From an English point of view, and narrowing the transaction to a dealing between England and Afghánistán, there was at the time much to be said in its favour. But it is impossible not to see that Shir Ali must have regarded it as selfish and unfriendly, as indicating a determination of the English to side only with the members of his family who for the time should be the strongest.

The question may be asked, how should the English have acted? An armed intervention was out of the question. There was no certainty that Shir Ali would gain the day. By helping him, the English would have made an enemy of his rivals. And if his rivals had won?

There is but one natural reply to these questions. The only support that could be given to Shir Ali was moral support—support to him as the ruler we had recognised; compliance with his demands, so far as such compliance did not involve us in actual hostilities; and refusal to recognise his rivals until he should have been absolutely effaced.

The actual policy pursued may be stated in a few words. In the course of the nearly five years' contest which followed the rebellion of April 1864, the advances made by Shir Ali to the India Government were uniformly received with coldness; whilst his brothers, on obtaining temporary occupation of the capital and its environs, were successively recognised as *de facto* rulers of that portion of the country.

The actual course of the events of the rebellion may be thus briefly sketched. At the time of the death of the Amír Dost Mahammad, his son Afzúl Khán was at Balkh, governing Afghán Turkistán; Afzul's brother, Azím, was at Fort Kúrm, governing the districts of Kost and Kúrm, adjoining the British frontier; Sharíf Khán, brother by the same mother to Shir Ali, governed Farrah and Girishk; whilst the fourth, Amín Khán, similarly related to the Amír, governed Kandáhár.

At first none of these four brothers showed any inclination to question their dead father's will. But at the end of August 1863, the Amír heard, when at Ghazní, that all was not right in Kúrm. He accordingly turned his course into that country, and forced Azím Khán to swear fealty to him. During the remaining months of 1863 order remained undisturbed throughout the country.

In April of the following year, both Afzúl and Azím rebelled. The Amír boldly met them, crushed, by means of one of his generals, Mahammad Rafik, the insurrection of Azím, whom he forced to take refuge in British territory; and, crossing himself the Hindú Kúsh, marched upon Afzúl.

The advance guard of the Amír's army engaged indecisively the advance guard of Afzúl Khán's army at Bájgah—the Bájgah so famous in 1840. Two days later, Mahammad Rafik joined the Amír, and Afzúl sued for peace. The Amír was merciful—too merciful —for he not only granted Afzúl peace, but restored him to his government.

But whilst the Amír yet remained in Afghán Túrkistán, on good terms with Afzúl, intelligence reached him that the son of Afzúl, Abdúl Rahmán, whom he had summoned to his court, had fled across the Oxus to Bokhára. Suspecting this evasion to be part of a preconcerted plot, he instantly caused Afzúl Khán to be seized and fettered. In his place he nominated his nephew, Fathi Mahammad, to be governor of the districts south of the Oxus.

The Amír was now apparently triumphant. But the insult offered to his father rankled in the mind of Abdúl Rahmán, and he incited the Amír of Bokhára to espouse his cause. Before the winter snows of 1864–65 had melted in the passes of the Hindú Kúsh, Shir Ali knew that the coming spring was pregnant with danger.

The danger came, first from the side of Kandáhár, caused by the revolt of Sharíf Khan. The tribes of the Kúrm country were at the same time roused by Azím Khán, who, on a sign from the conspirators, had crossed the British border.

Again did the Amír boldly face the danger. Mahammad Rafik cleared Kúrm whilst he marched on Kandáhár. The rebels, led by two of his brothers, Sharíf and Amín, and a nephew, Jalál-ú-dín, met him at Kújbaz, near Kalát-i-Ghilzai. The battle that followed was most hotly contested. In the height of the conflict the Amír's eldest son, Mahammad Ali, fell by the hand of his uncle, Amín Khán. Instantly the uncle paid for the bloody deed with his life, and the rebel army, disconcerted, fled in disorder.

This victory, great as it was, decisive as it might have been made, was more than tarnished, in the eyes of the Amír, by the death of his son. "It clouded all his joys;" it plunged him into a state of melancholy almost akin to madness. For months he paid no attention to affairs. In this state he remained, at Kandáhár, indifferent to all around him, not roused to action even by the intelligence that the rebels, gathering heart, and reinforced by levies from Túrkistán and Bokhára, were marching upon Kábul, and that his own friends were falling from him. But at last, when his lethargy had seemed to attain the condition of confirmed lunacy, the news of the occupation of Kábul by the rebels roused him to action. He then set out to meet them.

Who were these rebels? The victory of Kújbáz had been decisive enough to break up the conspiracy. On its morrow Sharíf Khán sued for pardon, Azím Khán had fled to plot renewed treason in British territory. The Amír, despite of his bitter grief, had been merciful—he had pardoned the revolters.

But, during his lethargy, Abdúl Rahmán, the exile at Bokhára, had been active. Aided by the Amír of that country, he raised levies, crossed the Oxus, corrupted the lieutenants of Shír Ali in Afghán Túrkistán, drew over to himself the Amír's best general, Mahammad Rafik, and, joined by the plotter Azím Khán, from his asylum in British territory, entered Kábul, 2nd March 1865.

This was the intelligence which roused the Amír from his stupor. With a force of about fourteen thousand men, five thousand of whom were horsemen, and twenty-five guns, he marched by way of Ghazní on the capital, and on the 9th May came up with the rebel army, strongly intrenched at Shékhábád.

The rebels had the advantage of numbers, of position, of fighting behind intrenchments. Shir Ali had in his favour the inspiration which attack always confers. He led his troops against the intrenchments with a valour not to be surpassed. Thrice repulsed, he charged a fourth time with so much vigour that the position was almost forced, when, at a critical moment, the levies he had raised at Kandáhár went over to the rebels. This desertion lost the Amír the battle. He fled from the field, followed by only five hundred horsemen.

Up to this time his half-brother Afzúl had been a prisoner—latterly in Ghazní. The commandant of that fortress, shutting its gates in the face of the defeated Amír, released the prisoner and restored him to his son, Abdúl Rahmán. From that moment Afzúl Khán assumed his position as chief of the triumphant conspirators. Entering Kábul, he usurped the dignity and office of Amír. The Múnshi, who then represented the Government of India at Kábul, received, shortly afterwards, instructions to present himself to the usurper and offer him the usual congratulations.

Meanwhile Shir Ali, collecting his partisans at a place beyond Ghazní, had assured them that, whilst under no circumstances would he renounce the office of Amír, he left them free to follow their inclinations. He then continued his flight to Túrkistán, raised there a second army, and marched with it towards Kábul. From the capital, to meet him, issued Abdúl Ráhman, son of the usurper Afzúl. This chief manœuvred with so much ability that he managed to interpose between the two corps into which the Amír had divided his army, fell upon that not led by the Amír, at Kila Alladád, on the 13th September 1867, and totally defeated it. The Amír, disheartened by this fatal mishap, hastily retreated through the passes.

Three weeks after this battle the usurper, on whose behalf it had been fought, died. Before his death the British Government had informed him that whilst they could not recognise him as ruler of provinces, such as those of Kandáhár and Herát, still in the possession of Shir Ali, they would be glad to have him as a friend if he were able to consolidate his power in the country.*

Afzúl Khán was succeeded in his usurpation by his brother Azím Khán, whose accession was likewise recognised by the Government of India. But his tenure of Kábul did not last long. In January 1868, the Amír left Túrkistán for Herát, and advanced on Kandáhár in the month of June following. There he was received as a deliverer. His generals, marching thence on the capital, took the Bálá Hissar by storm. He

* The concluding words of the British despatch are: "My friend! the relations of this Government are with the actual rulers of Afghánistán. If your Highness is able to consolidate your Highness's power in Kábul, and is sincerely desirous of being a friend and ally of the British Government, I shall be ready to accept your Highness as such, but I cannot break the existing engagements with Amír Shír Ali Khán, and must continue to treat him as the ruler of that portion of Afghánistán over which he retains control. Sincerity and fair dealing induce me to write thus plainly and openly to your Highness."

followed thither shortly after, forced the usurper* to seek refuge once more in British territory, inflicted upon Abdúl Rahmán, in January 1869, a crushing and decisive defeat, and recovered all the dominions bequeathed to him by his father. The credit for the success of the Amír in this victorious campaign was due mainly to three of his nearest relatives; to his son Yákúb Khan; to his brother Aslam Khán; and to his nephew Ishmáil, son of Amín Khán.

Thus, without external assistance, in spite of the recognition by the British of his rivals in the hour of their temporary success, did Shir Ali vindicate the prescience of his father and win by the sword the throne to which he had succeeded by right—as right is known to the Afgháns. In 1869 he was undisputed Amír of Afghánistán—a ruler stronger, more to be dreaded as an enemy or courted as an ally, than had been the Shir Ali of 1863.

With the triumph of 1868 closes the first troubled period of Shir Ali's reign. To understand the remainder it will be necessary to devote a chapter to the consideration of Russian policy in Central Asia from the year 1854 to the present time.

* He, Azím Khán, died subsequently in exile.

CHAPTER XII.

HISTORICAL.

RUSSIAN AND ENGLISH POLICY IN CENTRAL ASIA.

In a previous chapter of this history I have stated that it was the phantom of Russian aggression which caused the expedition to Kábul in 1839. Whatever ideas the Czar may have entertained on the subject of an eastern extension of his empire prior to that period, his frontiers were too remote, the intermediate distance to be traversed by his legions was too great, to necessitate action on the part of the British, politically premature, and in a military point of view unsound. It must always be recollected, when referring to the policy of 1838–41, that Afghánistán was then separated from India by three powerful and independent states: by the Panjáb, by Sind, and by Bilúchistán. Granting, too, as I am prepared to grant, that the idea of the conquest of Central Asia had taken in the mind of the Czar the form of a project to be accomplished in a distant future, it is certain that he never entertained the idea of immediate action, deeming the possession of Constantinople or the breaking-down of the barriers of the Caucasus an indispensable preliminary to its execution.

The Czar struck his blow for Constantinople in 1854, failed, and died. The idea did not die with him. But the road to Constantinople being temporarily barred, his successor, the present Czar, the inheritor of all his father's projects, made a determined effort to overthrow the barrier which shut from him the plains and the deserts, the cities and the rivers, of Central Asia. Hurling, in 1856, one hundred and fifty thousand troops against the passes of the Caucasus, the Czar resolved that this time there should be no playing at soldiers. The consequence was that less than three years after the signature of the Peace of Paris, Schamyl Khán was a prisoner; the strongholds of the Caucasus had been stormed; and the mountaineers, who for long preceding years had successfully defied Russia, had abandoned their native fastnesses to seek shelter in the dominions of the Súltán.

Nor, whilst thus engaged in breaking down the mountain barrier, had Russia been unmindful of the ulterior issues. For some years previously she had been working her way across the low undulating plains which lie between the Alatan range and the Jaxartes. The moment that she had succeeded in pacifying the conquered Caucasus she made the long-considered move in advance. Up to 1863 she had contented herself with creeping along the banks of the Jaxartes. In that year she made her spring across that river. The Khanate of Khokand, with a population of three millions, was the first object of her attack. The capture of the important city of Tchemkend brought her into collision with the troops of Bokhára—a collision which resulted in the defeat of the Amir of that place and the capture of the town of Túrkistán.

This sudden aggressive move on the part of Russia caused considerable anxiety to the governments of England and India, and the Russian government was addressed on the subject. The reply of Prince Gortschakoff, in the form of a manifesto, may be styled, judged by the light of later events, as truly Russian. The capture of Tchemkend and Túrkistán the Prince justified, in that document, on the plea that such a measure had been necessitated by the nomadic and predatory character of the populations on the Russian frontier. Prince Gortschakoff proceeded to imply that the point up to which necessity had forced Russia to advance had been reached. Russia was now, he said, "in the presence of a more solid and compact, less unsettled and better organised social state; fixing for us with geographical precision the limit up to which we are bound to advance and at which we must halt."

This State paper doubtless afforded, as it certainly was intended to afford, great satisfaction to the British Government of the day. If the reader will bear in mind its date, November 1864, and will recollect that at that time the Amír, Shir Ali, was on the eve of the great internecine struggle which lost him for a time his kingdom, he will see additional reason for the intense satisfaction with which the British Government received the assurances of the Russian Chancellor.

"But," as Sir Henry Rawlinson has truly recorded, "the ink was hardly dry with which this manifesto was written, before its pacific promises were completely stultified." The Russians, on the pretext that certain Russian officers, sent to Bokhára to negotiate, had been detained in that city, renewed hostilities with the Amir with greater bitterness than ever. By June 1865 they had conquered Tashkend. Again declaring (September 1865) that the Czar had no desire to add further to his dominions, they resumed hostilities in 1866, captured Khojend, the key of the Jaxartes, and overrunning Khokand, at once annexed one half of that province to their empire, placing the remaining moiety in the hands of a native chief, Khúdyár Khán, to be administered by him on terms which made him a vassal of Russia. Forgetting, or choosing not to remember, his Chancellor's famous manifesto of November 1864, the Czar, by a ukase dated July 1867—a period, be it remembered, when Shir Ali was still struggling for his kingdom,—formally annexed the newly conquered territories to the Russian empire.

Russia had now become the nearest neigbour to Bokhára. Under the pretext of protecting his recently acquired territories, the new Russian commander, General Kaufmann, established a fortified post at a point almost within reach of Samarkand. This constituted a challenge which the Amír of Bokhára could not refuse without sacrificing his independence. He accepted it, and was beaten. The consequence was that Samarkand was occupied by Russian troops, and as the occupation of that place affected the supply of water to Bokhára, the Amír of that place found himself forced to agree to become a tributary of the Czar.

I have now brought the historical sketch of the proceedings of Russia in Central Asia to the time (18th January 1869) when the Amír of Kábul, having vanquished, unaided, all his rivals, had established himself as undisputed ruler of Afghánistán. The four to five years occupied by him in repressing rebellion within his borders had been spent by the Russians in making the phantom of 1838 a reality, in bringing their borders within very easy distance of the river covering the Amír's northern frontier,—the Oxus.

The proximity between the Russian frontier and the frontier of the country which has ever been the outwork of Hindústán, in 1869, would seem to have roused the attention of the British Government, for it was in that year that Lord Clarendon suggested to the Russian Chancellor his famous plan of constituting Afghánistán a neutral zone. Prince Gortschakoff received the idea with enthusiasm, and declared that his master, the Czar, "looks upon Afghánistán as completely outside the sphere within which Russia may be called upon to exercise her influence." The Government of India having objected, and wisely objected, to an arrangement which removed Afghánistán completely from the sphere of British influence, the negotiations on the subject were prolonged for two years, the Russian Government continuing to protest, by the mouth of its Chancellor, that "Russia had no intention of going further south," and that "extension of territory was extension of weakness." Ultimately, Russia agreed to accept the line of the Upper Oxus as the boundary of Afghánistán.

It has since transpired, that whilst Russia was making these and similar protestations, she was planning an expedition against Khiva. Charged with the fact, she denied it over and over again. So explicit in his denial was the Russian Chancellor, that he imposed on the British Ambassador at St. Petersburg. But the truth gradually eked out. In 1872 Lord A. Loftus informed the British Government that he had gained the conviction that such an expedition had been decided upon, and would take place as soon as weather and circumstances would permit. Still the government of the Czar, and the Russian ambassador in London, continued to evade and to deny. Forced at last to admit that there was to be an expedition, they pleaded pathetically that it was to be a very little one. It was to consist of "but four and a half battalions to punish acts of brigandage." "Not only," added the Russian ambassador, "was it far from the intention of the Emperor to take possession of Khiva, but positive orders had been prepared to prevent it." What was the actual result? A few months later, 10th June 1873, Khiva fell; the whole of its territory on the right bank of the Oxus was annexed; the suzerainty of Russia was forced, and an enormous indemnity was imposed, upon the Khán! So much for the solemn promises of Russia! I must beg the reader to bear in mind that it was the fall of this place, and the means by which it fell, that impelled Shir Ali, terrified for his own country, to implore the close alliance of the Viceroy of India, Lord Northbrook, in 1873!

The manner in which the virtual annexation of Khiva, despite the solemn assurances of Russia, was received by the British Government of the day, is astounding. The Secretary for Foreign Affairs, Lord Granville, not only declined to examine "too minutely how far these arrangements were in strict accordance with the assurances given in January by Count Schouvaloff," but, hopeful still, he again addressed the Russian Chancellor on the subject of a clear and frank understanding between the two governments regarding their respective positions in Central Asia. The people of England, knowing what they know now, will not be at all surprised to learn that Prince Gortschakoff expressed in reply his "entire satisfaction" at the "just view Lord Granville had taken."

Having now reviewed the Russian policy in Central Asia up to the crucial year of 1873, I propose to inquire the steps which the Government of India had taken during that period to meet the insidious approach of their country's rival. I have called the year 1873 a "crucial" year not only because it witnessed the capture of Khiva by Russia, but because, also, it roused the keen apprehensions of our ally, Amír Shir Ali, to the danger which was threatening his territories.

In the preceding chapter I have brought the history of Shir Ali up to the year 1868. In the autumn of that year the Amír, having firmly established himself in Afghánistán, requested the Lieutenant Governor of the Panjáb to inform the Viceroy that, with a view to cement a good understanding between the two Governments, it would be a satisfaction te himself if the Viceroy of India would consent to a personal interview with him on the frontier, or at Pesháwar.

Lord Lawrence was willing to grant the interview, but before his reply to that effect could reach Kábul, the throne of the Amír was again jeopardised by the last invasion of Abdúl Rahmán. It was the Amír, then, who was forced by the necessities of his position to decline, for the moment, the interview he had requested.

Only, however, for the moment. The Amír drove Abdúl Rahmán across the Oxus, and in the spring of 1869 he cordially accepted an invitation, transmitted to him by the new Viceroy, the late Earl of Mayo, to meet him at Ambála.

Lord Mayo was, in every respect, a worthy representative of the Queen. To a noble presence, a dignified bearing, an irresistible charm of manner, he added a tact that was perfect, and a judgment of character rarely at fault. He received the Amír at Ambála, and, though unable to guarantee the cordial reciprocity desired by his guest, he won his regard and convinced him of his good will. It was unfortunate that before Lord Mayo had set foot in India the ministry which selected him had been displaced. He was therefore in the position of a Tory agent of Liberal masters. The result was that though he accomplished all that, under the circumstances, could have been accomplished, the actual results fell short of the hopes which the Amír had allowed himself to entertain.* The consequences of that interview and the restraints by which it was accompanied have been clearly set forth by the highest living authority on the Central Asian question. "The visit of Shir Ali to Ambála in 1869," writes Sir Henry Rawlinson,† "on the invitation of the Viceroy, forms an important epoch in the Afghán drama. Had our appreciation of the gravity of the crisis been as matured at that time as it is at the present, the epoch might have been a decisive one; for Shir Ali, though still brooding over his supposed wrongs, was not by any means alienated. He had conceived certain definite hopes and fears, not unreasonable in themselves, and a frank and full acceptance of the position on our part might have won his confidence for ever. Had we been prepared, indeed, in 1869, to undertake the same responsibilities, with a view to retaining a dominant influence at the court of the Amír, to which we have become reconciled

* In his despatch dated May 14, 1869, the Duke of Argyll was even inclined to view "not without some concern" "the expressions used in certain paragraphs of your Excellency's letter to the Amír, which, in so far they stand alone and apart from the verbal explanations I have referred to, may some day be construed by the Amír or by his successors as meaning more than, with those explanations, they were intended to convey." Although the reply of the Earl of Mayo was considered by the Duke to be satisfactory, the fact that the point was raised shows how narrowly his communications with Shir Ali were watched by the Liberal Government.

† "The Nineteenth Century," December 1868.

by later events—had the same terms indeed been offered to Shir Ali at Ambála that have been recently offered at Peshávar—there can be no doubt that we should have heard nothing of Russian interference in Kábul for the present generation at any rate; but public feeling at that time had not been educated up to the point required, and our statesmen, as usual, waited upon public feeling, adhering in the meantime to the old principle of reducing our liability to intervene to the lowest possible limit. The result accordingly of the conference at Ambála, though successful in its main features—inasmuch as Shir Ali, strongly impressed with the magnificence and cordiality of his reception—returned to Kábul a firm and true personal friend of the Viceroy's—cannot be said to have satisfied either one party or the other. The British Government having learned from experience that it was impossible to maintain close relations with the Afghâns, or even to acquire due information of what was passing in the country, except through the agency of its own officers, would have willingly revived with such modifications as the lapse of time rendered necessary, the fourth article of the treaty of 1857 with Dost Mahammad, which provided for the establishment of British officers at Kábul, Kandáhár, and Balkh; and communications in this spirit were accordingly opened with Shir Ali's confidential advisers at Ambála. But although the proposition, which was of far more practical importance to us than any amount of mere friendly profession, appears to have been acquiesced in to the extent of admitting British officers anywhere but at Kábul, still no definite engagement was taken; and ultimately Lord Mayo, finding that the measure was not particularly agreeable either to Shir Ali or his ministers, desisted from its further discussion. Nor did Shir Ali meet with better success in pressing his own personal objects. He had come to Ambála intent on forming an offensive and defensive alliance with the British Government. He expected, on the one hand, to be assured of full protection against Russian aggression which he saw looming in the distance, and, on the other, to be guaranteed against a renewal of his domestic troubles; but on both these heads he was disappointed. All that he could obtain was a vague and general assurance of support. He was told, firstly, that any attempt on the part of his rivals to disturb his position would be viewed by the British Government with 'severe displeasure'; and he was told, secondly, with regard to the risk of external pressure that, 'he would be strengthened from time to time as circumstances would seem to require,' and his applications for assistance would always be received 'with consideration and respect.' And it may be added, as a proof how completely up to this time the home authorities had failed to realise the importance of the Afghán alliance, that even this modified promise of support, barely sufficing as it did to prevent a break-down of the Ambála conference, was very coldly received in England — the Viceroy indeed being directed to discourage any possible expectation of our armed intervention in Shir Ali's favour."

It had been possible at that period, had Lord Mayo's

hands been free, to do much with Shir Ali. I have already stated that he owed the recovery of his throne mainly to three of his closest relatives: to his son, Yákúb Khán; to his brother, Aslam Khán; and to his nephew, Ishmáil Khán. But already, standing in British territory, the suspicion had crept over the mind of Shir Ali, that it was in the power of men who had done so much for him to work as effectually against him. Not at Ambála, not at Pesháwar, not at the entrance to the Khaibar pass, did he feel absolutely certain that he would be permitted to return to his rocky throne. His conduct, when having mustered the necessary resolution, he proceeded to and reached Kábul, betrayed the doubts which had tormented him when in British territory. How did he then treat the three close relatives who had restored him to his throne? Yákúb Khán he enticed, under the most solemn promises of safety, from Herát to Kábul, and then threw him into the dungeon, in which he still lingers. Aslam Khán he caused to be strangled.* Ishmáil Khán, he drove an outlaw to Láhor, where

* The murder of this noble was attended with circumstances of marked brutality. On a sign from the Amír two of his relatives, Kasím Khán and Hásán Khán, proceeded to the dungeon, carrying a rope. As they entered, Aslam Khán, seeing that his hour was come, prepared, in the manner of the Mahomedans, to meet his fate with dignity. The two noble ruffians immediately turned the rope once round his neck, then, each taking an end, they began to pull at it. But in the process their nerves forsook them, their strength failed them, and leaving their work half-done, they went out to procure assistance. A little later, with the aid of two semi-Chinese executioners, they accomplished the horrible deed.

he died. Another brother, Húsén Khán, share the fate of Aslam.

Had the Viceroy been then authorised to guarantee to the Amír and to his dynasty his throne, it is certain that his mind would not have been incited to commit these crimes; and it is not impossible that, uncertain of his throne as he then was, he might have been induced in return for the guarantee, to accept the over-lordship of the British Government.

Still, although neither the Government of India nor Shir Ali obtained all the concessions that either required, the Ambála conference was so far a success that it did obliterate from the mind of the Amír the more bitter recollection of his grievances, and it did induce him to lean upon the British as the power whose interest it was to accord him support. This was clearly proved when, on the capture of Khiva by the Russians in 1873, he instinctively stretched out his hand to the Viceroy and implored him for aid should he too be invaded.

Lord Northbrook was then Viceroy of India—a Liberal serving a Liberal Government. The telegraphic correspondence between the two shows clearly how the situation was appreciated by either.

The following were the messages exchanged:—

"*Telegram from Viceroy to Secretary of State.—Simla, dated 26th July* 1873.—Ameer of Cabul alarmed at Russian progress, dissatisfied with general assurance, and anxious to know how far he may rely on our help if invaded. I propose assuring him that if he unreservedly accepts and acts on our advice in all external relations we will help him with money, arms, and troops, if necessary, to expel unprovoked invasion. We to be the judge of the necessity. Answer by telegraph quickly."

"*Telegram from Secretary of State to the Viceroy.—India Office, dated 26th July* 1873.—Cabinet thinks you should inform Ameer that we do not at all share his alarm, and consider there is no cause for it; but you may assure him we shall maintain our settled policy in favour of Afghánistán if he abides by our advice in external affairs."

In his distress the Amír despatched a special envoy to the Viceroy. Lord Northbrook held a first interview with this envoy on the 12th July, and a second on the 30th. The result of these interviews was that the Amír was informed by letter that the Viceroy did "not entertain any apprehensions to your Highness's territories from without," but that "the British Government will endeavour from time to time, by such means as circumstances may require, to strengthen the Government of your Highness, to enable you to exercise with equity and justice your rightful rule, and to transmit to your descendants all the dignities and honours of which you are the lawful possessor." In the same letter the Amír was reminded of the assurances previously given by Russia as to his country being completely out of the zone of her influence. In his report of these proceedings to the Secretary of State, Lord Northbrook stated that the envoy of the Amír had been informed that "if, in the event of any aggression from without, British influence were invoked, and failed by negotiation to effect a satisfactory settlement, it was probable that the British Government would afford the Amír material assistance in repelling an invader, but that such assistance would be conditional on the Amír following the advice of the British Government, and having himself abstained from aggression." Further, that "as the subject is one of great importance, and the envoy appeared to doubt how far his instructions justified him in committing himself to any definite arrangement, we considered it advisable to postpone the settlement of it to a more favourable opportunity."

Such was the cold comfort given to the Amír in his extremity! Such the solace to the alarm caused in his mind by the capture of Khiva by the Russians! What did the reply of England amount to? To a virtual profession of belief in the assurances of Russia —to a vague promise, not of relief itself, but of the probability of relief!

To paint exactly the effect of this reply on the mind of the Amír, I must again quote from Sir Henry Rawlinson. The Amír "foresaw," says that high authority, "that there must ultimately be a collision between England and Russia in Central Asia; that he must, therefore, make his election between the opposing forces, and cast in his lot either with the assailants or the defence. Our hinted support would not meet the exigency of the case. An unlimited support we were not prepared to grant, and, moreover, to accept such support, administered as it must have been by British officers, would be to sacrifice his independence and to sink for ever to the level of the vassal princes of India. To connect himself, on the other hand, with Russia would be to secure the safeguard of a European guarantee against further pressure from England, whilst the distance and comparative weakness of the guaranteeing power would leave him free from any real control; and there would also be the prospect of a share in the spoils, and even of an increase of territory, in the event of a successful descent on India by the allies. Shir Ali may not have jumped to this conclusion at once, nor, indeed, have been exclusively influenced by such considerations in determining his future course; but it would certainly appear that his studied and sustained discourtesy to us from the time of the Simla conference was the result of deliberation and not of accident, and was as much due to encouragement held out to him from beyond the Oxus as to pique and disappointment at the treatment he had received from England. At this time, indeed, commenced that interchange of friendly communication, both by letter and agents, between Tashkend and Kábul, which, in spite of the official assurances five times repeated at St. Petersburg, that Afghánistán was altogether beyond the scope of Russia's Asiatic relations, was ever afterwards actively maintained, and which has recently culminated in the establishment of a Russian mission at the court of the Amír."

In describing, then, the year 1873 as a crucial year for the relations between the British power and Afghánistán I am fully justified by the facts of the case. In that year Russia, in despite of her solemn promises to the contrary, seized Khiva. The British Government, by the hand of Lord Granville—by the hand which had written that he saw "no practical advantage in examining too minutely how far these arrangements"—the annexation by Russia of a moiety of the Khivan territory and her suzerainty over the remainder —"were in strict accordance with the assurances given in January by Count Schouvaloff," condoned that breach of a solemn promise. The British cabinet and its agents in India, appealed to by the Amír to aid him against Russia, replied to him in a manner so half-hearted and so uncertain, pretending confidence in Russia which he knew to be undeserved, that it severed the last link which still bound him to the English alliance, and caused him to drift, partly in despair, partly in desperation, towards the rival who was courting him.

Many circumstances, prominent amongst them his contemptuous rejection of offered subsidies, soon occurred to prove that from the date of the return of his envoy in 1873, Shir Ali regarded the alliance with England as dissolved. It is scarcely necessary to enumerate the various instances in which this sentiment showed itself. It betrayed itself in acts, in writings, and in words. "Under this circumstance of the case," he wrote to Lord Northbrook in November 1873, in reply to that Lord's assurance that he would maintain the policy of Lord Lawrence and Lord Mayo, "under this circumstance of the case, it was not necessary to hold all these conversations with Syud Núr Mahammad Shah at Simla." "I am determined," he said on another occasion, "to receive no more favours from the British."

In the beginning of 1874 a Tory ministry succeeded the Government under whose administration the Amír had been allowed to drift into the arms of Russia. The new ministry lost no time in endeavouring to heal the breach made by their predecessors, but their efforts were rendered unavailing by the opposition offered to their schemes by the Government of India. Notwithstanding the well-ascertained fact that an active correspondence was going on between the Governor of Russian Túrkistán and the Amír, in spite of the knowledge that the political position of Afghánistán had been wholly changed since the period when the policy of "masterly inactivity" had been initiated, Lord Northbrook and his Council still clung with the obstinacy of *doctrinaires* to the last rag of a worn-out system. Russia, then, during the two years which succeeded the crucial period of 1873, enjoyed opportunity to work without opposition on the mind of Shir Ali. She used that opportunity to the utmost, at the same time that, under the pretence of sending out expeditions "to explore the old bed of the Oxus," she despatched a Cossack force to ensure the submission of the tribes occupying the territory between the Atrek and the Súmbar.

In the spring of 1876 Lord Northbrook was succeeded as Viceroy by Lord Lytton. The month of February of that year had witnessed the absorption by Russia of the remaining moiety of Khokand—the principality of Karatighin alone being permitted to retain a condition of semi-independence. The English Government, more than ever anxious regarding the fate of a country which has been well described as the glacis of the fortress of Hindústán, empowered the new Viceroy to offer to Amír Shir Ali the active countenance and protection which he had previously solicited at the hands of the British Government.* But before the native aide-de-camp selected by Lord Lytton to carry this message of reconciliation could reach Kábul—before even, I may say, Lord Lytton had set foot in India—the fatal rebuff of 1873—coinciding with an adverse decision, pronounced by British officers, on the subject of the Amír's dispute with Persia regarding Sistan; and with the urgent pleadings of the Government of India on behalf of Yákúb Khán—had driven Shir Ali into a condition of irreconcileable hostility towards England.

* Lord Cranbrook's despatch to Lord Lytton, 18th November 1878, para. 10:—

"Accordingly, on your Excellency's departure from England to assume the Viceroyalty, her Majesty's Goverument instructed you to offer to Shere Ali that same active countenance and protection which he had previously solicited at the hands of the Indian Government. It was clearly impossible, however, to enter into any formal engagement in this sense without requiring from the Ameer some substantial proof of his unity of interests with the British Government. Whilst her Majesty's Government, therefore, authorised your Excellency to concede to his Highness substantial pecuniary aid, a formal recognition of his dynasty, so far as it would not involve active interference in the internal affairs of Afghánistán, and an explicit pledge of material support in case of unprovoked foreign aggression, you were directed not to incur these heavy reponsibilities unless Shere Ali, on his part, were prepared to allow a British agent, or agents, access to positions in his territories (other than at Cabul itself), where, without prejudicing the personal authority of the ruler, they could acquire trustworthy information of events likely to threaten the tranquillity or independence of Afghánistán."

He was no longer capable of listening to reason. He refused, then, the offer of the Viceroy, and declined to receive an envoy. And though the conciliatory language of the Viceroy induced him to assume politeness so far as to depute an envoy to meet a British officer at Pesháwar, he gave to that envoy instructions fatal to the success of his mission.

The interview which took place in the early part of the year 1877, between Sir Lewis Pelly and the Afghán envoy, made it abundantly clear that the time had gone by when any cordial co-operation could be hoped for on the part of the Amír. His language and conduct, so long dubious, became at this period so openly hostile, that the Viceroy wisely took advantage of the death of the Kábul envoy to discontinue negotiations, the bases of which had been rejected.

From that moment the Government of India resolved, in accordance with instructions from England, "to maintain an attitude of vigilant reserve until such time as the Amír might better realise his own position and interests." This policy was persevered in for twenty months. During that time the aggressive action of Russia continued to develop itself. It is a well authenticated fact, that had the negotiations of the summer of 1878 terminated in a rupture between England and Russia, the latter power was prepared to follow in the footsteps of Nádir Shah—to threaten from the base of a friendly Afghánistán the empire of Hindústán. Under these circumstances, and with the intentions of Russia in its possession, it was impossible that the British Government should remain tranquil when—a breach between England and Russia seeming to be a question not of days but of hours—the Amír received with remarkable ostentation an embassy despatched to him by the Czar.

Yet though it was impossible that the British Government should allow to pass without notice an act which constituted a breach of the engagement existing between the two powers—an engagement, accepted by the Amír on his accession and confirmed by him at Ambála—which bound him to be the friend of the friends and the enemy of the enemies of England—the notice which the Viceroy did take of it was remarkable for its moderate scope. He simply required that the Amír, having received an embassy from the Czar, should welcome to his capital an envoy from himself. The Amír was informed at the same time that his refusal would be construed as an act of hostility.

The conduct of the Amír on the receipt of this friendly letter from the Viceroy was more than discourteous. It was hostile. Leaving unanswered the letter of the Viceroy, he directed the officer commanding his advance posts to refuse admission to the English envoy, and, if necessary, to repel him by force. The envoy attempting to enter the Khaibar pass was refused admission—and returned.

Still reluctant to proceed to extremities, the British Government, carrying moderation to a limit which, among Eastern nations, is not generally regarded as a sign of conscious strength, decided, before proceeding to hostilities, to allow the Amír time to return to his right mind. The Viceroy, therefore, under instructions from England, addressed to Shir Ali, in temperate language, a demand for a full and suitable apology within a given time for the affront he had offered to the British Government within his territories. The Amír was likewise informed that unless a clear and satisfactory reply were received by the 20th November, his intentions would be regarded as hostile, and he would be treated as an enemy.

The date, the 20th November, fixed for the receipt of the reply, allowed the Amír six clear days to consider and to reflect, before arriving at a decision. By allowing that time to pass by he accepted the alternative, and declared himself an enemy of England.*

Such was the origin of the second Afghán war. A hard and unelastic principle of policy, designed in its origin to deal with an Afghánistán bounded on the north and north-west by wild and independent tribes, had been rigorously applied to an Afghánistán watching with beating heart the steady and gradual absorption of those independent tribes by the perfidious disturber of the peace of the world. In her agony Afghánistán appealed, and appealed fruitlessly, to the Liberal Cabinet which governed England. In vain did she point to the fact that the great kingdom on her north-

* Subsequently the Amír sent a reply dated the 19th. It reached the Viceroy several days after hostilities had commenced, and was neither clear nor satisfactory.

west border had been swallowed up; that, virtually, she was threatened; that already the head of the monster was turned in her direction. The doctrinaires who governed England and India at that period, fascinated by a principle which allowed the foreign policy of their country to slide, declared their utter disbelief in the absorbing tendencies of Russia, their determination not to scan too closely the means by which, despite of her plighted word, she had swallowed up Khiva. They answered then the entreaties of Afghánistán by evading compliance with her demands; by citing the promises of Russia—promises analogous to those which she had often made, and as often violated. Baffled in her hopes of real help from England, it appeared to Afghánistán that the only chance of safety remaining to her was to ally herself with the encroaching disturber whom, it was clear to her, England feared. In cementing this alliance she deliberately defied her former protector, for she placed the glacis of the fortress of Hindústán virtually in the hands of the enemy of England. It is true that many excuses existed for her conduct. It is true that England had repelled her, and that she acted as she did act because she believed that, equally with herself, England dreaded the absorbing monster on her frontier. When, in 1876, England, better counselled, endeavoured to re-cement the broken friendship, Afghánistán had committed herself too far. The rebuff of 1873 had been too keenly felt. She had been driven to become Russian.

Thenceforward there was but one course to pursue;

and the Government of Lord Beaconsfield pursued it. The occupation of the salient angles of the outwork will be England's practical demonstration to Russia and to the world, that "cunning is not caution, and that habitual perfidy is not high policy of State."

APPENDIX.

The Rev. T. P. Hughes, of the Church Missionary Society's Mission to the Afghâns at Peshâwar, now on a visit to England, has assured me that I have erred in stating, at page 39, that the Pathâns are not Afghâns. Mr. Hughes, than whom it would be difficult to find a higher authority on all that relates to the Afghân people, writes to me on the subject as follows:—

"The national appellation of the people of Afghanistân is either *Afghân*, *Pathân*, *Pashtún*, or *Pukhtun*. The word *Afghân* is said to be derived from Afghânah, the supposed ancestor of the Afghân people, although according to Akhund Darweza, a celebrated local authority, it is from the Persian *fighán*, a complaint, or lamentation, as indicating the turbulent character of the people. It may, however, be derived from *fighán* (pl. of *fugh*) idols, *i.e.* idolaters. The origin of the word *Puthán*, according to the Persian history of Ni'amat Ullah, is as follows:—Abdur Rashíd, or Kais (the first descendant of Afghanah who embraced Islam), put seventy of the Koraishites to death, and the

Prophet predicted that God would make his issue so numerous, that they, with respect to the establishment of the faith, would outvie all other peoples; and that they would be in strength like the wood upon which they lay the keel of a ship when in course of construction, and which is called *Pathán*. The Prophet therefore conferred on Abdur Rashíd the title of Pathán. *Pashtun*, or as it is pronounced in Eastern Afghanistán *Pukhtún*, is said by native historians to be derived from a place in hills called Pasht or Pusht, although it seems more probable that the word can be traced to the Persian *Pushta*, a hill, *i.e.* the dwellers in hills, for in India the Afghans are still called *Rohillah*, or the people from Roh, the name given to the mountains between Pesháwar and Cabul."